Advanced Financial Reporting and Analysis

Advanced Financial Reporting and Analysis

John Dunn
Margaret Stewart

WILEY

Library of Congress Cataloging-in-Publication Data

Dunn, John, 1959-
    Advanced financial reporting and analysis / John Dunn, Margaret Stewart.
      pages cm
    Includes bibliographical references and index.
    ISBN 978-0-470-97360-8 (pbk.) – ISBN 978-1-118-82404-7 (ebk) – ISBN 978-1-118-82394-1 (ebk)
1.   Financial statements. 2.   Accounting.   I. Stewart, Margaret, 1956- II. Title.
    HF5681.B2D7796 2014
    657'.3–dc23

                                                                                          2013042819

ISBN 978-0-470-97360-8 (pbk)
ISBN 978-1-118-82404-7 (ebk)
ISBN 978-1-118-82394-1(ebk)

A catalogue record for this book is available from the British Library

Set in 11/13pt GoudyStd by Thomson Digital, India

Printed in Great Britain by Bell & Bain Ltd, Glasgow

Contents

A Brief Introduction
to the Text

Contents

Introduction

This chapter provides a brief overview of the text and will, hopefully, provide an idea of the best approach to the study of financial reporting at the advanced level.

It is always dangerous to generalise, but our experience of teaching financial accounting suggests that there is a natural progression:

- First year classes focus on the mechanics of bookkeeping and the basics of preparing financial statements. That is a difficult set of skills to master, and the secret is to practise on as many questions as possible to develop the necessary number-crunching skills.
- Second year classes start to relate the material from first year to the preparation of financial statements in the real world. Accounting standards appear for the first time. The jump from first year to second is very pronounced and can often appear more daunting than the initial learning curve of dealing with first year material. Again, it is necessary to practise constantly in order to develop the mechanical skills that are required in order to prepare a set of financial statements.
- Third year classes mark a turning point. Firstly, the jump in complexity from second year to third is rarely as daunting as the jump from first year to second. Secondly, a typical third year class will focus on topics in financial reporting and

so it is unlikely that you will have to prepare a full set of financial statements in its entirety. A typical third year class will cover a range of specific topics, some related to practice and others related to obtaining a deeper understanding of the role of accounting in society. There is still scope to practise on numerical questions, but the secret to succeeding in a third year class is generally about being open to ideas and being ready and willing to develop and express opinions.

It is envisaged that most readers of this text will be in their third year of study, although that will vary from course to course.

The Basic Structure of This Text

The next two chapters deal with important matters to the members of the accountancy profession, although it is debatable whether they are directly related to accountancy.

Chapter 2 deals with the question of professional status, the manner in which accountants have worked to obtain recognition as professionals and the manner in which the accountant is portrayed in popular culture. Typically, students are attracted to a career in accountancy because of the opportunity to be respected as 'professionals', but the question of why some groups are regarded as professionals and others are not is often overlooked. It is no accident that accountants are regarded as professional people.

Chapter 3 deals with the question of ethics. We all have to make decisions and those decisions can have consequences for many different people. Accountants frequently have to offer advice or prepare reports that can require some considera-tion of different parties' interests. For example, the treatment of a particular transaction could affect reported earnings and so affect an entity's ability to raise finance. Accounting choices could threaten jobs if a pessimistic view is taken or lead to lenders accepting unacceptable and unreported risks in the event of optimism. Chapter 3 explores the ethical dimensions of accounting and discusses some of the findings of studies into the manner in which accountants address ethical dilemmas.

Chapters 4 to 8 deal with a range of technical matters that affect the preparation of financial statements. Each of these chapters deals with a particular area that will affect the reported profit and/or reported financial position.

Chapter 4 addresses some of the 'problem areas' in financial reporting. The chapter argues that many of these issues arise because of difficulties in defining the boundaries of the reporting entity and also in setting realistic figures for the 'fair value' that is frequently the basis for reported asset and liability figures. The role of accounting is open to a degree of debate and the fact that certain hard decisions have not been taken has led to a lack of clarity in other areas.

Chapter 5 addresses governance issues and the manner in which they interact with accounting. The chapter commences by highlighting the economic causes for the conflict between the interests of shareholders and those of company directors. The role of accounting in resolving those conflicts is discussed. It is clear that accounting is only part of the solution, but it is nevertheless an important part. The chapter moves on to the accounting treatment of executive share options, which has been one of the more contentious areas in which accounting has been implicated in the problems associated with governance. The accounting treatment of options also raises questions about the need for consistency and the application of the principles underlying the International Accounting Standards Board's (IASB) *Conceptual Framework for Financial Reporting*.

Chapter 6 deals with accounting for post-retirement benefits, mainly pensions. This has been a contested area for accounting for many years. Very large amounts are involved, many of which are difficult to determine with any certainty. The accounting treatment of certain types of pension scheme is very complicated and standard setters have had to make some very difficult decisions. Furthermore, changes in the accounting rules have been blamed for the withdrawal of a type of pension arrangement that has been very popular with employees. Employers have used the changes to the accounting rules as a justification for doing so, even though the arguments that have been offered make no real economic sense.

Chapter 7 offers a diversion into the more esoteric question of the choice of a measurement basis for the preparation for financial statements. This is an important area because the choice of methods has implications for the usefulness of financial statements to different user groups. It has also been an interesting area in terms of the politics of setting and enforcing accounting standards. Different models for financial reporting have the capacity to increase or decrease reported profit figures when prices are rising (and it is a historical fact that prices do generally rise).

Chapter 8 concludes by addressing the question of accounting for financial instruments. Financial instruments that are issued in order to raise finance have been a controversial area in accounting for many years. There is a massive industry in 'financial engineering', with practitioners attempting to create instruments that make liabilities look like equity for reporting purposes. If successful, the overall effect is to reduce gearing ratios, thereby making the companies look less risky than they are. If anything, the accounting treatment of financial instruments held as assets has been even more controversial. There has been a boom in the creation of complex derivative instruments, many of which are sold in order to manage risk in a responsible manner. These instruments have also been purchased in order to create exposures to risks in order to speculate on market movements. The accounting treatment of financial instruments has been blamed, at least in part, for the 2007 Credit Crunch.

Chapters 9 to 13 deal with aspects of the preparation of group accounts. Readers may or may not have studied this topic before and so chapters 9 and 10 offer an overview that assumes no prior knowledge. It is a good idea to read these chapters even if the material is familiar because the process of preparing consolidated financial statements is still worth practising.

Chapter 11 deals with some of the more complicated ways in which control can be obtained. For example, a parent company can control a subsidiary through indirect shareholdings, with different group members owning shares in the subsidiary. There are also other forms of relationship that are worth considering, including the associates and joint arrangements. These relationships create their own problems and have to be included in the group accounts in different ways.

Chapter 12 deals with the question of changes in the group, with additional investments in group members and disposals of investments requiring some further thought about the mechanics of preparing consolidated financial statements.

Chapter 13 deals with the problems associated with accounting for items that are expressed in foreign currencies. This is essentially a continuation of the discussion of consolidations because the primary issue is translating the financial statements of foreign subsidiaries whose figures are expressed in a different currency. Those figures have to be restated to make them compatible with the parent company's financial statements. The problem is that there are different approaches to the translation process and each provides different figures for profit and financial position. This has been a highly controversial area.

Chapter 14 provides an overview of the issues associated with comparative financial reporting. It might be assumed that the acceptance of International Financial Reporting Standards (IFRS) as the basis for financial reporting, at least for quoted companies, in many countries would mean that there is no need to consider international differences. That is not, however, the case. There are cultural differences between countries and those differences affect the attitudes and behaviour of accountants.

Chapter 15 provides an overview of the implications of sustainability for financial reporting. Attitudes have hardened towards irresponsible behaviour by businesses who overlook their impact on the environment or who abuse the interests of employees or other stakeholders. Accountants have claimed a role in the process of reporting on these matters. Whether by accident or design, this topic has been adopted as an accounting matter.

Chapter 16 brings the text to a conclusion by offering some thoughts on planning and conducting a student dissertation. Many readers will be involved in dissertations at this stage in their studies. It is hoped that this final chapter will encourage some to write their dissertation on a topic that is related to financial reporting.

A Concluding Thought

The preceding overview has made repeated mention of problems and controversies. Accounting is not a straightforward mechanical process. Choices have to be made and those responsible for making the choices will be accountable to groups of stakeholders with different priorities. That can be frustrating to those students who would prefer to be told what the correct answer is, but it is hoped that this will be an encouragement to readers to explore the background to financial reporting. Accounting is interesting because it affects behaviour and relationships, both of which are endlessly fascinating subjects for study.

We hope that you enjoy working through this text.

Margaret and John

Professions and Professionalism

Contents

Learning Objectives

After studying this chapter, you should be able to:

- explain what it means for an occupation group to be classed as a profession;
- describe the professionalisation project and its implications for accountants;
- discuss the role of professional accountancy bodies;
- discuss the implications of the status granted to professional accountants.

Introduction

The reputation of accountants and the accountancy profession varies between countries and also over time. It is generally fair, however, to say that accountancy is regarded as a desirable occupation. Accountants usually enjoy a reasonable standard of living in return for their labour and are respected by friends, neighbours and others as 'professional' people.

This chapter will argue that it is no accident that accountants enjoy a positive reputation. History suggests that occupation groups can and do capture professional status as a conscious and deliberate programme of working to capture the right to self-regulate and also to exclude potential rivals. Professional status imposes many obligations, but these are more than compensated for by the rights that are granted to professionals.

The discussion of this process should be of interest to most readers of this text because, it is hoped, most will wish to enter the accountancy profession. Hopefully the opportunity to study the profession's success in obtaining and retaining professional status will encourage that ambition.

Why Do You Want to Be an Accountant?

The question of professional status is one that is likely to be of interest to the target audience for this book. Asked why they chose to study accountancy, generally the first (and frequently the only) response from a lecture theatre full of accountancy students is that they expect to earn a large salary. If it is pointed out that there are other well-paid occupations, the two factors that emerge as secondary considerations are that accountants are generally unlikely to be unemployed and that it is regarded as prestigious to be an accountant.

The status granted to accountants (and other occupations) varies from country to country. In the UK, a career in accountancy is often regarded as more prestigious than a career in engineering. In Germany the opposite is likely to be the case. There is no point in debating whether such rankings are valid or whether they reflect the actual contributions to society made by various occupation groups. It is, however, worth considering the manner in which accountants seek to protect and further their interests.

In the interests of avoiding accusations of elitism, this chapter makes no specific claim that accountants are in any way 'better' or 'more deserving' than other occupation groups. One of Douglas Adams' Hitchhiker's Guide series of satirical novels describes a society that exiled its telephone hygienists, only to learn the true value of that occupation group when the entire population died from an epidemic of a disease that had originated from a single dirty telephone. That said, there is no denying that accountants are generally better paid than telephone hygienists and that they generally enjoy greater status. The place of the accountant in society is a phenomenon that is worthy of academic study regardless of whether such status is justified.

Badges of Professionalism

In the distant past, sociological studies identified a profession by the so-called 'badges' of professionalism. These could be presented as lists of benefits and obligations associated with professional status:

Obligations	Benefits
Focus on service to society	Restriction of trade
Achieving and maintaining competence	Self-regulation

To be recognised as a profession, an occupation group had to be willing to put the needs of society and the specific stakeholders who used the profession's services before self-interest. For example, a medical doctor would treat a sick patient outside of normal working hours and a lawyer would advise a client on the basis of the best overall outcome for the client rather than the greatest possible legal fee for the lawyer. Society would generally feel confident that a professional person would behave with integrity and would view personal interests as secondary to service.

There is also an expectation that professionals will offer services that are of very high quality. A professional person will be educated and will have sufficient practical experience to ensure that any work will be done to an appropriate and acceptable standard. That generally means that there will be stringent conditions imposed on the right to practice as a professional person.

The benefits granted to professionals were viewed as compensation for the restrictions imposed by the obligations. There would be very little incentive to enter into an extensive training programme that led to a career of service and sacrifice if there were no commensurate benefits.

Professionals are generally free to offer their services without the risk of competition from other parties. That is clearly an important safeguard because it prevents the public from being misled by unqualified practitioners. It is also a significant economic benefit because the professionals are only required to compete with the others who share their professional accreditation. The laws of supply and demand suggest that restricting the right to supply a product in this way will generally lead to it being sold at a higher price. Sometimes the law prevents those who are not accredited professionals from practising. For example, in many countries only a medical doctor can prescribe medicines classed as 'prescription only'. Sometimes the law restricts itself to limiting the right to use a particular title. There are alternative therapists, such as chiropractors, who can offer treatments that are complementary to traditional medicine and many lay people are trained to provide first aid in the event of an emergency. Those therapists and first-aiders can treat patients but they cannot claim to be medical doctors in the process of doing so.

Self-regulation is also a significant benefit of professional status. Essentially, this means that the state leaves the regulation of the professions and their activities to the professionals themselves. Professionals are free to use their expertise to best advantage in serving society's needs. There is less risk of the professions being constrained by inflexible legislation and so professional rules and regulations can be far more responsive to changing circumstances. Clearly that also implies a great deal of trust in those professionals because they are effectively operating with relatively little oversight from the state.

Professions and Professional Bodies

From a practical point of view, all professions must be represented by one or more professional bodies. These bodies provide a focal point for their members and are an aid to the recruitment and training of new members. They also provide a means by which interested parties, primarily the government, can communicate and negotiate on areas of mutual interest.

Typically, anyone wishing to pursue a career in accountancy will join a professional body. In 2012, the magazine *Financial Director* published an analysis of the backgrounds of the finance directors of the UK FTSE 100 finance directors (Singh, 2012). Only 15 of them were not professionally qualified accountants and eight of those worked in mining or gas exploration, which is an industry with a history of appointing finance directors from non-traditional backgrounds.

Accountancy bodies generally require their members to pass a series of exams, often after first completing a degree. It would be unusual for an accountancy body to offer entry to anyone who has not passed, at the very least, the final level of professional exams. In addition, membership generally requires a period of professional experience, typically three years or more, working under the supervision of one or more qualified accountants. Thus, professionally qualified accountants can claim to have demonstrated that they have both the technical expertise required to pass professional exams and some practical experience.

The UK is typical of most countries in that there is more than one accountancy body to choose from. The most prominent of these are the six 'chartered' bodies:

- Chartered Association of Certified Accountants (ACCA)
- Chartered Accountants Ireland (CAI)
- Chartered Institute of Management Accountants (CIMA)
- Chartered Institute of Public Finance and Accountancy (CIPFA)
- Institute of Chartered Accountants in England and Wales (ICAEW)
- Institute of Chartered Accountants of Scotland (ICAS).

Each of these bodies can trace its origins back to one of 18 accountancy bodies that were created during the period from 1853 to 1919. A series of mergers has taken place since then to reduce the numbers to the six bodies listed above.

The original bodies were created by practitioners who wished to have a forum for the exchange of ideas and also in order to enhance their status. For example, the origins of ICAS lie in societies of accountants that were established in Glasgow and Edinburgh. These bodies merged to form a national society that has grown and prospered in the period since.

ACCA's earliest origins were in bodies that were created by professional accountants who did not meet the entry requirements for ICAEW's predecessors. Those somewhat negative beginnings have since been overtaken by the development of a global accountancy body that carries considerable influence in many countries.

The UK's accountancy bodies have had to learn to cooperate to the extent that they can offer a collective identity to government and to society at large. For example, an accountant who commits a serious offence may be subject to investigation and censure by a joint disciplinary board. Despite that, the bodies do compete with one another for members and for status. For example, ICAS offers training to large numbers of professional students in England who might otherwise have joined ICAEW.

There is a certain amount of specialisation in the services offered by members of different bodies. For example, the CIMA qualification focuses more on management accounting, whereas CAI, ICAEW and ICAS focus largely on financial reporting. However, most bodies would claim that their members are capable of fulfilling almost any role that is typically associated with accountancy.

There is an increasing tendency for accountancy bodies to operate internationally. For example, ACCA and CIMA recruit and train members from many countries and their examinations typically have more overseas candidates than UK.

The Professionalisation Project

Sociological studies of professions tend to start with the idea that professional status is desirable for virtually any occupation group. That status is essentially granted by society at large, but particularly by the state. Historical studies tend to present the process of obtaining this recognition as a deliberate project, acted out by the senior members of the bodies whose members constitute the profession.

Willmott's (1986) groundbreaking study of the development of professional bodies provides both a discussion of the theoretical approach that can be taken to the study of professions and an exploration of the development of the major accountancy bodies in the UK, from their creation through to the early 1980s.

Willmott argues that, 'professional [accountancy bodies] are *primarily*, but not exclusively, political bodies whose purpose is to define, organise, secure and advance the interests of their . . . members' (Willmott, 1986).

Willmott's exploration of three of the approaches that may be taken to the study of the history of the professional bodies finds value in all three (see Table 2.1).

Willmott acknowledges the merits of each approach. The most important issue for our purposes is that any study of the professions will be influenced by its theoretical perspective. There is no single or 'correct' reading of a set of events or of the historical development of a professional accountancy body.

Willmott prefaces his history of the professional accountancy associations by describing them as political bodies. He argues that they provide the means to advance the interests of their members. The bodies may promote the impression of competence and integrity on behalf of their members, but the intention will be to increase the market value of the services they offer. This can be achieved both by restricting the supply of accounting services by limiting the numbers of professionally qualified accountants and also by stimulating the demand for the services offered.

Willmott's history of the development of the accountancy bodies has been rather overtaken by the passage of time. However, his paper raises a number of important and enduring arguments:

• The emergence of an organised occupational group of accounting specialists coincided with the Industrial Revolution. The complexities of industrial (or capitalist) society created a demand for more sophisticated, standardised, specialised and complex accounting techniques.

• Market forces for labour can be complex and may not always operate freely. For example, trade unions may constrain the ability of employers to use the laws of supply and demand to reduce the wages on offer. Professional bodies can take this a stage further by creating a mystique concerning the services on offer and establishing a monopoly over the supply of those certified as competent in the provision of those services. Professional associations have sought to create monopolies of labour by restricting entry, by determining the type and duration of training and by regulating the mode and standards of practice.

• The interaction between the professions and the state is absolutely critical. Willmott argues that the relationship between professional associations and the state is best characterised as one of interdependence and tension in which each party enables as well as constrains the other. The state has the ultimate authority in terms of legal and physical compulsion. The professions require the endorsement and support of the state and the state will typically develop a dependence on the professions. Thus, the dynamic of the relationship between the state and the professions is one of mutual dependence.

Table 2.1 Three approaches to the study of professional bodies

Approach	View of professional bodies	Asks
Functionalist	Focuses on the tasks undertaken by professions. Professionals possess 'esoteric knowledge, independence, altruism and self-discipline'.	What do professionals do?
Interactionist	Focuses on professions as interest groups that strive to convince others of the legitimacy of their claim to professional recognition. Regards the professional body as 'a basic organisational instrument for defining and securing a respectable and valued social identity'.	How do professional bodies behave?
Critical	Focuses on professions as a resource that can be used by those whose exercise power and control over society. The Marxist view identifies ownership and control of the means of production as the key issue in understanding society. The division of labour is but one of the aspects of the resources controlled by capital. The activities of professions and professional bodies must be understood within the wider context of organising capitalist society.	How does a capitalist society present, promote and use the professions to further the interests of capital?

Source: Willmott (1986)

Studies of Professionalisation

The process by which the accountancy profession has sought and won influence has been studied in a variety of ways. The most obvious approach is to follow the development of the accountancy profession in a specific country.

Öhman and Wallerstedt (2012) discuss the responses of the Swedish accountancy profession to changes in the law. More specifically, they describe how audit regulation and the development of the auditing profession influenced each other from the end of the 19th century to the end of the 20th century.

Öhman and Wallerstedt describe the development of legislation requiring company audit and the associated development of the audit profession. The intriguing issue is the fact that the paper starts at the very foundation of company audit, with unqualified auditors being elected from and on behalf of the shareholders, and continues to the development of codified auditing standards and the effects of Sweden's entry to the EU in the closing years of the 20th century.

Uche (2002) provides an intriguing and sophisticated analysis of the development of the Nigerian accountancy profession. The Nigerian context is affected by the country's ties to the UK, which led to professionally qualified accountants being recruited from the UK and company accounts being audited by members of ICAEW. The paper charts the development of an autonomous accountancy profession and provides a very clear explanation of the political and social background to the changes. There is also an ongoing contest between competing accountancy bodies for influence and recognition.

Yee (2012) develops an interesting analysis of the recent development of the accountancy profession in China, with particular focus on the relationship between the accountancy bodies and the state. Her paper reprises the theme of the mutual dependence of the state and the professional bodies in terms of providing one another with support and legitimacy.

The literature also contains studies of the ways in which the accountancy profession has sought to protect its interests by claiming areas of expertise from which others should be excluded. For example, the process of winding up insolvent and bankrupt businesses and estates is an area in which accountants and lawyers have struggled for primacy. Walker (2004) studies the effects of changes to bankruptcy law in the 19th century and finds that accountants organised themselves in response to moves by the legal profession to exclude accountants from the lucrative opportunities created by the Bankruptcy Act 1869. The Act required the appointment of a trustee to administer the affairs of bankrupt estates. The legal profession was keen to capture this source of revenue. Established accountants were keen to compete and also to exclude the threat from inexperienced accountants who were being attracted into business by the prospect of these new sources of income. Walker puts forward compelling arguments for linking the creation of the

Incorporated Society of Liverpool Accountants (one of the founding bodies that were amalgamated into ICAEW) as a means of organising the accountancy profession so as to meet these challenges. One of the intriguing aspects of this paper is that there was a clash between the interests of the accountancy profession and those of the legal profession. Another issue is that Walker is extremely open about the complexity of analysing such sequences of events, and acknowledges that the Bankruptcy Act was not the only factor that came into play in the creation of the Incorporated Society of Liverpool Accountants.

Sikka and Willmott (1995) analyse the manner in which the accountancy profession uses claims of independence as the basis for protecting its jurisdiction. Accountants provide a variety of services and one of the accountancy profession's strategies for maintaining its claims of competence in these areas is the stress placed on the accountant's ability to offer an independent perspective. Sikka and Willmott attribute much of the accountancy profession's success to the capture of the external audit and the associated claims of acting independently in the provision of expert audit services. This highly visible role lends credibility to accountants in the other roles that they occupy. Criticisms of external audit may have a disproportionate impact on the profession's credibility. The authors analyse the accountancy profession's responses to a number of episodes involving criticisms of audit and auditor independence, and conclude that a number of tactics have been developed in order to respond to those criticisms. These tactics include revising the ethical guidance offered to accountants, introducing new disciplinary procedures, and mobilising support from politicians, the media and others in discrediting challenges to the claim of independence.

Educating Professional Accountants

Part of the accountant's claim to professional status resides in the fact that the professional bodies set stringent academic entry qualifications. These vary from country to country, although entry requirements are generally high. For example, a Danish student who wishes to enter into professional training for the principal auditing qualification must have a Master's degree and must have completed three years of practical training under the supervision of an authorised public accountant or approved public accountant. There are two days of written exams and an oral exam at the end of that training period.

It is fairly common for accountancy bodies to restrict entry to graduates, but that is not always so. For example, ACCA offers flexible entry routes to membership, including a series of foundation exams that can be taken without any prior study of accounting and that do not specifically require a degree or diploma for entry. That does not imply a lower level of academic performance than the bodies that specify a graduate intake because ACCA claims that its final-level examinations are of an equivalent standard to those on a Master's degree.

The International Accounting Education Standards Board (IAESB), a sub-committee of the International Federation of Accountants (IFAC), has a series of International Education Standards (IES). These are intended to assist member bodies around the world to fulfil their responsibilities with respect to the education and training of professionally qualified accountants. The IES set out a number of minimum education requirements. For example, an individual entering professional training should meet entry requirements that are at least the equivalent to those required for a university degree or its equivalent (IES1; IAESB, 2004a). The final assessment of capabilities and competence is normally in addition to purely academic qualifications and is beyond undergraduate degree level (IES6; IAESB, 2004b). In other words, the IAESB requires that all professional bodies set exams that are compulsory, even for those with accountancy degrees. The bodies' exams should be both more practical and more rigorous than those set by universities.

The final exams set by professional bodies tend to have relatively low pass rates. For example, year on year from 2007 to 2011, the first-time pass rates recorded by Chartered Accountants Ireland in the final examination has varied from 55% to 82% (Professional Oversight Board, 2012).

There is always a certain tension between setting high entry standards in order to signal quality, and encouraging a strong intake. For example, ICAS restricted entry to graduates for almost 30 years in order to claim an all-graduate membership. That policy was overturned in 2011 when a direct entry route was established in order to enable accountancy firms to train school leavers for membership. Gammie and Kirkham (2008) established that this route was regarded as less prestigious by students but clearly offers some flexibility to employers. In particular, many smaller accountancy firms will be able to offer ICAS training without incurring the costs associated with recruiting and employing graduates. It could previously have been desirable for a small accountancy firm whose partners were ICAS members to employ school leavers with a view to funding their study for ACCA. Such arrangements would have cost ICAS potential members.

A Very Brief Word about Training Contracts

Accountancy undergraduates often ask which of the accountancy bodies they should aim for after graduation. The advice that is offered in response is often biased in favour of whichever body the person being questioned belongs to. A member of the Association of International Accountants is unlikely to recommend joining any other body, and likewise most members of the Hong Kong Institute of Certified Public Accountants will claim superiority for their institution.

Ideally, any employer should be prepared to offer the necessary study leave and tuition fees associated with working towards membership of a professional accountancy body. Most professional qualifications are a sound basis for a career in accountancy. Most employers have a preferred qualification for their trainee accountants. On that basis, it is unlikely that you should reject a job offer on the basis that your prospective employer expects you to join one accountancy body rather than another.

Public Perceptions – Accountants at the Movies

There is a long history of accountant characters in films. The portrayal of accountants in popular culture could be viewed as an opportunity to measure the success of the accountancy profession's attempts to present itself in a positive light. Arguably, any stereotyped image will only be useful to a film-maker if it is recognised and understood by the audience. If nurses are perceived as kind and sympathetic, for example, then saying that a character is a nurse will be an easy way to establish that the character is kind and sympathetic.

It is fair to say that the portrayal of accountants has not been particularly positive. Dimnik and Felton (2006) identify five stereotyped images of accountants in their study (see Table 2.2).

Table 2.2 Stereotyped images of accountants

Dreamers	Naïve optimists who tend to be out of touch with the reality of their situation. They are generally timid, not overly intelligent and not concerned or even aware of how others perceive them.
Plodders	Hardworking and dedicated, but stuck in boring, low-level jobs with little status or power.
Eccentrics	Generally outgoing individuals who have strange personalities. Not many accountant characters fall into this classification and it is suggested that part of the intention is to create a humorous contrast between the accountant's occupation and personality.
Heroes	Individuals who rise to a challenge or otherwise win the day. They are usually characters the audience can relate to and identify with.
Villains	Characters who are cold, insincere, devious, greedy, uncharitable and impatient.

Source: Dimnik and Felton, 2006

Dimnik and Felton conclude that most of the films they reviewed presented accountants as ordinary and conventional individuals. The eccentric image was used in a tiny minority of the films and accountants were usually portrayed in a manner that fitted one of the other four stereotypes. There was often a hint of humour, with the accountant character presented in an unflattering way or used as a comic device. For example, in the film *The Untouchables*, the accountant who is drafted in to assist the FBI finds a technicality in the gangster's tax returns in order to secure a conviction and then provides one of the film's most memorable touches of humour by arming himself with a very large gun in order to participate in the gangster's arrest.

It may be that the events surrounding the scandals of Enron and other alleged accounting failures of the 1990s have slightly changed the accountant stereotype. For example, Thandie Newton plays a glamorous accountant who is employed by the head of a ruthless criminal gang in the 2008 film *RocknRolla*. The 2005 comedy *Fun with Dick and Jane* has an accountant character who wears the stereotypical boring grey clothes and depends on heavy drinking to deal with life. He is also heavily implicated in a major fraud that has cost the film's heroes, along with their co-workers, their jobs and their pensions. An accountant character in the television series *Weeds* helps the heroine to raise the finance to embark on a career as a drugs dealer and then helps her to launder the proceeds of her crime. This anecdotal and partial list echoes the sense that there has possibly been a shift in society's attitude towards accountants, with a little more emphasis on the accountant as a crooked facilitator who helps to hide criminal activities. For example, Carnegie and Napier (2010) report a change in the descriptions of the accountancy profession in business books written since the Enron scandal, and this could be matched by changes in the public attitude.

Summary

Accountants are professional people. It is no accident that they are, because there has been a concerted effort to create and maintain the status that has been granted to accountants by the state and by society as a whole. Accountancy is not alone in this respect; virtually all of the professional occupations have had to work through the same process at some time in their history.

Professional status is worth having from a purely economic perspective because it amounts to having the right to protect sources of revenue without having to submit to undue supervision from regulators.

It is worth reflecting on the factors that have led to accountancy enjoying this degree of recognition, because the project is ongoing. Professional status has been hard won and it could, in principle, be lost if the accountancy bodies do not maintain their vigilance. One area in which this process is extremely visible is the nature and extent of competition between bodies whose jurisdictions overlap.

For example, there are several highly regarded accountancy bodies in the UK, all of which are keen to recruit members and occupy positions of authority. None of these bodies can afford to compete too vocally, though, because to do so could undermine their credibility, to the detriment of all.

It can be interesting and even amusing to see how accountants have been portrayed on television and in the cinema. There are various stereotypical images of accountants that are used to great effect in these works of fiction.

Tutorial Questions

Question 1

Describe the reasons behind your decision to study accountancy.

Question 2

Study the website for the accountancy body that you would most like to join after you graduate. Identify the claims that the body makes on behalf of its members.

Question 3

Professional accountancy bodies have been criticised for occupying conflicting and even contradictory roles. On one hand, they seek to promote the status of their members and increase demand for their services. On the other hand, they are responsible for monitoring behaviour and taking disciplinary action against members who fall short of their standards.

Discuss the implications of this potential conflict of interest.

Question 4

Discuss the advantages and disadvantages of restricting entry to professional accountancy bodies to graduates.

Question 5

Discuss the implications of global accountancy bodies such as ACCA and CIMA for the governments of the countries in which they operate.

Question 6

Describe an accountant character in a film or television programme that you have seen. Explain whether that character gave a positive or a negative impression of accountants and accountancy.

Question 7

Explain whether negative characterisations of accountants in popular fiction matter.

References

Carnegie, G.D. & Napier, C.J. (2010) Traditional accountants and business professionals: Portraying the accounting profession after Enron. *Accounting, Organizations and Society* **35**(3) pp. 360–376.

Dimnik, T. & Felton, S. (2006) Accountant stereotypes in movies distributed in North America in the twentieth century. *Accounting, Organizations and Society* **31**(2) pp. 129–155.

Gammie, E. & Kirkham, L. (2008) Breaking the link with a university education in the creation of a chartered accountant: The ICAS story. *British Accounting Review* **40**(4) pp. 356–375.

IAESB (2004a) IES 1 *Entry Requirements to a Program of Professional Accounting Education.*

IAESB (2004b) IES 6 *Assessment of Professional Capabilities and Competence.*

Öhman, P. & Wallerstedt, E. (2012) Audit regulation and the development of the auditing profession: The case of Sweden. *Accounting History* **17**(2) pp. 241–257.

Professional Oversight Board (2012) *Key Facts and Trends in the Accountancy Profession.*

Sikka, P. & Willmott, H. (1995) The power of 'independence': Defending and extending the jurisdiction of accounting in the United Kingdom. *Accounting, Organizations and Society* **20**(6) pp. 547–581.

Singh, R. (2012) FTSE 100 FDs: Secret to their success. *Financial Director*, **26** April. Available at www.financialdirector.co.uk/financial-director/feature/2169195/ftse-100-fds-secret-success (accessed 24 September 2013).

Uche, C.U. (2002) Professional accounting development in Nigeria: Threats from the inside and outside. *Accounting, Organizations and Society* **27**(4–5) pp. 471–496.

Walker, S.P. (2004) The genesis of professional organisation in English accountancy. *Accounting, Organizations and Society* **29**(2) pp. 127–156.

Willmott, H. (1986) Organising the profession: A theoretical and historical examination of the development of the major accountancy bodies in the UK. *Accounting, Organizations and Society* **11**(6) pp. 555–580.

Yee, H. (2012) Analyzing the state-accounting profession dynamic: Some insights from the professionalization experience in China. *Accounting, Organizations and Society* **37**(6) pp. 426–444.

ETHICS

Contents

Learning Objectives

After studying this chapter, you should be able to:

- discuss the ethical dilemmas associated with accounting;
- frame ethical dilemmas as positive or negative duties;
- explain what is meant by moral development;
- discuss the role of the IESBA Code;
- explain the duties of professional bodies with regard to teaching ethics;
- identify the problems faced by qualified accountants in dealing with ethical dilemmas.

Introduction

Accountancy is often associated with sharp practice and unethical behaviour. Whether that reputation is justified or not, a great deal of attention has been paid to the whole question of regulating and educating accountants so that they behave more ethically.

This chapter will discuss the ways in which the accountancy profession and the academic accounting community have approached ethics. The profession has developed a host of rules, some of which appear to be more concerned with maintaining the appearance of ethical behaviour rather than its actual fact. Research studies suggest that accountants are relatively underdeveloped in terms of their ethical development. That raises questions about whether greater attention should be paid to teaching ethics as part of professional accountancy qualifications.

Is 'Accounting Ethics' an Oxymoron?

There is a common perception that accounting is a technical subject that must be practised in terms of debits and credits. First year students often state that they chose a degree in accountancy because they love the sense that they have arrived at the correct answer when the numbers that are supposed to balance do so. That ignores a number of important facts about accountancy.

Accounting numbers have the capacity to affect the actions of those who read them. That is strongly implied by the formal statement of purpose at the beginning of the International Accounting Standards Board's (IASB) *Conceptual Framework for Financial Reporting* (IASB, 2013):

> The objective of general purpose financial reporting is to provide financial information about the reporting entity that is useful to existing and potential investors, lenders and other creditors in making decisions about providing resources to the entity.

The fact that the statements are intended to inform decisions suggests that the entity may be affected by the impression that the statements create. If the company appears to be making losses or very small profits, then investors may decide to sell their shares; and if the financial position looks weak, then lenders may either refuse to make loans or demand a high rate of interest. Conversely, a company that appears to be both strong and profitable will have no difficulty in attracting resources.

Where do ethics come into accounting? That really depends on the extent to which the preparers are willing to compromise on matters other than technical accounting choices. For example, suppose an accountant is preparing a set of financial statements that will be submitted in support of a forthcoming loan application. It could be argued that the financial statements are intended to reflect the reality of the entity's performance and financial position. If the accountant takes that view and is prepared to adhere to it no matter what the consequences, then the process of preparing the financial statements is largely about the mechanics of accounting and the application of professional judgement in arriving at the most realistic set of figures. Ethical dilemmas can, however, creep into that process in several ways.

At one level, the accountant could feel pressured by the consequences of truthful reporting. If it is unlikely that a truthful set of accounts would impress the lender, then the accountant could feel a sense of responsibility for the parties who will be affected by the failure of the loan application. The shareholders could lose the money they have invested if the company fails because it cannot borrow; or the employees could lose their jobs. There could be a feeling that the interests of those stakeholders are more important than those of the bank and so it is acceptable to manipulate the figures in order to secure the company's future. The accountant faces an ethical dilemma whenever it is felt that an action will affect two or more interested parties in different ways.

The accountant could feel pressured at a personal level. If the loan application fails then the accountant could be removed from office, either because the directors are unhappy that the figures were not distorted in order to satisfy the bank or because the company failed through a lack of funding. That creates scope for a dilemma in terms of the accountant feeling a conflict between the need to protect his or her self-interest (and the interests of any dependent family members they may have) and the need to provide users with accurate figures.

Contributing to those pressures is the fact that the figures will, in any case, be affected by accounting choices and estimates. It could be argued that accounting often requires the selection of one figure from a range of potential outcomes and that it is not particularly dishonest to select a figure that happens to best suit the reporting entity's interests. For example, it could be argued that there is no particular reason to select the longest realistic estimate of the expected useful life of an asset, provided the figure that has been chosen remains realistic.

The extent to which accountants have given in to pressures to push accounting numbers in a particular direction has been summed up in a number of studies. Searching the academic literature using phrases such as 'earnings management' or 'aggressive accounting' throws up a large number of papers. For example, Li, Selover and Stein (2011) studied earnings management in China and found that the practice of pushing reported earnings in a particular direction was more pervasive in China than in mature market economies such as the United States. They observed that Chinese firms appear to follow a 'keep silent, make money' strategy by managing their reported earnings to zero, presumably in response to the regulatory environment in that country (Li *et al.*, 2011). Conversely, Ching, Firth and Rui (2006) found that family-owned firms are more likely to bias discretionary accruals in the period prior to certain types of share offer in order to attract a higher selling price. Those choices tended to have the effect of delaying the recognition of some expenses until the following accounting period, so that profit is boosted in the short term (just prior to the share issue) with a corresponding decrease in the following year when the costs are recognised (Ching *et al.*, 2006).

One important point about earnings management is that it tends to be associated with the distortion of estimates and assumptions, or the careful reading of accounting rules and regulations. Entire books have been written on the subject of so-called 'creative accounting' (for example, see Jones, 2010). The objective of creative accounting is to abuse the flexibility inherent in accounting to achieve some desired result in the financial statements. For example, if a company was concerned that it appeared to be making excessive profits and faced the risk of its market being regulated by government, then it might start to assume very pessimistic expected useful lives for its property, plant and equipment. In the short term, at least, that would depress reported earnings. In the event that this distortion came to light, the directors could insist that their estimates were realistic at the time and that any subsequent correction was the result of an innocent error or misunderstanding. Some authors extend the definition of creative accounting to include fraudulent misstatement of the figures, but the major accounting controversies tend to be far more frequently concerned with the ways in which users can claim to have been misled by financial statements that remain within the rules.

Creative accounting can be far more sophisticated than merely pressing an estimate to the very limits of credibility. For example, Chapter 11 discusses the manner in which third parties have assisted companies to create 'special purpose entities' (SPEs) whose purpose can include the exclusion of liabilities from the statement of financial position. In other words, banks and other financial institutions employ consultants whose job involves identifying loopholes in accounting regulations and designing financial instruments or company structures that can be used to exploit those loopholes. While that may appear to be possible only because of bad rules that do not cover every eventuality, these schemes are generally very artificial and there can be no doubt that they breach the spirit of the rules, even if they do not break the letter of the law in any way.

A Diversion into Philosophy

Most individuals face ethical dilemmas throughout their lives. It can be difficult to decide what the correct course of action is. A true ethical dilemma involves deciding between the competing interests of two parties (one of whom could be the decision-maker).

For example, suppose an accountant is preparing a set of financial statements in the knowledge that the company will use those as the basis for an application to extend a loan. If the application fails then the company will be unable to continue and its workforce will lose their jobs. The accountant knows from experience and from studying correspondence with the bank that a truthful report concerning the company's performance and financial position will not satisfy the bank's lending criteria. The accountant knows that it would be possible to manipulate the financial statements using an extremely misleading creative accounting technique to satisfy the bank.

In this case, the accountant could feel that there is an ethical dilemma between her duty to the bank (which requires a truthful report in order to make a decision about the important matter of whether to continue the loan) and her duty to the workforce (which requires her to manipulate the financial statements in order to protect the jobs that are at risk).

There is a long-standing argument that ethical duties can be categorised as either positive or negative and that such a distinction can sometimes simplify the whole process of resolving ethical dilemmas (Table 3.1).

In this case, the accountant can view the dilemma as a choice between a positive duty to preserve the jobs of the workforce and a negative duty to avoid misleading the bank by supplying misleading information. Happily (or otherwise), the philosophers have provided us with an argument that negative duties tend to outweigh positive duties whenever they come into conflict.

Table 3.1 Positive and negative ethical duties

Positive duties	A positive duty involves acting to do some good. The decision-maker is attempting to pursue some desirable outcome. This approach is sometimes described as 'teleological'.
Negative duties	A negative duty involves refraining from acting unethically. It is based on the idea that certain actions (such as lying) are inherently wrong and that they should not be undertaken. This approach is sometimes described as 'deontological'.

Relentlessness

Positive duties can never be discharged entirely. That suggests that any ethical decision-maker should not be burdened with a positive duty because it will never be possible to discharge it.

In our example, the workforce will always face the threat of losing their jobs. It may be possible for profits to be raised through redundancies, automation or relocation of factories. If the accountant wishes to prevent that from happening then it will become necessary to manipulate and distort both internal and external reports in order to mislead the shareholders and the directors. The threat of job losses will never disappear altogether and so any positive duty to preserve jobs will never be fully discharged.

Certainty of Outcome

Positive duties are largely about creating benefit. It could be argued that the desired outcome could occur in some other way. For example, the bank could be willing to grant the loan, even if the financial statements are prepared honestly, if management can make a convincing argument to the effect that the company is sound. Or the jobs could be preserved if the company can obtain funding to repay the loan from some other source. The accountant cannot know with absolute certainty that manipulating the accounts is the only way to preserve the jobs that are at risk.

Breaching a negative duty will always involve an ethical failure. It is always wrong to lie (or to cheat, kill, break the law, or whatever). If the accountant falsifies the figures to be presented to the bank then there is no doubt that an unethical act has occurred (even if it is motivated by a sense of compassion or concern for the workforce). Furthermore, there is no certainty that the positive outcome could not have been obtained in some other way.

Responsibility

We may be responsible for doing good, but we are not always responsible for pursuing every good outcome on every occasion. It could be argued that the accountant may have a responsibility for working towards the wellbeing and security of more junior colleagues, but it is highly unlikely that it is genuinely part of the accountant's direct responsibility to provide all staff with lifelong employment opportunities.

We are always responsible for any unethical acts that we perpetrate. The accountant is clearly responsible for the dishonesty involved in lying to the bank (again, regardless of the motive for doing so).

The question of responsibility can be complicated by the circumstances in the sense that, say, an employee may have a contractual duty to pursue the best interests of an employer. That may be sufficient to justify an act that breaches a negative duty. For example, a driver may be ordered to follow a route that wastes fuel but avoids a toll bridge. The driver may feel that saving the employer's money is a positive duty and avoiding unnecessary emissions by burning fossil fuels needlessly is a negative duty. Even so, it would probably be acceptable for the driver to follow the designated route and leave the ethical dilemma of cash versus the environment to his employer. That would be justified on the basis that the driver accepted that he would follow such orders when he signed his contract of employment. That argument does not absolve the driver of all responsibility. If the employer ordered the driver to do something illegal, such as driving a vehicle that was not properly insured to be on the road, then the driver could not simply delegate the responsibility for breaking the law to the company. In that case, the driver's negative duty to avoid breaking the law would override the positive duty to maximise the employer's profit.

Is That All There Is to It?

Clearly, the distinction between positive and negative duties may help in some cases, but it can be a clumsy and inappropriate distinction. For example, a trivial negative duty may not override a significant positive duty. It is potentially dangerous to classify a professional duty as 'trivial', but suppose our accountant had promised to meet a friend for lunch and honouring that arrangement would delay the submission of the application for the loan renewal so that the application would be automatically rejected because it arrived after a very strict deadline. If we define the dilemma strictly in terms of the positive duty to protect the employees' jobs against the negative duty to refrain from breaking a relatively insignificant promise to a friend then there can be little doubt that the positive duty outweighs the negative duty on this occasion. (There could be other ways to frame the deadline dilemma – it could be argued that insisting on a lunch break at a time when the company really required the accountant's presence was in itself a breach of the accountant's employment contract.) This topic is explored in more detail in Ruland and Lindblom, 1992.

More about Ethical Decisions

Rest, a theorist who has contributed to the psychological study of ethical decision-making, proposed the following four steps associated with making an ethical decision (Rest, 1986):

• Firstly, the decision-maker must recognise that there is a moral issue involved in the decision. That normally requires an understanding that the selection of a particular course of action will affect the welfare of other interested parties. If decision-makers are not sufficiently sensitive to ethical considerations then they will act in accordance with habit or by considering the technical aspects only. For example, suppose a commercial bank has approached a company's finance director with details of a complicated and potentially misleading creative accounting scheme. If our finance director lacks sensitivity, then that approach may be evaluated on the basis of the technical accounting arguments and the bank's fee. It may not even occur to the finance director that ethics are involved in deciding whether to adopt the scheme.

• Secondly, the decision-maker must be able to select an appropriate action. That may require the use of a decision aid, such as framing the decision in terms of positive or negative duties or it may be a matter of seeking advice or acting upon conscience. It may not be clear to our finance director whether it is more important to report truthfully or to maximise the company's share price.

• Thirdly, the decision-maker must attach priority to moral values. In other words, the decision-maker may choose to ignore the fact that the chosen course of action has been identified as 'wrong' and may act out of greed, fear or some other form of self-interest. The finance director may decide that a larger personal bonus is more important than providing the shareholders with accurate accounting information.

• Finally, the decision-maker must have sufficient moral strength to implement the resolution identified in the previous three steps. There is a difference between setting out with the intention of behaving 'properly' and actually making the sacrifices that are usually involved in doing so. Our finance director could reject the bank's scheme initially, but could then be pressured by the rest of the board if the projected financial statements appear disappointing. It is relatively easy to behave correctly when there is no cost associated with doing so. It may be difficult to adhere to principles if doing so creates the risk of being dismissed or losing a large bonus.

Research into ethical decision-making has tended to become quite focused on the manner in which ethical dilemmas are resolved. One reason for doing so is that research instruments have been developed in order to establish how decisions are arrived at. That is not to say that this step is necessarily any more important than any of the others, but it is likely to be the most accessible for any study. For example, moral strength is very difficult to observe in practice. Even if decision-makers could be persuaded to answer interview questions on the matter, they would not necessarily know whether they would be willing to make whatever sacrifices putting the morally correct course of action into effect would require.

Moral Development

Lawrence Kohlberg developed a framework that can be used to study the manner in which moral decisions are arrived at. His argument was that every individual passes through a series of stages that are distinguished in terms of the manner in which ethical dilemmas are resolved. Individuals start at the first stage and progress until they reach their limits. Progression from one stage to the next is influenced by experience and education. Most individuals fail to progress much beyond the middle stages.

The first two stages are associated with behaving in a self-interested manner that focuses on avoidance of punishment or a desire to earn some sort of reward. Such behaviour traits will be familiar to anybody who has ever observed the behaviour of a young child. Collectively, these stages are referred to as the 'preconventional' level.

The third and fourth stages make up the 'conventional' level. By this level, individuals recognise that they have a place within a society that imposes rules and norms. Generally, ethical dilemmas are dealt with in terms of those rules and norms, although that is not necessarily because of fear of punishment. There could also be a sense that obeying the law is the right thing to do for the sake of society. Those individuals who are at this level can be thought of as rule-followers who do not generally consider dilemmas in terms of personal principles or conscience.

Finally, the fifth and sixth stages comprise the postconventional level. Essentially, those at this level tend to respect society's rules, but they may be prepared to set aside any rules and norms that they perceive to be unjust and base any decisions on their principles.

Progression through the stages determines the manner in which a moral judgement is made. It is largely a matter of attitudes toward rules rather than a sense of those at the higher levels behaving in a more correct or ethical manner. An individual who operates mainly at the conventional level will not necessarily be any less moral or ethical than an individual who operates at the postconventional level. The conventional thinker will be more likely to resolve a problem in terms of rules and regulations while the postconventional thinker may be prepared to think beyond the rules.

The Defining Issues Test

Rest built upon Kohlberg's work by developing a test instrument, called the Defining Issues Test (or DIT), to measure respondents' tendency to operate at the postconventional level. This instrument presents a series of moral dilemmas and asks respondents to answer a series of questions concerning their reactions to the problem. The questions are designed to bring out the manner in which the respondent deals with the dilemma and there are internal checks that are designed to pick out inconsistent answers from respondents who are trying to raise their scores by misrepresenting their attitudes. The DIT has been used in many hundreds of published studies by academics from a huge variety of fields, including accountancy.

The DIT instrument is frequently described by summarising the first dilemma from the original version of the test. 'Heinz's dilemma' involves a man whose terminally ill wife requires a drug that Heinz cannot afford to buy. A number of questions deal with the question of whether Heinz should steal this drug. These are designed to determine whether the respondent is motivated most by fear of the penalties for theft (preconventional), a desire to uphold the law (conventional) or a willingness to engage in a principled consideration of the relative importance of life over property rights (postconventional).

The original instrument has been replaced by an updated version (DIT-2). In this version, Heinz's dilemma has been replaced with a scenario concerning a poverty-stricken father who must decide whether to steal food from a rich man's warehouse in order to feed his starving family. The dilemmas are all designed to be accessible to almost any reader so that they can be used to evaluate respondents from all sorts of backgrounds.

The DIT test generates a P score statistic that equates to the respondent's tendency to operate at the postconventional level. It is important to note that moral development should be thought of in terms of tendencies and so an individual with a low P score may still refer to principles on some occasions, just as an individual with a high score may rely on rules for certain decisions.

An early publication by Rest (1994) summarised the use of the test by listing average scores from different social groups (Table 3.2).

Generally, each person has an innate limit to his or her moral development. Everybody starts at the preconventional level and progresses through being exposed to moral dilemmas until that limit is reached. Exposure to dilemmas is generally related to a combination of age and experience, although education can also play a part in accelerating that process. It is unusual for moral development to decline once an individual has reached his or her potential.

Accountants' P Scores

The DIT test has been used to measure accountants' P scores at various stages of their professional development, from university right through their careers and in several different countries. The most consistent finding is that accountants generally report very low P scores. For example, Figure 3.1 illustrates a fairly typical set of findings.

Table 3.2 Average DIT score by social group

	P score
Moral philosophy doctoral students	65
Theology students	60
Advanced law students	52
Practising medical physicians	50
Average college students	42
Average adults in general	40
Average senior high students	32
Average junior high students	22
Institutionalised delinquent 16-year-old boys	19

Source: Rest (1994)

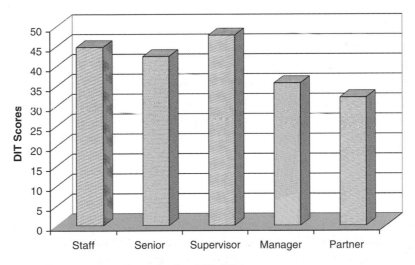

Figure 3.1 Cross-sectional results for 180 CPAs
Source: Based on Ponemon (1992)

The two features of the diagram in Figure 3.1 are that the scores reported across the various stages of career progression are relatively low, with accountants generally being lower than those who have participated in higher education. There is also a concerning trend for the scores of managers and partners to be lower than those of their junior staff. That trend could be read in a variety of ways. One possibility is that those with higher scores tend to leave through choice and another is that those with higher P scores tend to find it difficult to obtain promotion.

The low P score is a fairly robust finding in this area of research, which tends to suggest that accountants are generally rule-followers. (There is a useful summary of some of the accounting studies that make use of the DIT test in Bailey, Scott and Thoma, 2010.)

So What Are the Rules?

The International Federation of Accountants (IFAC) has a standard-setting body called The International Ethics Standards Board for Accountants (IESBA), which sets ethical standards for professional accountants. IESBA has published a Code of Ethics, which is supported by a 150-page handbook (International Federation of Accountants, 2010). The Code is split into three sections:

- Part A – General Application of the IESBA Code
- Part B – Professional Accountants in Public Practice
- Part C – Professional Accountants in Business.

The Code of Ethics comprises a general discussion of ethical behaviour in accounting in Part A and then expands on that in Parts B and C. Arguably, accountants in public practice are likely to encounter different problems from those in business and so there is an argument for having two separate sets of guidance for each of those situations. For example, an accountant in public practice may be responsible for preparing reports on behalf of third parties and that may create different pressures than those that affect an accountant who is employed within an entity and reports to its directors.

Fundamental Principles

Part A of the Code of Ethics sets out the fundamental principles that should govern an ethical accountant's decisions:

• Integrity – accountants should be straightforward and honest in their professional and business relationships.

• Objectivity – accountants should not permit bias, conflict of interest or undue influence to affect their professional or business judgements.

• Professional competence and due care – accountants should maintain their professional knowledge and skill and should keep up to date with any developments. Their work should reflect those technical standards.

• Confidentiality – accountants should not disclose information gathered in the course of professional and business relationships to third parties without proper authority.

• Professional behaviour – accountants should comply with relevant laws and regulations and should not act in a manner that will discredit the accountancy profession.

The first point to notice about the fundamental principles is that they reduce ethics to specific aspects of behaviour that say little or nothing about the morality of an accountant's behaviour. If, for the sake of argument, an accountant felt that there could be a moral justification for misstating the information in an application for a bank loan then the principles of integrity and objectivity would tend to avoid any consideration of that concern because they would both require a truthful report.

Another issue is that the duties are not absolute. For example, an accountant is required to treat all information obtained in the course of employment or a professional appointment as confidential. The Code of Ethics does permit some fairly significant exceptions to that duty. For example, it is acceptable to disclose information in order to comply with a quality review undertaken by a professional body or in order to offer a defence against any legal proceedings. Thus, an accountancy firm could make confidential files available regardless of the duty of confidence. The accountant may also disclose when disclosure is required by law. For example, UK accountants are required to report suspicions of money laundering to the authorities and so an employer or client cannot expect to hide behind this duty of confidence.

Overall, the principles appear to be designed to protect the credibility of the accountancy profession. That is most obvious in the principle of professional behaviour that forbids accountants from making negative comments about, say, competitors.

Public Practice

Accountants in public practice fulfil many roles, but it could be argued that the most important of these is the external audit of financial statements. External auditors gather evidence and form an opinion on the financial statements prepared by the company's directors. Their report enhances the credibility of the financial statements and reassures users of the accounts that they can rely on them for stewardship and decision-making purposes.

There are particular threats associated with public practice that have the potential to undermine the application of the fundamental principles. For example, the accountant's fee income is typically dependent upon retaining business from clients. That is frequently dependent upon avoiding any form of conflict with the directors, even when the appointment is to ensure that the directors have not abused their authority. The best example of this is the annual external audit. In many countries, including the UK, the external auditor is appointed by the shareholders. In theory, that prevents the auditor from being removed from office unfairly by the directors. The reality is somewhat different, with the shareholders seeking the advice of the directors on matters relating to the appointment and retention of the auditor.

Many of the examples in this section deal with the accountant as external auditor, but there are other aspects of public practice. For example, accountants frequently offer tax advice and that can include ensuring compliance both with the tax laws and with tax planning. These activities raise ethical issues in terms of deciding how far to press an opportunity to reduce a tax liability. At one extreme, telling an outright lie to evade tax on behalf of a client is clearly unethical. At the other extreme, choosing the least expensive option offered by tax law is perfectly legitimate. In between are various grey areas, such as the creation of artificial tax planning schemes that exploit loopholes in the rules.

The Code of Ethics deals with several threats to the ethical behaviour of an accountant in public practice, shown in Table 3.3.

The Code requires that accountancy firms should develop safeguards to prevent such threats from materialising. These safeguards can include strong and responsible leadership, with senior management demonstrating their commitment to ethical behaviour.

The Code also sets out a variety of detailed provisions concerning the ethical behaviour of accountants in public practice. These cover a number of very specific matters:

- professional appointment
- conflicts of interest
- second opinions
- fees and other types of remuneration
- marketing professional services
- gifts and hospitality
- custody of client assets
- objectivity – all services
- independence – audit and review engagements
- independence – other assurance engagements.

Table 3.3 Threats to the ethical behaviour of accountants in public practice

Self-interest	This threat arises when there is a conflict of interest between the wellbeing of the accountant and that of the client. That could arise if the accountant has a financial interest in the client and acts in order to protect that interest rather than protecting the client. Or the accountant could be motivated by the fee income and could protect that revenue stream at the client's expense.
Self-review	Self-review can arise when the accountant undertakes more than one appointment for the same client and is effectively checking the accounting firm's own work – for example, when the same firm advises on the preparation of financial statements and then audits the resulting figures.
Advocacy	There is the possibility that an accountant could be asked to lobby on behalf of a client. For example, if assisting with a share issue, there could be times when the accountant is acting as both an independent adviser and actively promoting the shares to the public.
Familiarity	A long-serving association with a particular client can lead to both a sense of identity with that client and a tendency to take too much for granted. The accountant may not even realise that this is causing an ethical problem.
Intimidation	Intimidation is related to self-interest. There could be times when the client or the client's directors will attempt to bully or manipulate the accountant into behaving in an unacceptable manner.

Source: International Federation of Accountants (2010)

These sections of the Code of Ethics set out some very detailed regulations. For example, an accountant in public practice cannot accept a professional appointment without first considering whether the firm has sufficient technical skill and can accept an appointment of that size without creating an undue self-interest risk. Furthermore, the accountant must write to the outgoing firm and ask whether there are any reasons, professional or otherwise, for refusing the appointment. The appointment must be refused if the outgoing firm replies that the client will not grant permission to give a full and honest reply. That has the effect of giving all accountants the opportunity to write to their prospective replacements and warn them of any concerns. For example, the outgoing firm may feel that the directors are dishonest bullies and that they are being replaced because they refused to compromise their professional standards.

The rules give an insight into some practices that have caused problems in the past. For example, the section on second opinions deals with a practice called 'opinion shopping', whereby a company's directors would ask a firm of accountants for a written opinion on the suitability of a particular accounting policy or whatever, in a given set of circumstances. That written opinion could then be used to exert pressure upon the audit firm to accept the directors' views on that accounting policy. There are now rules in place to restrict opinion shopping. For example, the firm should have the opportunity to write to the auditor directly to explain the limitations of the opinion and to minimise the extent to which the auditor will be threatened by the prospect of being replaced by a more compliant competitor.

Professional Accountants in Business

The Code of Ethics also sets out specific rules on the behaviour of accountants who are in full-time employment or otherwise engaged within an entity. Basically, the fundamental principles still apply to accountants who are committed to an entity in this way, although the circumstances are clearly different. Society is entitled to expect professionally qualified accountants to behave honestly and with integrity, no matter what.

The same threats to the accountant's ethical behaviour still apply, although the circumstances may alter the response. For example, there is a clear self-interest threat created by the need to protect one's employment. It may also be regarded as acceptable for an accountant to have a financial interest arising from shares and share options granted to employees and managers.

The Code of Ethics sets out a number of sections that deal with specific areas:

- potential conflicts
- preparation and reporting of information
- acting with sufficient expertise
- financial interests
- inducements.

For example, an accountant could face a conflict arising from a request to set aside an International Financial Reporting Standard (IFRS) in order to overstate profits. The accountant should be prepared to respond to such a request, ideally by negotiation with the employer's senior management. It is clearly unacceptable for such a request to be granted.

Teaching Ethics

IFAC has a committee that deals with the education of professionally qualified accountants. The International Accounting Education Standards Board (IAESB) publishes International Education Standards (IES) to which professional accountancy bodies must adhere in the development of their educational programmes and assessments.

IES 4 was published in 2004. It requires IFAC's member bodies to ensure that their educational programmes provide a framework of 'professional values, ethics and attitudes' when educating their students (IAESB, 2004).

IES 4 acknowledges that local cultures and values must be reflected in any ethics programme, but lists a number of topics that must be covered in the overall programme of ethics education:

- the nature of ethics;
- differences of detailed rules-based and framework approaches to ethics, their advantages and drawbacks;
- compliance with the fundamental ethical principles of integrity, objectivity, commitment to professional competence and due care, and confidentiality;
- professional behaviour and compliance with technical standards;
- concepts of independence, scepticism, accountability and public expectations;
- ethics and the profession: social responsibility;
- ethics and law, including the relationship between laws, regulations and the public interest;
- consequences of unethical behaviour to the individual, to the profession and to society at large;
- ethics in relation to business and good governance;
- ethics and the individual professional accountant: whistle-blowing, conflicts of interest, ethical dilemmas and their resolution.

Comparing the above list to the topics covered in the IESBA Code of Ethics suggests that IES 4 is looking for a much fuller understanding of ethics than would be implied by a close reading of the Code. The Code sets out a number of fundamental principles and then provides some very detailed rules that are intended to support these. IES 4 goes into much greater detail on the principles that must be covered.

Bodies have to strike a balance between ensuring acceptable coverage of ethics and presenting ethics as a separate topic that is divorced from the actual practice of accounting. Thus, there is scope for combining both stand-alone ethics papers with integrating ethical dilemmas into more technical papers. The former will ensure that students have an adequate background in ethics while the latter will demonstrate that accountants face ethical dilemmas in answering technical dilemmas. For example, a make or buy decision in a management accounting question could be presented as simply finding the cheapest way to produce the item, but there could also be a question about the implications for the employees whose jobs will be lost if production ceases.

Qualified Accountants

Professional bodies offer their members basic advice on the resolution of ethical dilemmas associated with their working lives. Such advice is necessarily limited in scope because of the potential costs associated with getting directly involved in a whistleblowing scandal.

The ACCA's website (www.accaglobal.com) offers members an electronic guide to lead them through any ethical dilemma. Essentially, this amounts to determining whether any of the fundamental principles would be breached to a material extent by the action that is being contemplated. Where that would occur, the member is advised to refrain from that action.

Clearly, the problem that remains is the potential cost to the accountant who is forced to refuse to act in this way. In an ideal world, the accountant will be able to explain that the behaviour is unethical and the manager or director who made the request will withdraw it. At the other extreme, it is possible that the accountant will be forced to choose between compliance and dismissal if his or her employer refuses to withdraw the instruction.

On a related note, the accountant may also be faced with the problem of knowing that an entity is engaged in wrongdoing that is damaging to the public interest: for example, when an employer is misleading customers when selling financial services. Such knowledge has the potential to create a conflict between the accountant's duty to protect the public interest and the duty of confidentiality.

A number of countries have introduced legislation to protect so-called 'whistleblowers' in the event that they divulge confidential information in order to safeguard the public interest. Such actions are generally complicated because the employee must be able to demonstrate that the report was made in good faith. The disclosure must also be made to the appropriate person or authority. There may be internal mechanisms for dealing with such matters and the whistleblower must have taken the possibility of using those into account before reporting the matter externally.

Whistleblowing is generally a costly thing to do. It would be very difficult to retain one's job after breaching confidentiality in this way. Indeed, it may be very difficult to find another job in the aftermath of a major (e.g., see Lewis, 2008).

Summary

Accountancy is associated with a number of major scandals that have highlighted the costs associated with misleading financial reporting and auditing. The accountancy profession's response has included the development of rules that set out the fundamental principles of good ethical behaviour.

Accountancy is a complicated professional activity. The dilemmas that affect accountants are complicated too. For example, the accountant may have conflicting responsibilities and it may be necessary to weigh up one ethical duty against another.

The accountant's ethical behaviour has been researched and investigated thoroughly. The results of that research indicate that the accountant is typically a rule-follower and does not have the same capacity as most similarly educated professionals to resolve dilemmas using principles and reason.

Professional accountancy bodies are required to educate their student members to deal with ethical dilemmas. The bodies also provide their members with active encouragement to behave in an ethical manner, to the extent of resigning from jobs that would force them to behave unethically and to report any serious misbehaviour to the appropriate authorities.

Tutorial Questions

Question 1

An accountant has been asked to prepare some calculations to determine whether it would be cheaper to close a factory in the home country and move production to a developing country that has lower labour costs.

Discuss the extent to which this assignment involves an ethical dilemma for the accountant.

Question 2

Critically evaluate the assertion that creative accounting is morally justified because users of financial statements can frequently see that the figures have been adjusted in this way.

Question 3

A standard-setting body is considering tightening up the reporting requirements to prevent liabilities from being excluded from the financial statements. It has been argued that the new rules will make it impossible for many companies to raise further finance.

Explain whether the duty to tighten up the standard is a positive or negative duty and use that as the basis for an argument about the correct treatment.

Question 4

Discuss the assertion that it is not necessarily a bad thing for accountants to be rule-followers.

Question 5

The partner of an accountancy firm receives an invitation to have lunch with the finance director of a major client. The partner discovers that the lunch will be in a very expensive restaurant run by a famous chef.

Discuss the ethical implications of accepting this invitation.

Question 6

Would you feel comfortable about having ethics taught to you as part of an assessed course?

Would you feel differently if the ethics component was not assessed?

Questions with Answers

Question 1

A tax adviser's largest and wealthiest client has read about a complicated tax avoidance scheme that would make it possible to pay no tax on more than half of his income.

Discuss the extent to which it is morally acceptable for the accountant to assist in devising such a scheme.

Question 2

Frame the duties associated with offering tax advice, as discussed in question 1 above, as either positive or negative and use the result of your analysis to determine whether it would be appropriate to advise the taxpayer on ways to reduce the tax bill so dramatically.

Question 3

It has been established that staff employed by different accounting firms have different levels of moral development.

Discuss the suggestion that firms ought to use the DIT test to identify staff whose moral development is in line with the firm's average.

Question 4

Explain whether it is acceptable for an audit partner to accept a copy of a client company's calendar as a gift.

References

Bailey, C.D., Scott, I. & Thoma, S.J. (2010) Revitalizing accounting ethics research in the neo-Kohlbergian framework: Putting the DIT into perspective. *Behavioral Research in Accounting* **22**(2) pp. 1–26.

Ching, K., Firth, M. & Rui, O. (2006) Earnings management, corporate governance and the market performance of seasoned equity offerings in Hong Kong. *Journal of Contemporary Accounting & Economics* **2**(1) pp. 73–98.

IAESB (2004) IES 4 *Professional Values, Ethics and Attitudes.*

IASB (2013) *The Conceptual Framework for Financial Reporting.* London: IFRS Foundation/IASB.

International Federation of Accountants (2010) *Handbook of the Code of Ethics for Professional Accountants.* International Ethics Standards Board for Accountants. Available from www.ifac.org (accessed 14 September 2013).

Jones, M. (2010) *Creative Accounting, Fraud and International Accounting Scandals.* Chichester: John Wiley & Sons.

Lewis, D. (2008) Ten years of public interest disclosure legislation in the UK: Are whistleblowers adequately protected? *Journal of Business Ethics* **82**(2) pp. 497–507.

Li, S., Selover, D.D. & Stein, M. (2011) 'Keep silent and make money': Institutional patterns of earnings management in China. *Journal of Asian Economics* **22**(5) pp. 369–382.

Ponemon, L.A. (1992) Auditor under-reporting of time and moral reasoning: An experimental lab study. *Contemporary Accounting Research* **9**(1) pp. 171–189.

Rest, J.R. (1986) *Moral Development: Advances in research and theory.* New York: Praeger Publishers.

Rest, J.R. (1994) Background: Theory and research. In J.R. Rest & D. Narváez (eds) *Moral Development in the Professions*, pp. 1–26. Hillsdale, New Jersey: Lawrence Erlbaum Associates.

Ruland, R.G. & Lindblom, C.K. (1992) Ethics and disclosure: An analysis of conflicting duties. *Critical Perspectives in Accounting* **3**(3) pp. 259–272.

An Overview of
Accounting Problems

Contents

Learning Objectives

After studying this chapter, you should be able to:

- discuss the difficulties faced by accounting standard-setters because of a lack of agreement over recognition and measurement;
- discuss the difficulties arising from the lack of clarity over the boundaries of the reporting entity;
- describe the difficulties arising from the reporting of fair values in financial statements;
- discuss the problems arising from the abuse of professional judgement by preparers of financial statements.

Introduction

The purpose of this chapter is to look ahead to a number of the issues that will be covered in future chapters. The basic argument is that there are some enduring problems that make it difficult for standard-setters to prevent accounting scandals in which financial statements that have complied with all of the rules are still found to be misleading. The message is not totally bleak because it argues that slow progress is being made. The International Accounting Standards Board (IASB) is not afraid to impose changes that will prove unpopular. The initiative will always lie with the preparers who wish to think creatively about ways to work around the rules and so it is somewhat unfair to blame all of accounting's problems on the standard-setters.

Two basic problems are highlighted in this text. The first is that there are unanswered questions about the precise role that accounting should have. These questions amount to deciding who the primary readers of financial statements are. Unless there is absolute clarity on that, then we will always be unsure about exactly how the reporting entity should be defined and how the facts and figures that are disclosed are to be measured. The only alternative would be to resurrect the idea of multiple sets of financial statements, each prepared on a different basis and so useful for its own purpose.

The second basic problem is that some accountants are willing to go to great lengths to find ways to manipulate the impression created by the financial statements. Actually breaking the rules would leave them open to sanctions ranging from disciplinary action by their professional bodies all the way through to possible criminal charges. Exploiting a loophole to publish figures that comply with the rules while creating the desired impression in readers' minds is far less risky.

It should be stressed from the outset that it would be grossly unfair to accuse all company directors and all accountants of being willing to mislead shareholders and other stakeholders. The only sense in which it is possible to generalise is that some preparers of financial statements have behaved in this manner and that has led to a situation where confidence in financial reporting has been damaged.

The More Things Change . . .

Tweedie and Whittington (1990) open their paper with the following paragraph:

Financial reporting has been an area of exceptional innovation in the UK and elsewhere during the past five years or so. Such issues as off-balance sheet financing, accounting for complex capital issues and, more recently, accounting for brand names have become matters of considerable contention and are widely regarded as 'problems' with which the standard setting bodies should deal. The object of this paper is to examine a number of these problems and to identify their common characteristics. We then consider possible systematic principles which the standard setters might adopt in order to cope with these common characteristics and thus eliminate, or at least alleviate, the problems.

One of the most intriguing things about this is that it was published in 1990. Arguably, replacing the reference to accounting for brand names with a more generic reference to accounting for fair values[1] would render the document as current, almost 25 years later, as it was when it was first written. To be fair, the paper then goes on to describe a number of specific matters that have since been addressed by accounting standards before addressing the 'common characteristics of current problems'. These can be classified as 'recognition problems' and 'measurement problems'.

Recognition problems arise largely from difficulties associated with defining the boundaries of the accounting entity, a problem that persists until the present day. It can be difficult to apply the definitions of the elements of accounting because assets are defined in terms of resources controlled by the entity and liabilities are defined in terms of obligations by the entity.

Measurement raises two issues: the issue of valuation and that of the capital maintenance concept. These issues will be discussed in Chapter 7. For now, it is sufficient to state that there are important choices that have to be made. For example, valuation can be expressed in terms of historical cost, replacement cost or market value. Capital maintenance is a matter of deciding when gains and losses in value should be recognised.

Tweedie and Whittington (1990) go on to offer possible remedies, with an emphasis on designing accounting standards that deal with the deeper issues rather than tackling individual problems as and when they arise. Perhaps standards should be broadly defined, with support from detailed interpretations as and when required. Tweedie and Whittington note the tendency to report economic substance as one way to address the problems, but it is not sufficient in itself to ensure comparability between different companies' financial statements.

Both authors have played significant roles in dealing with the problems that they addressed in their paper. Tweedie became chairman of the UK's Accounting Standards Board (ASB) and subsequently went on to head the IASB. Whittington served as academic adviser to the ASB and was a member of the IASB. The standard-setting process has since attempted to address the issues that Tweedie and Whittington highlighted, with significant effort being invested in clarifying the boundaries of the entity and with the introduction of fair value accounting to address many of the concerns relating to measurement. Unfortunately, both problems have been difficult to eradicate entirely.

The Reporting Entity

At the time of writing, the definition of the entity was an ongoing project. The only formal statement on the reporting entity is enshrined in an Exposure Draft (IASB, 2010). This document was issued as one part of a wider project, being conducted jointly between IASB and the Financial Accounting Standards Board (FASB), to both align and strengthen the two bodies' Conceptual Framework documents. The reporting entity was identified as requiring attention because existing documents lacked 'a robust concept of a reporting entity' (FASB, 2008).

The need for review stems partly from the decision as to whether to prepare financial statements on an entity basis or a proprietary basis. Under the entity basis, the reporting entity is deemed to have substance of its own, separate from that of its owners. Under the proprietary basis, the reporting entity does not have substance of its own separately from that of its proprietors or owners.

The proprietary perspective can be seen to have some relevance in accounting for a sole trader or a small partnership, where the owners' interests are being furthered through the use of the resources that they have invested. Any claims by lenders effectively reduce the equity in a very direct and obvious manner.

Virtually all companies of any size have separated ownership from control to such an extent that the proprietary perspective has very little relevance. It makes far more sense to view the business as a separate entity in its own right, one that manages the resources that have been entrusted to it with little or no regard as to whether those resources have been provided by debt or equity.

The International Federation of Accountants (IFAC) and FASB agree that the entity perspective is a far more relevant basis for the preparation of financial statements. The question that follows on from this is the extent to which that decision affects the development of accounting standards. It is relatively easy to argue that the entity perspective can be useful in identifying the primary users of financial statements and the objectives of accounting. The question that remains is whether the decision to adopt the entity perspective has any further significance in the development of accounting standards.

The IASB Exposure Draft (ED) defines the reporting entity as follows (IASB, 2010):

A reporting entity is a circumscribed area of economic activities whose financial information has the potential to be useful to existing and potential equity investors, lenders and other creditors who cannot directly obtain the information they need in making decisions about providing resources to the entity and in assessing whether management and the governing board of that entity have made efficient and effective use of the resources provided.

The ED identifies three features that arise from this definition (IASB, 2010):

• The entity conducts, has conducted or will conduct economic activities.
• The entity's economic activities can be distinguished from those of other entities and from the entity's economic environment.
• Financial information about the entity's economic activities has the potential to be useful in making decisions about providing resources to the entity and in assessing whether its management has made efficient and effective use of the resources provided.

It is acknowledged that these conditions are necessary, but not always sufficient, to identify a reporting entity. To an extent, the definition is a little circular because the usefulness or otherwise cannot be discussed effectively without first providing a hypothetical boundary and considering the extent to which a set of statements for that 'entity' might be rendered more or less useful by expanding or contracting its limits.

There is a presumption that an individual legal entity is likely to be a reporting entity, but the entity may be defined more widely and may not necessarily be a separate legal entity. For example, the preparation of consolidated financial statements may already be familiar to some readers (and this topic will be developed in some detail in Chapters 9 to 13). It is possible to argue that a group of companies is an economic entity whose financial statements are of great value to its stakeholders, regardless of the fact that the group is not necessarily identifiable as a legal identity.

The circular nature of the various decisions that have to be made in setting accounting standards is highlighted by the definitions of assets and liabilities, which are themselves the basis for the definitions of equity, income and expense:

• An asset is a resource controlled by the entity as a result of past events and from which future economic benefits are expected to flow to the entity.

• A liability is a present obligation of the entity arising from past events, the settlement of which is expected to result in an outflow from the entity of resources embodying economic benefits.

So, the entity is defined in terms of economic activities, which are likely to be represented by elements such as assets, liabilities and other elements that will be identified in terms of the limits of the entity. One problem, identified by Tweedie and Whittington, is the meaning of 'expected to', because the degree of uncertainty that is implied will affect the extent to which certain assets and liabilities will be recognised. That, in turn, may feed back into the definition of the entity.

Fair Values

Valuation raises a host of questions about the criteria to be used in determining the most appropriate basis for the valuation of figures in the financial statements. The answers to those questions will have implications for the timing of recognition of profit as well as the amount attributed to assets, liabilities and equity in the statement of financial position. These arguments will be addressed in Chapter 7.

The discussion in this chapter will be restricted to the gradual phasing out of historical cost in favour of fair values for many of the figures in the financial statements. For example, IAS 16 *Property, Plant and Equipment* (IASB, 2001b) permits the use of historical cost less depreciation in certain circumstances, but the standard offers the alterative of reporting fair values instead. It is very common for companies to report fair values for their property, plant and equipment.

The prevalence of fair value accounting has led to the issue of IFRS 13 (IASB, 2011), which is devoted in its entirety to this very subject.

IFRS 13 defines fair value as:

the price that would be received to sell an asset or paid to transfer a liability in an orderly transaction between market participants at the measurement date

Underlying the definition is the notion that there are market forces that determine fair values and that those market forces must be visible if the resulting fair values are to have any meaning.

Fair values should be determined in terms of the asset's 'highest and best use', which could complicate the determination of an appropriate market valuation. For example, a factory may be worth a considerable sum to a house builder, who would demolish the factory building and replace it with houses for resale. Determining the value of the factory could, therefore, require a number of assumptions in order to arrive at a realistic fair value. Those assumptions may have little or nothing to do with the reporting entity's intentions.

IFRS 13 does not, in itself, require the use of fair values. Rather, it deals with the process of determining a fair value in circumstances where their use has been mandated by another standard.

Implications of Fair Value

Whittington (2008) articulates some of the implications of the fair value view of the world. He lists the following main features of the fair value view:

- The sole objective of financial reporting is usefulness for economic decisions.
- The primary users for general purpose financial statements are current and prospective investors and creditors.
- Users' principal information need is related to forecasting future cash flows.
- The primary characteristic required in financial statements is relevance.
- Reliability is less important and is better replaced by representational faithfulness, which implies a greater concern for capturing economic substance rather than statistical accuracy.
- Ideally, accounting information needs to reflect the future, not the past, and so past transactions and events are only peripherally relevant.
- Market prices should give an informed, non-entity-specific estimate of cash flow potential. Markets are generally sufficiently complete and efficient to provide evidence for representationally faithful measurement on this basis.

Whittington offers an 'alternative view' of accounting, which would have the following characteristics:

- Stewardship, defined as accountability to present shareholders, is a distinct objective for accounting, ranking equally with decision usefulness.
- The present shareholders have a special status as users of financial statements.
- Feedback from shareholders (and markets) in response to accounting reports may influence management decisions.
- Reliability is an essential characteristic because financial reporting relieves information asymmetry in an uncertain world.

• Past transactions and events are important both for stewardship and as inputs to the prediction of future cash flows.

• The economic environment is one of imperfect and incomplete markets in which market opportunities will be entity-specific.

Whittington offers this alternative view as a synthesis of arguments expressed by commentators who saw the need for change in accounting but who did not necessarily accept that markets are either complete or perfect. It may be argued that the imperfections of real world markets render the fair value view somewhat naïve. That is not to say that the alternative view is capable of offering simple or coherent solutions to the problems faced by accounting standard-setters, but it does provide a framework within which standards might be set, albeit with a greater need for judgement and the tailoring of solutions to the specific circumstances of entities or their industries.

Whittington does not claim that there is open debate between the proponents of fair values and the alternative view. Effectively, he claims that there has been a tendency for new IFRS to favour fair value as a measurement basis and that some commentators would not necessarily favour the use of fair value in every case. At the very least, reporting fair values will frequently create concerns about valuation.

A Word about Stewardship

The concept of stewardship is rather open ended. In its simplest form, stewardship is about demonstrating honesty in the handling of the company's assets. If the shareholders entrusted the managers with specific resources at the beginning of the year then a basic stewardship report would show whether or not those resources were still there at the reporting date. The valuation basis would make little difference if the objective was to demonstrate that the entity had three machines and a truck at the beginning of the period and that all were present and in good repair at the end. Stewardship could also require some demonstration that the managers had been good stewards, so that the shareholders could be reassured that the entity was making good use of the resources invested in it to create wealth. In that case, the financial statements would have to provide a little more in the way of value as a basis against which revenue and profit could be evaluated.

The distinction between stewardship and economic decision-making can be quite narrow, but it does exist. The UK court case of *Caparo Industries plc* v. *Dickman and Others* (1990) dealt mainly with the external auditor's duties to shareholders and other stakeholders, but a significant part of the court's deliberations in making a judgement on that case was the question of the nature of the decisions that the financial statements are intended to inform, at least in the eyes of the law. The basic decision was that the financial statements were prepared and audited in order to enable the shareholders to scrutinise the directors' financial stewardship. The shareholders as a body are entitled to study the audited financial statements in order to scrutinise the directors' behaviour, but individual shareholders are not entitled to make decisions about holding or selling their investments.

The Caparo case focuses on the specific legal question of whether the shareholders are entitled to sue their external auditor for negligence. Clearly, the case's findings cannot prevent any interested reader from obtaining the financial statements and putting them to any use that they wish. It should be borne in mind, however, that the major accounting firm that was under threat in this case offered the defence that the financial statements were not being prepared to inform economic decisions.

Determining Fair Values

The potential difficulties associated with determining fair values are highlighted by the fact that IFRS 13 offers a 'fair value hierarchy' that prioritises different inputs that might be called upon for measurement purposes (Table 4.1).

For our purposes, it is sufficient to note that fair values will vary in terms of their reliability, depending on their nature. Financial instruments that are freely traded on open markets have visible market prices and so it is easy to argue that they reflect the IFRS 13 definition of fair value being 'the price that would be received to sell an asset . . . ' (IASB, 2011). It may be far more difficult to attach a fair value to many assets for which there is no observable market in identical assets. For example,

Table 4.1 The IFRS 13 fair value hierarchy

Level 1 inputs	Unadjusted quoted prices in active markets for identical assets or liabilities that can be observed at the measurement date.
Level 2 inputs	Observable inputs other than level 1 inputs. For example, quoted prices for similar assets or liabilities in active markets or quoted prices for identical assets or liabilities in markets that are not active.
Level 3 inputs	Unobservable inputs, such as a valuation model that determines a fair value for an unquoted company's shares. That may involve making assumptions about future cash flows and determining a net present value.

properties may be subject to observable market forces, but the fair value of an office block cannot be readily observed. Even if similar properties have sold in that neighbourhood, they may differ in terms of size or proximity to amenities or the prices may not reflect current market conditions. In other words, for many assets and liabilities it will be necessary to report fair values determined using level 3 inputs that are, at best, open to corroboration against other sources.

A paper by Christensen, Glover and Wood (2012), which analysed the difficulties faced by external auditors in dealing with fair values, highlighted the dangers inherent in using management estimates of fair value in financial reporting. The authors estimated the level of estimation uncertainty in two companies that reported fair values for financial assets and compared the result with estimates of the auditors' materiality thresholds for the two companies. In both cases, the estimates indicated that the uncertainty in the valuation was material. The authors went on to argue that accounting information is becoming increasingly complex, but financial statements do not provide adequate disclosure of the resulting uncertainty.

Attitudes of Preparers

So far, this chapter has focused on the theoretical problems identified by Tweedie and Whittington (1990) as arising from a lack of clear agreement on the boundaries of the accounting entity and the difficulties associated with measurement. The remainder of the text will deal with the concerns arising from the phenomenon of earnings management.

Earnings management can comprise a host of different forms of behaviour. Ball (2009) lists a number of forms that the practice may take:

• structuring transactions with regard to their effect on the financial statements (leasing being a prominent example);
• timing asset sales to book gains in years with lower profits, and to book losses in years with higher profits;
• giving year end quantity discounts to major customers, generating sales 'pull forwards', but failing to disclose that they inflate current earnings and borrow against future earnings;
• knowingly failing to comply with GAAP.

Ball asserts that accounting frauds share three properties:

1. Inability to meet performance expectations
2. Personal costs – pecuniary or non-pecuniary – of failing to meet expectations
3. Being able to convince oneself that real performance will improve soon.

There would be relatively little point in fraudulent reporting if expectations will be met or exceeded anyway. Managers are generally keen to avoid exceeding expectations for fear of raising unrealistic expectations for the future.

The personal costs could arise from profit-related remuneration, but they could just as easily be reputational.

Many frauds will be difficult to maintain in the long term. For example, the Parmalat scandal in 2003 involved the booking of fictitious revenues, which the directors attempted to conceal by falsifying a bank balance of €3.95bn. Logically, there is a limit to the extent to which distortions can be concealed in the long term and so accounting manipulations may be motivated by a desire to survive a short-term setback, in the hope that the underlying business will recover before the fraud is discovered.

Ball's (2009) paper concludes with an extensive discussion of the role of both legislation and market forces in dealing with accounting fraud. He concludes with the rather chilling observation:

Markets need rules, and rely on trust. U.S. financial markets historically had very effective rules by world standards, the rules were broken, and there were immense consequences for the transgressors. The system worked surprisingly well in detecting but not in preventing the problem.

It should be noted, however, that many of the major accounting scandals have involved accounting practices that are by no means fraudulent. Indeed, most of Ball's list of earnings management practices would almost certainly be classified as misleading and unethical but would not actually involve breaking the rules or even failing to comply with IFRS.

Playing the Daft Laddie

One of the most effective approaches to manipulating the financial statements without actually breaking the rules is to pretend to misunderstand the situation.[2] For example, lease accounting is under review at the time of writing. A detailed discussion of accounting for leases is beyond the scope of this text, but the essence is relatively straightforward. In the dim and distant past it was relatively common for companies to finance the acquisition of property, plant and equipment by taking out long-term leases. There were several advantages to using leasing instead of taking out a straightforward loan in order to purchase the asset, one of which was the fact that the asset was never the lessee's property.

Most companies accounted for the lease by writing off the annual lease payments as an expense, without ever recognising either an asset or a liability in the financial statements. That meant that the gearing ratio and return on capital employed were both more attractive than they would have been if the company had borrowed.

This state of affairs could not continue because it was potentially very misleading. There were some accounting scandals in the 1970s that arose when lessees ran into difficulties because they could not keep up with their lease payments. One notable case was an airline that had leased its aircraft. Its finances looked strong, right up until the moment it collapsed unexpectedly, leaving many holidaymakers stranded with no way to get home. The airline had overcommitted itself to lease payments that it could not sustain from its operating cash flows.

The problem faced by standard-setters is that only some leases have the characteristics of debt. If a lease has the effect of granting the use of an asset to the lessee for the whole of its useful life then it is reasonable to assume that the lease payments will be similar in timing and amount to the payments of interest and principal on a loan, and so there is an argument that the lease should be accounted for as a loan from the lessor and the corresponding asset as an asset in the lessee's books.[3] Unfortunately, the same cannot be said of all leases. For example, it would make little sense to capitalise the cost of a van that had been rented for a week to provide extra delivery capacity during a busy period.

The Problem With Definitions

Leases that last the whole life of the leased asset can easily be classified as financing arrangements and those that last for a very short part of the asset's life cannot. Each is easy to classify. The problem is in deciding how to deal with an arrangement that falls somewhere in between. Suppose a van that has an estimated useful life of five years is leased for three. How should that be accounted for?

In the UK, the first standard dealing with leases was Statement of Standard Accounting Practice (SSAP) 21 *Accounting for Leases and Hire Purchase Contracts*, which was published in 1984.[4] SSAP 21 identified two categories of lease: finance leases and operating leases. If a lease contract committed the lessee to making payments that had a net present value in excess of 90% of the fair value of the asset, then it was classified as a finance lease and the value of the lease had to be capitalised as both an asset and a liability. If the lease did not meet the definition of a finance lease, then it was classed as an operating lease, which meant that the lease payments were simply written off as an expense as and when they were incurred.

The 90% threshold was a reasonable basis for distinguishing finance leases from operating leases. However, it became common for leasing companies to structure the lease contracts so that long-term leases that were essentially finance leases in nature were worth very slightly less than the 90% limit and so they could legitimately be treated as operating leases.

The fact that lessees were prepared to seek out such leases is significant because it makes it clear that some accountants are prepared to abuse loopholes in rules and regulations in order to present misleading financial statements. That attitude lies at the heart of the concerns expressed by Ball (2009).

The IASB addressed the problem of leases in IAS 17, *Leases* (IASB, 2001c) by describing a finance lease as 'a lease that transfers substantially all the risks and rewards incidental to ownership of an asset'. Thus, there is a clear statement of the spirit underlying the distinction between a finance lease and an operating lease. If the lessee has acquired the risks and rewards of owning the asset then it is a finance lease and there are some commonsense questions that can be asked.[5] In theory, that should make it difficult to structure a long-term lease that is effectively a finance lease so that it can be accounted for as an operating lease. (It could be argued that if there is any real doubt as to which type of lease it is, then it is probably a finance lease.)

Unfortunately, the application of IAS 17 suggests that defining the essence of a finance lease is not sufficient to ensure that finance leases are properly accounted for. In fact, the IASB (2012) is considering a revision to the rules so that any lease that has a duration of more than 12 months will be capitalised at the net present value of the lease payments as at the commencement of the lease. In principle, the distinction between finance and operating leases will be eliminated altogether.

When Definitions Fail

The point of this discussion is that accountants are apparently willing to abuse any scope that any accounting standard gives to manipulate the impression created by the financial statements. This tendency is so pronounced that standard-setters are considering the elimination of professional judgement from accounting for leases. Doing so will mean that genuine operating leases will now be accounted for in a manner that is not necessarily appropriate.

This will not be the first time that standard-setters have been forced to eliminate professional judgement. For example, IAS 1, *Presentation of Financial Statements*, (IASB, 2001a) states that 'An entity shall not present any items of income or expense as extraordinary items, in the statement(s) presenting profit or loss and other comprehensive income or in the notes'. In the past, it was possible to classify costs and revenues as 'extraordinary' if they were material, non-recurring and outwith the normal scope of business activity. Extraordinary items were disregarded when calculating the earnings per share ratio and a number of other figures. Indeed, profit was reported both before and after extraordinary items. Unfortunately, it proved extremely difficult to define extraordinary items in such a way that only truly 'extraordinary' events were treated as such. Many companies reported extraordinary items every year, almost always expenses, with the intention of overstating their earnings per share.

In theory, extraordinary events were meant to be so unusual that it would be impossible to fully appreciate the company's performance unless the event was treated separately. For example, a massive and catastrophic accident that led to massive uninsured costs would and should be regarded as extraordinary. In practice, anything that was mildly unusual would be classified as an extraordinary item. For example, costs associated with downsizing and restructuring were commonly treated as extraordinary even though many of the companies who did so were incurring such expenses on an annual basis.

The standard-setters attempted to define extraordinary items more narrowly in order to prevent this abuse, but the only solution that worked was to forbid the classification of any event as extraordinary. As with our earlier discussion of lease accounting, there was a clear understanding of what should be classed as extraordinary and what should not. Unfortunately, that was a matter for professional judgement and the response of many accountants was to abuse that judgement in order to overstate profit before extraordinary items. That does leave the possibility that there will be genuinely extraordinary occurrences that can no longer be accounted for in an appropriate manner because of the more restrictive regulations.

Summary

This chapter has dealt with some problems that have affected confidence in financial reporting. It has been necessary to focus on threats and scandals and, in the process, may have presented an unduly bleak picture of the state of accounting. As with most aspects of life, it is important to have a sense of perspective. Readers of financial statements should not accept everything that they read blindly, without considering the possibility that the figures are not necessarily prepared in a manner that suits their needs. The quality of the information is also dependent, to some extent, on the integrity of the people responsible for the preparation of the financial statements. It would be naïve to assume that company accounts are always prepared honestly and with the desire to state the truth. (It would also be just as naïve to assume that the figures are always prepared in a misleading way with the intent to mislead.)

The readings cited in this chapter have been written by authors who are both respected as academics and largely supportive of the accountancy profession. It would have been relatively easy to have found more extreme criticisms from authors whose research is theorised using a more disruptive political stance. The hope is that these arguments will lead to a more sceptical reading of the rules when working through future chapters rather than an outright rejection of them.

Tutorial Questions

Question 1

Is it acceptable for the chapter on the accounting entity to be missing from the IASB's Conceptual Framework document?

What are the implications for the credibility of the Conceptual Framework if a chapter can be withdrawn without immediate replacement?

Question 2

The debate concerning the choice of measurement basis arises partly because it is unclear whether financial statements should be prepared in order to assist with economic decisions or to demonstrate good stewardship.

Discuss the implications for the accountancy profession of focusing more on stewardship than on informing economic decisions.

Question 3

Discuss the relative merits of the entity and proprietary bases for accounting for each of the following companies:

- An engineer has a consultancy that is incorporated as a company. She owns 100% of the equity. The engineer is a recognised authority in her area of expertise and she is the only member of professional staff.
- An individual owns 100% of the equity in a company that employs three engineers who are experts in a particular field. The engineers are all employees of the company.
- A quoted engineering consultancy employs 200 engineering professionals to deliver advice about product design and development. The company has a widespread body of shareholders, but five of the most senior engineers founded the company and they own 18% of the shares between them.

Question 4

Discuss the potential advantages and disadvantages of accounting for assets on the basis of historical costs rather than fair values.

Question 5

A bank purchased a crane to a lessee's specifications. Discuss the extent to which it is likely that the lease is a finance lease, based on that information alone.

Question 6

Prepare an argument that justifies the use of a loophole in accounting standards to enhance the reported profit figure.

Discuss the extent to which you are convinced by your own arguments.

Questions with Answers

Question 1

A company's draft statement of profit or loss shows operating profit of $100m and its statement of financial position shows equity of $400m and debt of $250m.

An internal report shows that these figures were prepared on a basis that complies with the letter of IFRS, but not their spirit. The application of the spirit of the standards would increase operating profit by $2m and debt by $60m.

Calculate the return on capital employed and gearing ratio for this company using both the draft figures and 'corrected' figures based on the spirit of the rules.

Comment on the results.

Question 2

Discuss the argument that dishonest accountants will always be found out and that market forces will deter the abuse of loopholes.

Question 3

Discuss the argument that the IASB could defeat manipulative accounting practices by eliminating accounting choices, as proposed for lease accounting and as happened in the case of accounting for extraordinary items.

Endnotes

1. The basic argument about accounting for brand names could be reduced to the question of whether these assets' fair values could or should be reported in the financial statements.

2. Scottish people refer to this strategy as 'playing the daft laddie'; in other words, winning an unwinnable argument by pretending not to understand the other party's position and refusing to enter into a debate.
3. This is also very consistent with the IASB's definition of an asset. If the lessee is free to use the asset as it wishes for its entire useful life then the lessee has control and so the asset should be recognised. This definition was not available at the time of the initial debate about lease accounting.
4. Statements of Standard Accounting Practice were published by the UK's Accounting Standards Steering Committee (latterly renamed the Accounting Standards Committee) from 1971 to 1990.
5. Who is responsible for maintaining the asset and insuring it? Who will bear the loss if it is lost or damaged? Can the lessee cancel the lease if the asset is found to be unsuitable or surplus to requirements or if it becomes obsolete?

References

Ball, R. (2009) Market and political/regulatory perspectives on the recent accounting scandals. *Journal of Accounting Research* **47**(2) pp. 277–323.

Christensen, B.E., Glover, S.M. & Wood, D.A. (2012) Extreme estimation uncertainty in fair value estimates: Implications for audit assurance. *Auditing: A Journal of Practice and Theory* **31**(1) pp. 127–146.

FASB (2008) *Conceptual Framework for Financial Reporting: The objective of financial reporting and qualitative characteristics and constraints of decision-useful financial reporting information.* Exposure Draft 1570-100.

IASB (2001a) IAS 1 *Presentation of Financial Statements.*

IASB (2001b) IAS 16 *Property, Plant and Equipment.*

IASB (2001c) IAS 17 *Leases.*

IASB (2010) *Conceptual Framework for Financial Reporting – The reporting entity.* Exposure Draft ED/2010/2.

IASB (2011) IFRS 13 *Fair Value Accounting.*

IASB (2012) *Investor Spotlight: Potential changes to lessee accounting.* IASB, 14 December.

Tweedie, D., & Whittington, G. (1990) Financial reporting: Current problems and their implications for systematic reform. *Accounting and Business Research* **21**(81) pp. 87–102.

Whittington, G. (2008) Fair value and the IASB/FASB Conceptual Framework project: An alternative view. *Abacus* **44**(2) pp. 139–168.

ACCOUNTING AND CORPORATE GOVERNANCE

Contents

Learning Objectives

After studying this chapter, you should be able to:

- identify governance issues;
- explain the mechanisms that are often put in place to ensure sound governance;
- describe the role of governance codes;
- discuss the accounting issues arising from share-based payments.

Introduction

'Corporate governance' is a collective term used to describe the various issues arising from the management of companies and the relationships between stakeholders. The term came into common usage in the 1990s, in the aftermath of a number of corporate scandals.

At its core, corporate governance is a matter of dealing with the conflicting pressures faced by directors. Regardless of their honesty and integrity, there is always an opportunity open to a board of directors or an individual executive to profit from misbehaviour. There has been a relatively small number of major corporate frauds that have undermined confidence in company directors. The response has been the creation of new rules on governance mechanisms and disclosures.

This chapter provides a brief overview of some of the key issues associated with governance, focusing primarily on those that are likely to have an impact (direct or indirect) on financial reporting. Governance can be studied from a variety of different perspectives. Classes in auditing, finance and economics could just as easily deal with governance. Indeed, it is often taught as a discrete class in its own right.

The management of corporate governance is often a matter of managing conflicting objectives. The history of stock options is but one possible example. In the distant past, these were regarded as a threat to directors' integrity. More recently, they were popular with shareholders because they gave the directors an incentive to increase the share price. More recently still, they have been discredited by scandals involving the manipulation of share prices by dishonest directors. That has led to a parallel series of changes in the accounting treatment of share-based payments that has been designed to capture expenses in the financial statements that might otherwise have been excluded on the basis of both relevance and valuation difficulties.

What is Corporate Governance?

In the broadest possible terms, corporate governance is simply the collective term for the structures, processes, cultures and systems that are associated with the management of an organisation. The phrase came into common use during the 1990s, during a period when there were a number of major business scandals. The scandals resulted in a loss of confidence in company directors, which prompted attempts to reassure shareholders and other stakeholders.

A series of cases in the UK prompted the business establishment to form a committee, under the chairmanship of Sir Adrian Cadbury. The Cadbury Committee published a report that set out a series of recommendations for the management of UK quoted companies. That report has since gone through a series of revisions, including changes of title, culminating in the UK Corporate Governance Code, the most recent version of which was published in 2012 (Financial Reporting Council, 2012).

It is difficult to discuss corporate governance without focusing on mismanagement and dishonesty. The driving force behind many of the changes to regulation often boils down to the incidence of corporate failures and directors' mismanagement. That is unfortunate because reading about the reasoning behind the rules can create the impression that company directors are dishonest, incompetent or both. As with many walks of life, misbehaviour by a minority of directors has threatened the credibility of all of them.

Agency Theory

Limited companies make it possible for large numbers of shareholders to concentrate their wealth in investments in large and economically efficient entities. That makes it necessary to appoint full-time directors to manage those entities and for individual shareholders to delegate control to those directors. If the directors are keen to work in the shareholders' best interests, then that arrangement will be mutually advantageous to all concerned. The directors will have well paid and rewarding careers and the shareholders will receive profits through dividends and capital growth in their share prices.

The problems associated with this arrangement arise from the possibility that the directors will be tempted to act in their own interests to the detriment of the shareholders. In the most extreme and blatant cases, they may abuse their positions to defraud the shareholders. In the worst possible case, that could be sufficient to bring about the company's downfall. Less extreme forms of misbehaviour include the payment of excessive management remuneration. If the directors are left to manage the company as they see fit without any oversight, then each will be happy to vote for a salary structure that offers every board member a lavish reward. Self-interest could also make the directors reluctant to pursue opportunities that are in the shareholders' interests. For example, the directors may reject a slightly risky investment project that offers a realistic prospect of success because most of the benefit will be enjoyed by the shareholders. In the event that the project fails, the directors may be blamed for the *ex post* outcome, despite the fact that the *ex ante* analysis was promising.

Agency theory is a branch of economics that deals with the possibility that agents will act in their own self-interests rather than pursuing the interests of the principals who appointed them. To a large extent it is irrelevant whether those agents will actually misbehave because the principals will have to make decisions based on their perceptions. Thus, the suspicion that directors might abuse their positions may be sufficient to deter potential shareholders from investing.

Agency theory was described in some detail in a seminal paper by Jensen and Meckling (1976). Their study was followed by a host of papers that start with the basic agency relationship and study its implications.

In an ideal world, it would be possible to align the interests of agents and principals so that the agency problem was eliminated. It is difficult to do so in practice. For example, profit-related pay creates an incentive for directors to maximise profit, but it can be possible to abuse that mechanism:

- First of all, maximising short-term profits may not always be in the shareholders' best interest. For example, investing less on research or staff training could reduce costs in the short term, but the company could suffer in the longer term when products are out of date or there are too few trained staff.
- The directors may still profit from overspending. For example, first class travel for directors will reduce profits but the directors will enjoy 100% of the benefit from that expenditure and their profit-related bonuses are likely to be reduced by only a relatively small amount.
- The reported profit could be manipulated and so the directors' performance could be misunderstood.

It is clear that the agency threats have not prevented the creation of major multinational corporations, many of which are largely funded by shareholders' equity. In practice, these agency issues have been addressed in a number of ways. These will be discussed in the following section. It will be no surprise that accounting has played a major role in this.

Limitations of Agency Theory

It is worth noting that agency theory reduces people to mathematical formulae, whose behaviour can be predicted in terms of economic self-interest. The advantage of doing so is that human behaviour is endlessly complex and the purpose of any model is to simplify an issue so that it can be understood. It is clear, however, that the price of simplification is that the results may be open to distortion. Tinker and Okcabol (1991) deal with that to great effect in their paper on the limitations of agency theory.[1] For example, if management fraud and other forms of white collar crime are analysed using agency theory it seems illogical that company directors would ever refrain from fraud. There is only a slim chance of being discovered and the likelihood of a successful prosecution is even slimmer. Once convicted, the penalties are generally not as serious as for other major crimes. The authors' point is that very few individuals engage in this criminal behaviour and so they cannot really be modelled effectively using agency theory. (The authors are *not* recommending a life of crime or that readers should engage in any of the other forms of behaviour that could be shown to make rational economic sense according to this paper!)

Controlling Agents

A number of mechanisms have been developed to protect the interests of share-holders. A full discussion of these would take an entire book in itself (see, for example, Solomon, 2010). This section will outline some of the ways in which directors are made accountable.

Codes

Many countries have developed codes that deal with governance issues. Reference has already been made to the UK Corporate Governance Code (Financial Reporting Council, 2012). In the US, the Sarbanes–Oxley Act was introduced in 2002 in response to the financial and accounting scandals of Enron and WorldCom and the alleged failure of the accounting firm Arthur Andersen. The main aim of the act is to deal with core issues of transparency, integrity and oversight of financial markets.

The Sarbanes–Oxley Act imposes a host of onerous requirements:

- the disclosure of all material off-balance sheet transactions;
- the certification of annual and quarterly financial reports by the chief executive and chief financial officer of all companies with US securities registrations;
- criminal penalties imposed for knowingly making false certifications;
- the CEO and CFO must give assurances regarding the effectiveness of control systems within companies, with Section 404 of Sarbanes–Oxley requiring companies to state the responsibility of management for establishing and maintaining an adequate internal control structure and procedures for financial reporting; and
- an independent Public Company Accounting Oversight Board was established with responsibility for setting standards for auditing, dealing with quality control and auditor independence.

In South Africa, the King Report deals with governance issues. One interesting feature is that sustainability is included as a governance issue, in addition to matters relating to governance and strategy.

Just as the content of codes can vary from country to country, so can their enforcement. The Sarbanes–Oxley Act is enacted in the law. The directors of those companies that fall within its coverage may be charged with criminal offences if they breach its requirements. The UK Corporate Governance Code operates on a 'comply or explain' basis. Companies who choose not to comply with the provisions of the code must state that they have not complied and offer an explanation for non-compliance. It is then a matter for the stock markets to decide whether that breach is important. If it is, then the share price may decline.

Board Structure

A large company will typically have two senior managers to share the overall responsibility for management. The chief executive officer (CEO) will take responsibility for the management of the company's business. The chairman[2] is responsible for managing the board of directors. This creates a degree of mutual review because neither the CEO nor the chairman has unfettered power to make decisions.

Furthermore, the board will normally comprise a mixture of both executive and non-executive directors. Executive directors are usually full-time employees and each will have a specific role to play in strategic management. The executive directors will also play a role by sitting on the board and participating in the overall management and direction of the company. Non-executive directors will not be employed in a full-time capacity. Their role will be to provide oversight of the decisions being made by the executive directors. To that end, they will attend board meetings. There may also be sub-committees of the board that will be made up of non-executive directors.

The logic underlying the appointment of non-executive directors is that they will usually be men and women who have established reputations. They may have had extensive careers in the management of other companies or they may be former politicians. The expectation is that non-executive directors will wish to protect their reputations and will refuse to be associated with any underhand dealings. They will receive all of the information that is available to all directors and they will have the ability to request further information if the need arises. They may well be held liable along with the executive directors in the event that the company's behaviour is ever criticised. Thus, the non-executives are just as accountable as their executive counterparts but they have far less to gain from any dishonesty because they are only paid to act in a part-time capacity. The non-executives have been characterised as the board's 'conscience'.

Our discussion assumes a single, 'unitary' board, which comprises both executive and non-executive directors. In some European countries it is common to have two-tier boards comprising a management board and a supervisory board. The management board is usually made up of executive directors and the supervisory board of non-executives. As the title suggests, the supervisory board provides oversight.

Making the Board Accountable

The most effective deterrent against misbehaviour is the ability to monitor the activities of the board using credible financial statements. The publication of IFRS is just one example of the importance that is attached to the protection of shareholders and other interested parties by the provision of high quality accounting information.

The validity of the information in the financial statements is further supported by the external audit function. The external auditor is an independent firm of accountants who undertake a thorough check of both the bookkeeping records and the manner in which the resulting balances are presented. The external auditor's role is to state an opinion as to whether the financial statements 'present fairly' or give a 'true and fair view'. That opinion is expressed in the form of an audit report, which will typically occupy a page of the annual accounts. (The auditor's role and the manner in which the audit determines and reports an opinion are covered in Porter, Hatherly and Simon, 2008).

The auditor's role can lead to conflict with the executive directors because their natural inclination is to present the company in the best possible light and the auditor's task is to ensure that the financial statements are prepared in accordance with generally accepted accounting principles (GAAP). Most companies support the auditor by having an audit committee comprising non-executive directors. The audit committee's role is to liaise with the partner in charge of the audit and to consider any matters of judgement associated with the preparation of the financial statements. The fact that the committee members are non-executives means that they will be unlikely to agree to the publication of misleading or distorted financial statements.

Board Remuneration

There are basically two issues arising from the manner in which directors are rewarded for their efforts.

Firstly, many companies pay their directors generously. From time to time, that becomes a matter of principle and the shareholders rebel at the substantial amounts that are on offer. It is argued that company directors must be well paid, otherwise they will be tempted to leave for better-paid jobs with competitors. That does not necessarily reflect the fact that the directors of large companies are generally much better paid than most of the other employees.

Secondly, there is a strong desire for the executive directors' rewards to reflect their companies' successes and failures. The concern is that the directors will not be motivated to perform well unless their remuneration varies in line with performance. Ideally, performance should be measured in terms of dividends and share price movements so that the directors' rewards are aligned to shareholders' wealth.

Non-executives are generally paid fixed salaries, with no bonuses or other rewards. That means that they earn the same regardless of the company's performance and so they have no financial incentive to tolerate risky or underhand business practices.

It is difficult to avoid accusations that directors are overpaid. One approach is to establish a remuneration committee comprising non-executive directors. The remuneration committee will be responsible for agreeing the amounts to be paid to the executive directors in the form of salaries, bonuses, shares and share options. That introduces a degree of independence into the setting of executive pay, but the problem is that the non-executives will almost certainly have had careers as executive directors themselves and so they will have become accustomed to substantial payments.

One of the most controversial areas of executive remuneration has been the use of stock options. A call option confers the right, but not the obligation, to buy an asset at an agreed price on a designated date or within a designated period. An option to buy shares will become valuable if the share price exceeds the striking price of the option by the time of exercise. If that price is not achieved then the option will expire worthless.

Options have had a chequered past. In the aftermath of the 1929 Wall Street Crash, it was argued that stock market prices had been artificially inflated by directors buying options in their companies and manipulating the markets to artificially inflate share prices. Market confidence evaporated when it was realised that prices were overstated and the global economy was plunged into depression.

Options have the effect of increasing exposure. For example, it may be possible to purchase five options for the price of one share. If you are confident that share prices will exceed the option's striking price then you should be able to make five times the profit from investing in options rather than in the shares themselves. The downside is that the options will expire worthless if the shares do not reach the strike price and so investing in options can be very risky. For that reason, directors were forbidden from holding options in their own companies because it created a massive temptation to manipulate share prices.

With the passage of time, it was deemed desirable to reward directors by paying them with options. If the directors received options that were 'out of the money' at the time of issue then they had an incentive to work towards increasing the share price before the options expired. If the options had a 'vesting period' of, say, three years after the options had been granted, then the directors had an incentive to remain with the company otherwise their option rights would be forfeited. The value of an option is linked to the volatility of the underlying share price. The more volatile the shares, the more likely the directors will be able to exercise their options at a substantial gain. That gives the directors an incentive to be less risk-averse, which could be to the shareholders' advantage if it encourages the directors to accept positive net present value projects that they would otherwise be inclined to reject.[3]

Options became a popular means of rewarding executive directors. Unfortunately, the lessons of 1929 repeated themselves. The WorldCom scandal in the US involved the manipulation of share prices with the intention of increasing the value of executive stock options. Indeed many of the scandals that occurred during the late 1990s and early 2000s were blamed, at least in part, on the temptations arising from executive share options.

The accounting treatment of executive share options has been an interesting area of accounting. The remainder of this chapter will deal with IFRS 2 *Share-based Payment* (IASB, 2004), which has been developed with the controversy associated with executive share options as its background.

IFRS 2 – The Mechanics

IFRS 2 deals with share-based payment. Companies can issue equity shares in payment for any asset or service. The focus in this section will be on the accounting treatment of share-based payments to reward staff.

Equity versus Cash

Share-based payments can be settled using equity. For example, goods or services can be obtained in exchange for equity instruments, usually shares or share options.

The alternative is to settle the transaction with a cash payment based on the share-price at a specified date.

The transaction will be recorded at fair value in either case, but the credit that matches the debit to assets or expenses will go to equity if the payment is share-based or to liabilities if it is cash-based.

The fair value will normally be determined in terms of the fair value of the goods or services that are to be received. If the payment is to employees then the transaction is recorded at the fair value of the equity or liability at the grant date.

Grant Dates versus Vesting Dates

The grant date is the date at which the arrangement is agreed.

The vesting date is the date upon which the recipient becomes entitled to the payment.

For some transactions, the transaction will vest on the grant date. That would be unusual for the grant of executive share options (ESOPs), which do not usually vest for a period of at least three years after the grant date.

For example, a company's remuneration committee might inform an executive director on 20 February 20X3 that she is to receive one million share options as part of her remuneration for the year ended 31 December 20X2. The options will not vest until 31 December 20X5, which means that the director will not be entitled to anything unless she meets the vesting conditions, such as remaining in post until the end of 20X5 or meeting certain specific performance targets during the vesting period.

Equity-Settled Share-Based Payment

When employees are granted any form of share-based payment, the related equity instrument should be shown at its fair value as at the grant date. Ideally, that will be the market value of the instrument, but there will not be a market value if the instrument is not identical to one that is traded on an exchange.

ESOPs are not normally the same as any other instruments. It is possible to buy and sell standardised options on company shares, known as traded options, on the open market. Even when those exist, ESOPs will generally have different exercise rights and different strike prices and maturities from their traded counterparts.

One of the biggest controversies associated with IFRS 2 is that companies must determine fair values for financial instruments even though the instruments in question are often unique and have been designed for the specific purpose of making a share-based payment. That means that there are no observable market prices that can be used to determine whether the valuations that are reported are realistic.

IFRS 2 requires the selection of a valuation technique that is regarded as orthodox and is generally accepted. For example, options are frequently valued using the Black–Scholes model.[4] IFRS 2 requires a valuation to be shown even where it is felt that a fair value cannot be determined reliably.

Any market-related vesting conditions should be taken into account in determining the fair value of the instrument. That will often happen automatically when options are issued. For example, a target share price that has to be achieved will almost certainly be set as the striking price of the option, which will affect the valuation of the options at the grant date.

Non-market conditions are a little more complicated. The company should use the best available estimate of the number of instruments that are expected to vest under the arrangement and that figure will be adjusted as and when estimates are updated. For example, if 100 employees are each granted 1000 options on condition that they must remain with the company for the duration of the vesting period then the company should estimate the number of options that are likely to vest at the end of the period. That will require forecasts of the numbers of staff who are expected to leave during the period.

Perhaps paradoxically, IFRS 2 requires that the entity should account for the cost of services while they are rendered throughout the vesting period. That may prove confusing because the shares or options may have been granted as a reward for work undertaken before the grant date, but it is likely that most ESOPs and some other share-based payment schemes will require further effort in order to satisfy any vesting conditions and also to create any value from the financial instruments. It is common practice, for example, for options granted under most ESOPs to be out of the money at the grant date and so the recipients will be responsible for working to increase the share price in order to make those options worth exercising by the time they are vested and can be exercised.

An Example of an Equity-Settled Share-Based Payment

On 1 January 20X1, Y granted 1000 share options with a fair value of £12 per option to each of its 100 employees. The only vesting condition was that the employees had to remain with the company until 31 December 20X3, at which time the options would vest.

During 20X1, Y lost four employees and Y estimated that it would lose a further nine employees by 31 December 20X3.

A further six employees left during 20X2 and Y estimated that a further seven would leave before the end of 20X3.

During the year ended 31 December 20X3, the company lost a further five employees, which left $100 - 4 - 6 - 5 = 85$ employees who satisfied the vesting conditions.

This scheme had a vesting period of three years, so the expense associated with the employees' service would be spread over that period.

On a year-by-year basis, we have to estimate the number of options that will vest. That requires the estimate of the number of staff who will be eligible for the options to be updated from year to year until the situation is resolved at the end of the final year.

The fair value of each option as at the grant date was £12. That figure was not adjusted for any changes that occured during the vesting period.

So, by 31 December 20X1, Y had lost four employees and expected to lose a further nine employees during the remaining two years of the vesting period. That left $100 - 4 - 9 = 87$ employees who were expected to receive options.

Each eligible employee was expected to receive 1000 options, valued at £12 each. The total value was $87 \times 1000 \times £12 = £1\,044\,000$.

Only one third of the vesting period had expired by 31 December 20X1, so the total cost of the scheme recognised by that date was $1/3 \times £1\,044\,000 = £348\,000$. All of that cost arose during the year ended 31 December 20X1.

The expense was recorded using the following journal:

Debit Staff costs	£348 000	
Credit Shares to be issued		£348 000

The 'Shares to be issued' account is an equity balance.

The same logic applied to the year ended 31 December 20X2. There were $100 - 4 = 96$ employees in post at the start of the year. That number was reduced to 90 because of the six staff who left during the year and a further seven were expected to leave before the vesting date, so the estimated number of staff who would be eligible for these options was 83.

The total value of options expected to be issued at the end of the vesting period was $83 \times 1000 \times £12 = £996\,000$.

Two thirds of the vesting period had elapsed, so the total cost to be recognised was $2/3 \times £996\,000 = £664\,000$. That is a cumulative total that includes the £348 000 already recognised, so the cost for the year ended 31 December $20X2 = £664\,000 - £348\,000 = £316\,000$. The journal for the year was:

Debit Staff costs	£316 000	
Credit Shares to be issued		£316 000

That left a credit balance of £664 000 on 'Shares to be issued'.

By 31 December 20X3 it was known that 85 employees satisfied the vesting conditions, so the final cost to be recognised was $85 \times 1000 \times £12 = £1\,020\,000$. As before, that is a cumulative total, so the cost for the year was £1 020 000 − £664 000 = £356 000. The final journal entry was:

Debit Staff costs	£356 000	
Credit Shares to be issued		£356 000

The closing balance of £1 020 000 on the 'Shares to be issued' account remains in equity, regardless of whether the options are exercised or are left to expire. It is, however, acceptable to transfer the balance to another equity balance. For example, if the options lapse then the £1 020 000 could be transferred to retained earnings.

Cash-Settled Share-Based Payment

Cash-settled payments result in an outflow of cash. These could take the form of redeemable shares or share appreciation rights, which give employees the right to a future cash payment that is based on the increase in the share price over a specified period.

When the rights under the scheme are first granted, they are recorded at their fair value. That fair value is re-measured at each reporting date until the liability is settled, with changes in fair value going to the statement of profit or loss.

As with equity-settled payments, when services are received their costs are recognised over the period that the services are rendered. By the vesting date there should be a provision or a liability that is equal to the cash payment.

An Example of a Cash-Settled Share-Based Payment

On 1 January 20X1, Z granted 1000 share appreciation rights options with a fair value of £8 per right to each of its 100 employees. These rights would not vest until 31 December 20X3 and employees had to remain with the company until that date in order to be eligible.

The company lost two employees during 20X1 and estimated that a further six would leave before the vesting date. The fair value of the share appreciation rights was £9 at 31 December 20X1.

One employee left during the year ended 31 December 20X2 and a further four were expected to leave during the final year before the scheme vested. The fair value of the rights was £10.

Z lost a further three employees during the year ended 31 December 20X3 and the share appreciation rights were worth £11 each when they vested.

At 31 December 20X1, Z expected that $100 - 2 - 6 = 92$ employees would be eligible to receive the share appreciation rights. Their fair value as at that date was $92 \times 1000 \times £9 = £828\,000$.[5]

One third of the vesting period had elapsed, so the liability as at the year end $= 1/3 \times £828\,000 = £276\,000$. That is a cumulative total, but this was the first year of the scheme, so the journal required to record the liability and the associated expense was:

Debit Staff costs	£276 000	
Credit Provision for Share appreciation rights		£276 000

By 31 December 20X2, it appeared that rights would vest to $98 - 1 - 4 = 93$ employees. The associated fair value was $93 \times 1000 \times £10 = £930\,000$.

Two thirds of the vesting period had elapsed, so the liability as at 31 December 20X2 was $2/3 \times £930\,000 = £620\,000$. Increasing the liability to that level required a further journal entry of:

Debit Staff costs	£344 000	
Credit Provision for Share appreciation rights		£344 000

On 31 December 20X3, the scheme vested with $97 - 3 = 94$ eligible employees. Their rights had a fair value of $94 \times 1000 \times £11 = £1\,034\,000$. That required a further journal entry of:

Debit Staff costs	£414 000	
Credit Provision for Share appreciation rights		£414 000

That left a liability of £1 034 000 on the share appreciation rights account, which would be settled in cash.

Disclosure Requirements

The basic principle is that users must receive sufficient information to enable them to understand the nature and extent of share-based payment arrangements that exist during the period.

Detailed disclosures will include:

- a detailed listing of commitments, with numbers of instruments involved;
- information concerning the model used to value the fair value of any equity instruments granted;
- the amounts of expenses recognised and movements on balances.

In practice, that can lead to extensive notes concerning these schemes.

IFRS 2 and the Conceptual Framework

The preceding summary of IFRS 2 ignores some really significant issues relating to the accounting treatment of ESOPs. It could be argued that the IFRS is inconsistent with some of the principles set out in the IASB's own *Conceptual Framework for Financial Reporting* (IASB, 2013).

The treatment set out in IFRS 2 can be challenged in a number of ways.

What is an Expense?

The *Conceptual Framework for Financial Reporting* defines expenses in terms of 'outflows or depletions of assets or incurrences of liabilities that result in decreases in equity' (IASB, 2013). If a share-based payment is cash-settled then that definition clearly applies, but that is not so in the case of equity-settled payments.

If an entity makes a share-based equity-settled payment in the form of options then those options will either lapse, which will increase equity, or they will be exercised, which may result in additional shares being issued at a premium. The only situation in which an equity-settled arrangement will reduce assets and equity is when the entity buys existing shares on the open market for resale to the employee at the option's striking price.

If the entity settles the agreement with options that can be exercised in return for newly issued shares then the only cost to the entity is the administrative expense associated with issuing and registering the new shares if the options are exercised. The directors or employees will only exercise their shares if the striking price is less than the market price, so the market value of the shares will be diluted slightly. The shareholders will bear the cost of that dilution and it will have no direct effect on the operations of the company.[6]

In Chapter 4 of this text, we saw that the boundaries of the entity have yet to be finally decided by the IASB. At the time of writing, the IASB's Conceptual Framework has set aside Chapter 2 in order to deal with the reporting entity, but the chapter has yet to be written. An exposure draft of Chapter 2 (IASB, 2010) describes the entity in terms of the usefulness of accounting information relating to that entity and in terms of the entity's economic activities. It is clear that those economic activities can and should include the control of assets that are used to create wealth in the form of goods and services. It is less clear that the entity extends to the market capitalisation of its shares. One of the features of an entity proposed by the exposure draft (IASB, 2010) is that:

[its] economic activities can be objectively distinguished from those of other entities and from the economic environment in which the entity exists.

It could be argued that stock market prices and speculative gains and losses incurred by the shareholders are really features of the entity's economic environment rather than its economic activities.

Accrual Accounting

If the preceding argument that the costs are often borne by the shareholders and not by the reporting entity is set aside, that leaves the question of when the costs arising from a share-based payment ought to be recognised.

Chapter 1 of the Conceptual Framework makes it clear that accruals-based accounting requires the recognition of transactions when they occur. It is rarely clear when the effects of a share-based payment actually occur:

• At the grant date? It could be argued that awards are generally granted as an incentive to perform well during the period leading up to the grant date. That would suggest that the costs relate to that period.

• During the vesting period? Generally, there are further conditions that must be met, otherwise the rights that have been granted will be forfeited. In some cases, though, the obligations arising during the vesting period are not particularly onerous.

It is not always entirely clear whether share-based payments are rewards for past services rendered before the grant or an incentive to maintain standards during the vesting period. It is certainly difficult to argue that none of the payment should be recognised at the grant date.

The insistence that the value of any equity-settled payment be determined as at the grant date and is not adjusted further confuses the argument that the cost should be spread over the vesting period. Ideally, the value of the prospective payment will increase throughout the vesting period in response to the efforts that are being encouraged by the incentive scheme. Those increases in value will not be recognised under IFRS 2.

Recognition Criteria

The Conceptual Framework offers the following criteria for the recognition of a figure in the financial statements (IASB, 2013):

An item that meets the definition of an element should be recognised if:

(a) it is probable that any future economic benefit associated with the item will flow to or from the entity; and

(b) the item has a cost or value that can be measured with reliability.

The question of reliability has never been adequately addressed. IFRS 2 requires the use of a recognised model for the valuation of share-based payments. Unfortunately, there will generally be several competing models for the valuation of any given financial instrument. Each will require estimates and assumptions. The choice of a model and the determination of the parameters that are to be put into it will have a significant effect on the final figure.

The ultimate test of an arm's length fair value is whether the asset can be bought and sold at the proposed valuation. The rights arising from ESOPs are generally unique and so there is very little opportunity to check that the sums that are being disclosed are valid. A Finnish study (Ikäheimo, Nuutti & Puttonen, 2006) offers some evidence that the prices attributed to ESOPs are often lower than the value that could be determined using the Black–Scholes model.

Before IFRS 2 came into effect it was accepted that shareholders needed to know about options and other share-based payments granted to company directors. That information was generally provided in the form of notes to the financial statements that disclosed the details of ESOPs, including the number of options held and details such as striking prices and any outstanding vesting conditions that had to be met.

IFRS 2 – The Governance Debates

During the 1990s, there were two main reasons for directors to be rewarded with share-based payments such as options:

• The first was that the shareholders were keen to give their directors the greatest possible incentive to maximise the share price. Granting out of the money options meant that company directors could only benefit if they worked to increase the share price beyond their options' striking prices.

• The second issue was political. The market for executive compensation was pushing up rewards around the world and that led to a public outcry, with newspapers condemning directors for overpaying themselves. That led to the US government placing a cap of $1m per year on directors' remuneration. Options were not taken into account in applying this limit in the US and the granting of options in other countries did not appear to inflame the same degree of moral outrage at 'greedy' company directors.

From an agency point of view, the problem created by options is that they give their holders an incentive to manipulate share prices so that they can be exercised at a profit before they expire. In 2005, the chief executive of WorldCom was sentenced to 25 years in prison for his part in a securities fraud. It was alleged that he had used his position as CEO to inflate the company's share price in order to protect the value of his many millions of stock options.

The WorldCom scandal occurred at roughly the same time as many other major corporate scandals, including Enron. It was alleged that executives had fallen prey to the temptations created by their options. Perhaps illogically, commentators started to ask why the options were not appearing as expenses in the statement of profit or loss.

The role of lobbying on the accounting treatment of ESOPs was picked up in a study by Zeff (2002). The extent to which accounting arguments were influenced by public arguments in the media was picked up in a US study (Street, Fordham & Wayland, 1997) that tracked the development of the accounting regulations in response to press comment.

Summary

Corporate governance is a contentious area that encompasses a variety of issues relating to the management of companies. Developments in this area have generally been driven by scandals. The basic cycle is that a major event is analysed and its causes are established. Then a new set of rules is developed and enacted in law, stock exchange rules, or whatever. Some countries have formal codes of corporate governance that are kept up to date to deal with developments or changing circumstances.

The basic problem with governance is that company directors are in a position to abuse their authority. There have been some extremely serious cases where shareholders have suffered at the hands of unscrupulous directors. Every such event has the effect of undermining investor confidence. Developments in the regulation of governance are often intended just as much to restore confidence as to prevent a recurrence.

Tutorial Questions

Question 1

Download a company's annual report and come to class prepared to discuss the governance information that has been published.

Question 2

Find the external auditor's report for the company in question 1 and explain what assurances it provides. Are there any statements in the report that raise concerns?

Question 3

Discuss the extent to which it is fair to link executive remuneration to measures of success.

Question 4

HG granted 1000 share appreciation rights (SARs) to its 120 employees on 1 January 20X7. (An SAR is a cash-settled right.) To be eligible, employees must remain employed for three years from the grant date. The rights must be exercised in December 20X9.

In the year to 31 December 20X7, 12 staff left and a further 15 were expected to leave over the following two years.

In the year to 31 December 20X8, 8 staff left and a further 10 were expected to leave in the following year.

The fair value of each SAR was $15 at 31 December 20X7 and $17 at 31 December 20X8.

Required
Prepare the accounting entries to record the expense associated with the SARs for the year ended 31 December 20X8.

Question 5

FGH granted share options to its 600 employees on 1 January 20X7. Each employee would receive 500 share options provided they continued to work for FGH for four years from the grant date. The fair value of each option at the grant date was $1.48.

The actual and expected staff movement over the four years to 30 September 20X1 is given below:

20X7   20 employees left and another 50 were expected to leave over the next three years.

20X8   A further 25 employees left and another 40 were expected to leave over the next two years.

20X9   A further 15 employees left and another 20 were expected to leave the following year.

20X1   No actual figures available to date.

The sales director of FGH has stated in the board minutes that he disagrees with the treatment of the share options. No cash has been paid out to employees, therefore he fails to understand why an expense is being charged against profits.

Required
Calculate the charge to the statement of profit or loss for the year ended 31 December 20X9 and draft a journal entry to record this.

Draft a response to the sales director's statement.

Questions with Answers

Question 1

Discuss the argument that many of the provisions intended to ensure sound governance could simply create a false sense of security.

Question 2

Discuss the proposition that it is not necessarily either fair or logical to link executive remuneration to the company's performance.

Question 3

CVB granted 1000 share appreciation rights (SARs) to each of its 1500 employees on 1 January 20X0. To be eligible for the rights, employees had to remain with CVB for three years from the date of grant. The rights had to be exercised in January 20X3, with settlement due in cash.

86 employees left during the year ended 31 December 20X0 and a further 125 were expected to leave over the following two years.

53 employees left during the year ended 31 December 20X1 and a further 55 were expected to leave in the following year.

48 employees left during the year ended 31 December 20X2.

The fair value of each SAR was $8.50 at 1 January 20X0, $11.00 at 31 December 20X0, $13.00 at 31 December 20X1 and $14.50 at 31 December 20X2.

Required
Prepare the journal entry to record the expense associated with the SARs for the year ended 31 December 20X1.

Explain how the recognition and measurement of a share-based payment would differ if it was to be settled in equity rather than cash.

Endnotes

1. Take care when reading this paper. The authors are attempting to undermine the assumptions made by agency theory by taking them to their logical (or illogical) extremes.
2. 'Chairman' is the title that is normally used in this context, despite the availability of potentially less gender-specific titles.

3. Apart from the desire to avoid being blamed for a 'bad' investment, the directors will always have a different attitude towards risky investments. The shareholders can diversify their investments and so the risks associated with any given investment opportunity can be viewed in the context of a portfolio. The directors cannot diversify the interest in the companies that they manage and so they are far more heavily exposed to any and all risks associated with a project. Holding options gives the directors an incentive to take responsible risks because the options are more likely to be in the money if the project succeeds.

4. Most advanced finance texts will discuss this model. The Black-Scholes model is a very complex formula that can be used to value options and that takes into account the life of the option (time to maturity), the extent to which the option is in or out of the money (intrinsic value) and the volatility of the underlying asset. The longer the life, the larger any positive intrinsic value; and the more volatile the underlying asset, the higher the value attributed to the option by the Black–Scholes model.

5. Strictly, we should have estimated the cost of settling this scheme at 1 January 20X1 when the rights were granted, but that would then have required an adjustment as at the end of the first year, which would have led to the same net expense in the statement of profit or loss and the same liability in the statement of financial position.

6. It could be argued that the shareholders will welcome this dilution. The options were granted in order to motivate the board or the workforce to work harder in order to raise the share price beyond the options' strike price. If the hard work succeeds then the shareholders will benefit, even if some of their gains are subsequently shared with the option holders.

References

Financial Reporting Council (2012) *UK Corporate Governance Code*. Available at: www.frc.org.uk/Our-Work/Codes-Standards/Corporate-governance/UK-Corporate-Governance-Code.aspx (accessed 17 September 2013).

IASB (2004) IFRS 2 *Share-based Payment*.

IASB (2010) *Conceptual Framework for Financial Reporting – The Reporting Entity*. Exposure Draft ED/2010/2.

IASB (2013) *The Conceptual Framework for Financial Reporting*. London: IFRS Foundation/IASB.

Ikäheimo, S., Nuutti, K. & Puttonen, V. (2006) The 'true and fair view' of executive stock option valuation. *European Accounting Review* **15**(3) pp. 351–366.

Jensen, M.C. & Meckling, W.H. (1976) Theory of the firm: Managerial behaviour, agency costs and ownership structure. *Journal of Financial Economics* (October) pp. 305–360.

Porter, B., Hatherly, D. & Simon, J. (2008) *Principles of External Auditing* (3rd ed.). Chichester: John Wiley & Sons.

Solomon, J. (2010) *Corporate Governance and Accountability* (3rd ed.). Chichester: John Wiley & Sons.

Street, D.L., Fordham, D.R. & Wayland, A. (1997) Stock options as a form of compensation for American executives: Impact on accounting rules of themes and arguments reported in newspapers and business magazines, 1975–1993. *Critical Perspectives on Accounting* **8**(3) pp. 211–242.

Tinker, T. & Okcabol, F. (1991) Fatal attractions in the agency relationship. *British Accounting Review* **23**(4) pp. 329–354.

Zeff, S. (2002) 'Political' lobbying on proposed standards: A challenge for the IASB. *Accounting Horizons* **16**(1) pp. 43–54.

ACCOUNTING FOR POST-RETIREMENT BENEFITS

Contents

Learning Objectives

After studying this chapter, you should be able to:

- distinguish defined benefit from defined contribution plans;
- explain the logic underlying IAS 19's treatment of defined benefit plans;
- apply IAS 19's requirements to simple cases;
- discuss the alleged economic consequences of IAS 19.

Introduction

Pension costs are an emotive issue. From the employee's point of view, a pension is (or was) an anticipated reward for a lifetime of work and service. Employees contributed to pension schemes in the expectation of a financially secure retirement. From the employer's point of view, pensions have become a somewhat expensive commitment. Improved medical care and longer life expectancies have made it far more expensive to continue to guarantee employees' security for the duration of their retirement.

This chapter will discuss the accounting treatment of the different types of post-retirement benefits available to employees. The focus will be on the defined benefit pension because that has been the one that has caused the greatest controversy.

The accounting treatment of pensions has, and remains, complicated because of the difficulties associated with valuing the associated assets and liabilities. It has also been complicated by the fact that accounting regulations have been blamed for the tendency to close defined benefit pension plans and replace them with far less desirable defined contribution plans. This is a classic example of accounting standards being associated with significant major economic consequences, although it is debatable whether the accounting treatment has driven this change.

Types of Post-Retirement Benefit

This chapter will focus on pension costs. It is possible for employers to offer their staff a range of additional benefits payable from retirement but their accounting treatment should not be significantly different because of the nature of the benefit. For example, some employers provide their staff with private medical insurance and will continue to provide that after retirement, subject to the employee having met the employer's conditions in terms of length of service.

Post-retirement benefits can take a number of forms. In the most complicated case, the employer agrees that employees will receive a benefit that will commence upon retirement and will continue for the remainder of their lives. These benefits create commitments that are potentially substantial because paying a meaningful pension or covering an elderly retiree's healthcare costs will be expensive. The commitments will run for the remaining lives of the employees after their retirement and could continue for many years. These commitments will, therefore, be both material and difficult to value.

Types of Pension

The pensions industry offers a vast range of different products, but these can be simplified into two broad categories: defined contribution and defined benefit.

Defined contribution is the simplest form of pension arrangement. The employer agrees to pay a certain amount into a pension fund, possibly on a monthly basis, with the contributions calculated as a percentage of each employee's salary. Once the payment has been made the employer has no further commitment with respect to pensions. The pension fund is then responsible for investing the funds in order to provide the employees with their pensions when they retire. The value of the pension is likely to be determined in terms of the performance of these investments and so the employee bears the risk that weak returns will yield a poor pension.

Defined benefit is far more desirable for the employee. The employer makes regular payments to a pension fund, but the agreement is that the employee will receive a benefit that is linked to years of service and annual salary at the date of retirement. The precise formula varies from company to company, but it may be that the employee will receive one-fortieth of his or her salary at the date of retirement for every year spent with the company as an annual pension payment. That sum will be payable for the remainder of the employee's life, with an annual adjustment to allow for inflation. For example, an employee might be entitled to one-eightieth of her annual salary for every year of employment, up to a maximum of 40 years' service. If that employee has worked for 30 years and earned $40 000 at retirement then her initial annual pension would be 30/80 × $40 000 = $15 000. That sum would then be index-linked to adjust for inflation throughout the remainder of her life.

Defined benefit plans give employees the assurance of a realistic pension when they retire, but they impose substantial risks upon employers. If the returns from the investment of the pension contributions are poor then the employer may have to make additional contributions to the pension fund in order to ensure that the commitments to the employees can be met. The commitment itself can vary because of changes in salary levels and also, to be morbid, because of changes in life expectancy. If healthcare improves and pensioners live for longer, then their pensions will cost more.

Pensions can be arranged through third parties or can be administered by the employer. A funded plan involves making a payment to a separate fund, which will then make investments in assets that are expected to maintain their real value and offer some capital growth. Equity and property are the most obvious investments. It makes very little difference to the accounting treatment whether this fund is operated or managed by a third party or by the entity itself.

Unfunded plans do not involve setting aside any assets in order to pay pensions. Arguably, those funds are being invested in the company itself. This chapter will focus on funded plans throughout.

There are a number of legal matters that affect the operation of pensions, which we need not concern ourselves with. The law imposes restrictions in order to protect pensioners' rights. A 35-year-old employee will have pension contributions invested on his or her behalf for the next 30 years or more and must be protected against loss or fraud for the whole of that period. Once retired, pensioners rely on their pension funds for income. The law takes the protection of pensioners' interests very seriously.

The routine payments into the plan will generally be linked to employees' salaries. Some plans require the employees to make a contribution in addition to that paid by the employer. This does not affect the accounting treatment of the pension plan itself. If employees make a contribution then it will be deducted from their gross pay and paid into the plan by the employer along with the employer's contribution.

Individual pensioners may have complicated pension histories. Most employees will change jobs and move between employers in the course of their working lives and will possibly have the right to move their pension contributions into their new employers' pension plans in order to simplify their pension arrangements. That can be a complicated area because of the need to protect employees' interests in the course of such transfers and also because pension contributions often have tax implications and the law must prevent pension arrangements being abused to avoid the payment of tax on earned income. Fortunately, such transfers have very little impact on the financial reporting aspects of accounting for pensions and can be ignored for the purpose of this chapter.

IAS 19

IAS 19 *Employee Benefits* was issued in 1998 (IASB, 1998). This was mirrored by changes in the UK, which introduced FRS 17 *Retirement Benefits* in 2000 (ASB, 2000). These standards proved controversial because they essentially forced companies to reflect the risks associated with defined benefit pension plans in their financial statements. They imposed a requirement to recognise the estimated value of the liabilities arising from these plans in line with changes to those estimates.

One implication of these standards has been that many employers have used their implementation as an excuse for closing defined benefit pension plans and replacing them with defined contribution plans. We will explore these changes later in this chapter.

Knowing the Future

IAS 19 basically requires employers to recognise the true value of their pension commitments. The risks can be best understood by thinking about the challenges facing the employer who operates a defined benefit pension plan:

• The most fundamental responsibility is to ensure that the company can pay the employees' pensions for the remainder of their lives. The amount to be paid varies with the rate of pay as at the date of retirement. Future salary levels are likely to be roughly in line with those paid at present, adjusted for cost of living increases due to inflation. So estimating the annual future pension bill involves predicting rates of inflation into the long-term future.

• The duration of the pension payments is a function of the life expectancy of the employees. Fortunately, the insurance industry has conducted a great deal of research into mortality statistics and has a realistic basis for estimating life expectancies. Nevertheless, estimates can change over time because social changes affect life expectancies. For example, fewer people smoke tobacco than before and the average life expectancy has increased because of this.

• Pension payments may run into the distant future. The associated liability has to be discounted to its net present value. Changes in interest rates will have an immediate and potentially material effect on that net present value.

• Finally, the pension payments will be funded out of the returns from the investments in the pension plan. Returns can be volatile and expectations of future returns can vary significantly.

Essentially, the challenge is to ensure that there are sufficient assets in the pension fund to ensure that there will be an adequate cash flow to meet the commitments to the pensioners as and when they fall due. If the values of the assets and liabilities fall out of line then the employer may have to make an additional contribution to the pension fund in order to remedy any shortfall or may be permitted to reduce payments in the event that the assets in the fund are deemed to be more than adequate.

Part of the challenge from an accounting point of view is that the values of the assets and liabilities can be substantial. Any movement in these balances can have a significant impact upon reported earnings when those movements are taken to the statement of profit or loss.

The Role of the Actuary

Pension funds rely on actuaries for advice concerning the valuation of assets and liabilities. An actuary is essentially a highly qualified and respected statistician who can develop forecasts based on past experience. There is never any guarantee that a forecast will turn out to be accurate, regardless of who makes it, but an actuarial report on a pension fund is likely to reflect the best possible estimates of future outcomes.

The pension industry shares many similarities with the insurance industry and so actuaries have been gathering data on the factors that determine life expectancy for many years in order to set realistic premiums for life insurance policies.

Actuaries are also experts in the whole area of making economic predictions and forecasts.

In the real world, the accountants and auditors who prepare accounts that involve pension funds will work alongside the actuaries and will develop an understanding of the techniques and the issues involved. For the purpose of this chapter it will be sufficient to take the figures provided by the actuary as given.

Accounting for Defined Contribution Plans

Defined contribution plans are relatively straightforward from an accounting point of view.

The employer's contribution to the pension fund is treated as an expense for that year. The fact that the employee will not receive any payment until retirement is not relevant. The pension contribution is part of the remuneration package for the present year's employment.

Any balances that are due to be paid into the fund at the year end, whether for employer or employee contributions, are current liabilities.

The employer's contribution for the year must be disclosed in the notes to the financial statements. Employee contributions are simply part of the total employment cost and so no separate disclosure is required.

Under a defined contribution plan, the risks associated with changing economic circumstances are borne by the employees and so the reporting entity is not affected by movements in interest rates or changes in actuarial assumptions.

Some defined contribution plans include an additional payment into the fund that pays for a third party to provide the employees with what are, effectively, a defined benefit. Such a scheme should be accounted for as a defined contribution scheme because the employer's commitment is limited to the defined annual contribution. The third party is bearing all of the risks associated with the volatility and the estimates and assumptions described above.

Accounting for Defined Benefit Plans

The basic principle with a defined benefit plan is that the employer has a liability in the form of the long-term commitment to both employees and pensioners (who have already retired and are in receipt of their pension). That liability changes in value for the reasons that have already been discussed.

Offset against that liability, the plan will hold assets that are intended to yield the cash flows from which the pension commitment will be paid. Those assets will also change in value.

The statement of financial position will show the net value of the plan, which is arrived at by offsetting the pension plan's assets and liabilities.

The statement of profit or loss will show the movement in the net assets and liabilities as an expense.

The Plan Liability

The actuary determines the net present value of the commitments owed to past and present employees.

The liability will increase annually for two reasons:

• Firstly, an additional commitment will arise because current employees have earned further pension rights in return for their labour during the year.

• Secondly, the passage of time means that future payments that have already been committed are now a year closer to their payment. So their net present value will increase because of the dates of these payments 'unwinding'.

These liabilities can extend into the distant future and so it is appropriate that they should be discounted. The discount rate is based on the market yields offered by high quality corporate bonds.

The pension plan liability does not include any unpaid contributions arising from, say, the salary payment for the year's final month. These are treated as a current liability.

The Plan Assets

The assets will be valued at their fair value. Ideally, that will be based on observable market prices, but an estimate can be used when no observable price is available.

The plan actuary will typically advise on the value of assets as well as liabilities.

The Statement of Profit or Loss

There are several elements to the cost, shown in Table 6.1.

In principle, these elements could either be classified as a single expense or they could be split between different categories. IAS 19 does not prescribe a particular

Table 6.1 Elements of cost

Current service cost	Employees are entitled to additional pension because of the work undertaken during the current year. The net present value of the plan liability will increase because of that entitlement.
Past service cost	This will only arise when the benefits offered under the plan are enhanced. If the benefits associated with past service are enhanced then their net present value will increase.
Interest cost	The passage of time means that the liability associated with past service is a year closer to being paid and so the effects of discounting are less. The present value of the future payments will increase.
Expected return on plan assets	The expected return for the plan's assets for the current year. The expected return is used to ensure that the figures agree and balance. The difference between the expected return and actual return is dealt with under the heading 'actuarial gains and losses'.
Settlements or curtailments	These are gains and losses arising from major reductions to the number of employees in the plan or the benefits promised to them.
Actuarial gains and losses	These are increases and decreases in the asset or liability that occur either because the actuarial assumptions have changed or because of differences between the previous actuarial assumptions and what has actually happened ('experience adjustments'). This figure is determined as a balancing figure when analysing the net movement for the period.

classification and some elements could be viewed as operating expenses and others as financial. It could be argued that current and past services costs, and settlements or curtailments, arise from operating activities and could be treated as operating expenses. Interest cost and expected return on assets could be viewed as financial items. The classification of actuarial gains and losses will depend on the factors that caused them.

A Worked Example

A company has a defined benefit plan.

The plan's assets and liabilities both stood at $200m on 1 January 20X4.

The following information has been provided for the year ended 31 December 20X4. All transactions are assumed to have occurred as at the end of the year in which the occurred:

- Discount rate at the start of the year, 10%
- Expected rate of return on plan assets for the year, 11%
- Current service cost, $23m
- Benefits paid, $18m
- Contributions received, $24m
- Present value of plan obligations at 31 December 20X4, $231m
- Fair value of plan assets at 31 December 20X4, $223m

Accounting for this plan is easier if the calculations relating to the plan's liabilities are kept separate from those relating to the plan's assets.

The opening liability as at 1 January was $200m. By the end of the year, the commitments are a year closer to being paid and the interest rate is 10%. The interest cost for the year is, therefore, $200m × 10% = $20m.

The current employees are entitled to pension benefits with a present value of $23m for their labours, so the current service cost will increase the liability by $23m.

During the year the company made payments totalling $18m to past employees who have retired and so the plan's obligations will decrease by that amount.

By the end of the period, if all of the estimates and assumptions made by the plan actuaries were correct and did not require adjustment during the year, the liability would be $200m + $20m + $23m − $18m = $225m. The actual liability was $231m, which suggests that the plan's liabilities are greater than predicted. There is an actuarial loss of $225m − $231m = ($6m).

This working would normally be set out as a table:

	$m
Present value of obligation at 1 January	200
Interest cost (at discount rate for the year)	20
Current service cost	23
Benefits paid	(18)
Actuarial (gain)/loss on obligation (balancing figure)	6
Present value of obligations at 31 December	231

At a common sense level, we know the value of the liability as at the beginning and end of the year, and we can explain some of the movements in terms of transactions that have occurred and the additional commitment due to the current employees. That leaves an 'unexplained' adjustment of $6m, which may be due to changes in interest rates acting against the plan.

The biggest challenge would be the determination of the present value of the plan liability, which is likely to be entrusted to the plan actuary.

The treatment of the plan assets is very similar.

The opening fair value was $200m and that was expected to increase by 11% or $22m.

Contributions of $24m were received. In other words, cash was received from the company and the current employees for their respective pension contributions.

Benefits of $18m were paid out, which would deplete cash by that amount.

These figures suggest that the closing value of the plan's assets should be $200m + $22m + $24m − $18m = $228m. In fact the value was $223m and so there has been a further actuarial loss of $5m.

Again, it would be better to present the working as a table:

	$m
Fair value of assets at 1 January	200
Expected return on plan assets	22
Contributions received	24
Benefits paid	(18)
Actuarial gain/(loss) on obligation (balancing figure)	(5)
Fair value of assets at 31 December	223

At the beginning of the period the plan's assets and liabilities were both valued at $200m, so there was no net asset or liability. At the end of the period there is a net liability of $231m − $223m = $8m.

The statement of profit or loss will show a total pension cost of:

	$m
Current service cost	23
Interest cost	20
Expected return on plan assets	(22)
Net actuarial (gain)/loss recognised [$6 + $5]	11
Total charge	32

We can prove that these numbers fit together by taking the opening net asset or liability, adjusting for the total charge (which would increase the net liability) and adjusting for cash paid into and out of the plan. The cash inflow from contributions will increase the plan's assets. The cash outflow for benefits paid will decrease both assets and liabilities by the same amount and so they can be disregarded. That means that we can reconcile the various movements as follows:

	$m
Net (asset)/liability at 1 January 20X4 [$200m − $200m]	0
Total charge	32
Contributions received	(24)
Net (asset)/liability at 31 December 20X4 [$231m − $223m]	8

Why Pensions Matter

This example illustrates the problems that IAS 19 creates for companies that offer a defined benefit pension scheme. Basically, any volatility in the plan's liabilities and assets can have the potential to alter the pension cost so that the movements are taken directly to the statement of profit or loss. That problem is compounded by the fact that the values of the assets and liabilities can be substantial, so that any movement can have a major impact on the reported earnings.

There could be an argument that these adjustments are of relatively little concern in any case. For example, the fair value of the plan assets may not matter much in the short to medium term if the intention is to keep them as long-term investments that will yield cash to settle commitments that may not become payable for many years.

Reporting Actuarial Gains and Losses

Actuarial gains and losses arise in the context of defined benefit plans. It is these gains and losses that create much of the controversy over accounting for defined benefit plans, and so IAS 19 offers a limited opportunity to defer some of the gains and losses so that the impact of changing values is less pronounced.

IAS 19 used to offer three methods of accounting for actuarial gains and losses:

- immediate recognition in the statement of profit or loss;
- immediate recognition as 'other comprehensive income' and thereby included in equity;
- subject to numerical limits, the gains and losses could be spread over future periods.

Immediate recognition in income is generally consistent with the treatment of provisions for other losses. It also reflects the costs associated with providing these pension benefits, including the risks connected with the volatility associated with long-term investments and liabilities.

Immediate recognition in equity is generally consistent with the treatment of recognised gains on other assets. It reflects gains or losses in other comprehensive income in the period in which they arise. It avoids introducing the volatility into reported earnings.

Spreading gains and losses forward allows for the possibility that fluctuations in the short to medium terms will reverse and tend to cancel out over the longer term. It is, however, inconsistent with the treatment of other gains and losses arising on other assets and liabilities generally.

In any case, IAS 19 was modified in 2011 so that all actuarial gains and losses must be recognised immediately in the statement of profit or loss.

The Asset Ceiling

It can be possible for there to be a net pension asset. That is acceptable, but there is an upper limit to the resulting asset balance. This 'asset ceiling' is restricted to:

- unrecognised past service costs (see below); plus
- the present value of any economic benefits available in the form of refunds from the plan or reductions in future contributions to the plan.

This upper limit effectively limits the value of the recognised surplus to the extent to which it will be recoverable in the form of refunds or reduced contributions in the future. The company might be entitled to make such a recovery if the assets exceeded a prescribed threshold and that entitled the owner to either a refund of past contributions or the reduction of future contributions until the assets were brought into line with the prescribed limits.

For example, the following balances exist with respect to a company's defined benefit plan:

- Fair value of plan assets, $900m
- Present value of pension liability, $820m
- Present value of future refunds and reductions in future contributions, $15m
- Unrecognised past service cost, $30m.

Normally the surplus that would be recognised would be:

	$m
Plan liabilities	820
Plan assets	(900)
Surplus	(80)

The asset ceiling will restrict this to:

	$m
Unrecognised past service cost	30
Present value of future refunds and reductions in future contributions	15
	45

The ceiling restricts the surplus that can be recognised to 45.

The remaining $80m − $45m = $35m will have to be recognised as a loss immediately.

Settlements and Curtailments

Settlements arise when employees leave the scheme and a payment is made to redeem the company's obligation to them. For example, an employee changes jobs and requests that the amount due from the original employer's pension plan be transferred to the new employer's.

Curtailments arise when the entity commits itself to making a material reduction in the number of employees covered by the plan. For example, the company could make a large number of staff redundant. The plan's obligations could also be curtailed if the terms offered to current employees are altered so that they qualify for reduced benefits on future service.

If there is a difference between the fair value of any fund assets applied in the course of a curtailment or settlement and the associated reduction in the plan's obligations, then that difference should be recognised as a gain or loss when the curtailment or settlement occurs.

Past Service Costs

Employers may decide to enhance the benefits offered by the plan. Such enhancements may be retrospective, so that the additional benefits are paid for past service. The treatment of the additional costs associated with such enhancements depends on the conditions attached to them. The benefits are said to have 'vested' when the employees become eligible to receive them.

If the enhancements vest immediately then the associated costs should be recognised immediately in the fund liability.

If the enhancements vest over a defined period then the additional cost should be spread over the vesting period on the straight-line basis. The unrecognised element will be treated in a similar manner to unrecognised actuarial losses.

For example, a company's pension plan had previously entitled staff to an annual pension of one-fortieth of their salaries at the date of retirement for every year of service. The company has decided to improve these terms by giving one-thirty-fifth of final salary for every year. That additional benefit will vest immediately for employees who have more than six years' service and will be granted to other current employees once they reach six years.

The present value of the additional benefits payable to those employees with more than six years' service is $18m.

The present value of the additional benefits payable to the other employees is $12m. The average period to vesting for those employees is three years.

The $18m benefit that has vested immediately will be recognised as a cost and will increase the plan liability.

One-third of the $12m = $4m that will vest will be recognised as an expense every year over the three-year period. The unrecognised element (i.e. $8m in the first instance) will be treated as an unrecognised loss.

Disclosure Requirements

Pension disclosures relating to defined benefit plans are notoriously complicated. Indeed, the figures may be almost impossible for many readers to understand. The former head of the IASB once joked that the figures relating to deferred tax, pensions and goodwill should be combined so that there is only one meaningless number in the statement of financial position instead of three meaningless numbers.

Disclosures Relating to Defined Contribution Schemes

The amount recognised as an expense should be disclosed in the notes to the financial statements.

Disclosures Relating to Defined Benefit Schemes

The broad principle underlying IAS 19's disclosure requirements is that users of financial statements should be able to evaluate the nature of the company's defined benefit plans and the financial effects of changes in those plans during the period.

This is then supplemented with a detailed list of disclosures, which amount to the requirement to show all of the adjustments described in this chapter as components of the pension cost. There should also be detailed reconciliations of the opening and closing balances on the fund asset and liability figures.

It is debatable whether many readers of the financial statements will be able to make a great deal of sense of those disclosures.

For example, Volvo's annual report for 2011 has almost five pages of information on provisions for post-employment benefits. The fact that the company is multinational means that it has to make estimates and assumptions in virtually all of the countries in which it employs staff. Volvo makes most of its arrangements through defined contribution plans, but remains responsible for defined benefit plans that were put in place before the move towards defined contribution.

The importance of pension costs is underpinned by the fact that pension costs totalled SEK3471m, which is a material sum in comparison to the Volvo group's pretax earnings of SEK24 929m.

Disclosures include tables of actuarial assumptions made in Sweden, the United States, France and Great Britain. The group faced obligations that were valued at SEK40 358m from its remaining defined benefit plans.

Accounting Standards and the Demise of the Defined Benefit Pension – A Study of Economic Consequences

It is hardly surprising that most employees would prefer a defined benefit scheme to a defined contribution. Under defined benefit, there is a realistic expectation that the pension paid on retirement will be sufficient to provide a predictable and acceptable standard of living; and under defined benefit, the risks associated with weak investment performance and the like will be borne by the employer.

Defined benefit pensions have become increasingly uncommon in recent years, with many employers closing their plans to new employees. Dixon and Monk (2009) discuss the role that accounting standards have had to play in this phenomenon. They argue that defined benefit schemes have become increasingly expensive because of factors such as improving medical care leading to greater longevity. However, the authors also find a clear line of argument to suggest that changes to accounting requirements in the UK and the Netherlands had a significant role to play in the demise of defined benefit.

Prior to IAS 19 (and the UK's equivalent standard FRS 17), the accounting treatment of defined benefit schemes smoothed out much of the volatility associated with changes to the values of plan assets and liabilities. The new accounting regulations required a more immediate recognition of gains and losses and so reported earnings appeared to be more volatile. Losses associated with weak investment returns were reported in a more prominent manner than previously.

The intriguing conundrum is that these new accounting treatments had no real change on the economic cost of providing defined benefit pensions. They may have made the costs more visible to stakeholders, although pension funds are themselves major investors and they would have been very conscious of the costs and risks associated with pension arrangements before IAS 19. Similarly, company directors and their pension managers were aware of the values of their plan assets and liabilities before the accounting changes.

Napier (2009) provides an excellent overview of the development of accounting for pensions, accompanied by a clear and lucid exploration of the theoretical background to accounting for pensions. In the 19th century it was deemed acceptable simply to show the cash paid in respect of pensions as an expense. As time passed, the pension commitment began to be viewed as deferred pay and so more attention was paid to recording a realistic figure for the cost incurred. Over time, that led to a desire to report the liabilities associated with pension plans. The history of the developing standards in this area has been characterised by compromises that have had unintended consequences.

Kiosse and Peasnell (2009) deal with the arguments surrounding the withdrawal of defined benefit schemes in response to the introduction of IAS 19 and its equivalent standards. They conclude that the link between the accounting implications of the latest standards and the withdrawal of defined benefit plans has been overstated. It could be argued that the increased visibility of these costs because of the accounting regime has provided employers with a convenient excuse for switching to defined contribution.

Summary

Pensions and other post-retirement benefits can be difficult to account for. If the plan guarantees the employee a defined benefit upon retirement, then the financial statements must reflect a liability that requires many complicated estimates and assumptions. The resulting balance will be very sensitive to changes in those estimates.

The accounting requirements relating to defined benefit plans have developed so that the associated costs and risks are reflected in the financial statements. There are some very limited provisions for deferring losses arising from pension adjustments, but the rules set out in IAS 19 effectively require the recognition of any significant fluctuations in the assets and liabilities associated with defined benefit plans.

Meeting employees' expectations for a secure and comfortable retirement has been an increasingly significant commitment. It would appear that many employers have used the introduction of IAS 19 as an excuse to close their defined benefit plans to new employees and to replace them with defined contributions.

Tutorial Questions

Question 1

Download a company's annual report and come to class prepared to discuss the notes relating to pensions and any other post-retirement benefits.

Question 2

Discuss the implications for the IASB of the fact that the closure of many defined benefit schemes has been blamed on the introduction of IAS 19.

Question 3

A company operates a defined contribution pension plan. The company pays a contribution of 5% of employee gross salaries. In addition, employees pay a contribution of 3% of their gross salaries.

The gross salary bill is $400 000 per month, with the pension contribution paid monthly during the month after the related salary payment.

Calculate the pension cost for the year ended 31 December 20X4 and also the balance outstanding according to the statement of financial position as at 31 December 20X4.

Question 4

The following information relates to a defined benefit plan for the year ended 31 December 20X5:

Present value of plan obligation at start of year ($m)	240
Fair value of plan assets at start of year ($m)	220
Discount rate at start of year	8.5%
Expected rate of return on plan asset as at start of year	12.0%
Current service cost ($m)	46
Benefits paid ($m)	38
Contributions received ($m)	23
Present value of plan obligation at end of year ($m)	260
Fair value of plan assets at end of year ($m)	222

Explain what each of the items listed above means, using your own words.

Determine the figures that will appear in the statement of profit or loss and statement of financial position in respect of the pension plan.

Question 5

The following information relates to a defined benefit plan:

	31 December 20X1	31 December 20X2	31 December 20X3
Present value of plan obligation at start of year ($m)	470	535	655
Fair value of plan assets at start of year ($m)	455	472	468
Discount rate at start of year	9.2%	9.4%	9.6%
Expected rate of return on plan asset as at start of year	11.4%	11.1%	10.3%
Current service cost ($m)	92	89	86

Benefits paid ($m)	72	74	76
Contributions received ($m)	44	42	43
Present value of plan obligation at end of year ($m)	535	655	738
Fair value of plan assets at end of year ($m)	472	468	472

Determine the figures that will appear in the statement of profit or loss and statement of financial position in respect of the pension plan.

Questions with Answers

Question 1

The present value of the obligation arising from a company's defined benefit plan was €650m on 1 January 20X7 and the fair value of the plan's assets was €635m on that date.

The discount rate at the start of the year was 7.8%. The plan's actuaries predicted a return on the plan's assets of 11.5%.

The following figures were recorded during the year ended 31 December 20X7:

	€m
Current service cost	124
Benefits paid	128
Contributions received	70

The present value of the plan's obligation was €730m at 31 December 20X7 and the fair value of the plan's assets was €645m.

Determine the figures that will appear in the statement of profit or loss and statement of financial position in respect of the pension plan.

Question 2

The present value of a company's pension plan obligations was $1.2m at 1 January 20X3. The fair value of the plan's assets was $1.1m at that date. There were no unrecognised actuarial losses as at that date.

The following information relates to the plan:

	31 December 20X3	31 December 20X4	31 December 20X5
Discount rate at start of year	8.5%	9.1%	9.3%
Expected rate of return on plan asset as at start of year	9.8%	10.5%	10.3%
Current service cost ($m)	0.14	0.12	0.11
Benefits paid ($m)	0.51	0.50	0.49
Contributions received ($m)	0.77	0.75	0.72
Present value of plan obligation at end of year ($m)	1.07	1.01	0.98
Fair value of plan assets at end of year ($m)	0.95	1.20	1.49

Determine the figures that will appear in the statement of profit or loss and statement of financial position in respect of the pension plan.

Assume that the company is permitted to use any net assets that arise to reduce future pension contributions.

References

ASB (2000) FRS 17 *Retirement Benefits*.

Dixon, A.D. & Monk, A.H.B. (2009) The power of finance: Accounting harmonization's effect on pension provision. *Journal of Economic Geography* **9**(5) pp. 619–639.

IASB (1998) IAS 19 *Employee Benefits*.

Kiosse, P.V. & Peasnell, K. (2009) Have changes in pension accounting changed pension provision? A review of the evidence. *Accounting and Business Research* **39**(3) pp. 255–267.

Napier, C.J. (2009) The logic of pension accounting. *Accounting and Business Research* **39**(3) pp. 231–249.

INCOME, VALUE AND FINANCIAL REPORTING

Contents

Learning Objectives

After studying this chapter, you should be able to:

- discuss the importance of the choice of basis for the determination of income and value;
- explain the logic underlying historical cost accounting;

- explain the logic underlying replacement cost accounting;
- explain the logic underlying current purchasing power accounting;
- explain the logic underlying net realisable value accounting;
- explain the logic underlying real terms accounting;
- appreciate the factors that have affected the choice of accounting basis in practice.

Introduction

Financial reporting is intended to communicate useful information to users of financial statements. Users need to understand the performance and financial position of the entity, and that requires some thought to be given to how things will be valued. There is an almost unspoken tendency to value balances at their historical costs unless there is a specific reason for doing otherwise. It is possible, however, to argue that a number of other approaches are worthy of consideration.

This chapter will discuss some of the approaches that have been put forward as alternatives to historical cost accounting. This has been a contested and controversial area of accounting in the past and it may well emerge as an area for discussion in the future. It is important to appreciate that the arguments have continuing relevance, even if that is only because the move towards fair value accounting has some role to play in changing the basis of financial reporting.

Income, Economics and Accounting

Accountants and economists often explore the whole question of valuation and measurement differently. Economists generally provide information for internal decision-making and are relatively free of the need to have uniform rules and regulations that involve the development of standards.

From an economic point of view, it is possible to measure wealth or capital at the beginning and end of a period and determine income in terms of the increase or decrease. That calculation could be made for an individual or for a business. This gives the following simple equation:

$$\text{Income} = \text{Capital}_t - \text{Capital}_{t-1}$$

The formula assumes that the owners have made no further investments of capital and that nothing has been withdrawn by way of dividends.

If a company's capital at the end of a period ('time t') was $1000 and at the beginning of the period ('time t minus 1') it had been $800, then the increase of $200 for the period was income, assuming that the figures had not been affected by the injection of fresh capital or the withdrawal of capital through dividends or any other form of repayment.

This chapter will show how the different assumptions concerning the valuation of capital can affect the resulting figures for the measurement of income. These assumptions have fed into a number of arguments concerning the most appropriate systems for the accounting measurement of income and capital. The history of financial reporting includes a number of attempts to decide the most suitable arrangements for the measurement of capital and income.

Hicks' Definition

John Hicks was an economist who expanded upon our simple formula for the determination of income:

$$Y_e = C_t + (K_t - K_{t-1})$$
$$C_t = \text{consumption during the period from time } t - 1 \text{ to time } t$$
$$K_t = \text{net present value of future cash flows as at time } t$$

In theory, this model could be used as the basis for accounting statements. Shareholder wealth could be expressed in terms of the net present values of the assets and liabilities as at times t and t − 1. Consumption would be the value of any dividends paid, less any injections of capital.

This approach would raise a vast number of practical difficulties arising from the problems associated with calculating net present value. Apart from the complexity of the forecasts required for this calculation, there is also the risk that users of the financial statements will challenge the basis upon which the net present value has been determined. Users of the financial statements may compare the figures with the subsequent cash flows and may accuse the preparers of incompetence or deliberate bias if the actual results are poorer than expected.

Ex Ante versus Ex Post

It is often taken for granted that financial statements should be prepared on the basis of looking backwards at past events, but there is no reason why financial reporting must always be historical in nature. If C and K are determined using past results then this is known as 'ex post' income and capital. However, it is possible to base the figures on expected results in order to arrive at 'ex ante' figures:

$$Y_e \;=\; C'_t + (K'_t - K_{t-1})$$

C'_t = expected realised cash flow for period $t-1$ to t, anticipated at $t-1$.

K'_t = expected closing capital as estimated at $t-1$.

K_{t-1} = 'actual' opening capital as measured at $t-1$.

Ex ante and ex post income figures could be used to inform different decisions. For example, ex ante income would be useful to management in deciding what dividends the company could afford to pay out of the incoming year's profits.

For example, a company has been established to undertake a four-year project. It will be wound up at the end of the four years. Estimated net cash flows over the life of this project are as follows:

$t_0 - t_1$	£1000
$t_1 - t_2$	£2500
$t_2 - t_3$	£3700
$t_3 - t_4$	£7000

This company's cost of capital is 7%.

Ex ante income for the period t_0 to t_1 can be calculated as follows:

Expected cash flows $= £1000$

$$\text{Capital at start} = \frac{1000}{1.07} + \frac{2500}{1.07^2} + \frac{3700}{1.07^3} + \frac{7000}{1.07^4} = 11\,479$$

$$\text{Expected capital at end} = \frac{2500}{1.07} + \frac{3700}{1.07^2} + \frac{7000}{1.07^3} = 11\,282$$

$$\text{Income} = £1000 + (11\,282 - 11\,479) = £803$$

So, the directors know that they cannot afford to pay a dividend exceeding £803 during the first year of the project. If they do then they will erode the company's capital and the company may run into difficulties.

If the numbers never change, then the ex ante and ex post income figures will always be the same. Ex post income could be calculated as:

$$Y_e = C_t + (K_t - K'_{t-1})$$

C_t = realised cash flow for period $t - 1$ to t, anticipated at $t - 1$.

K_t = closing capital as estimated at t.

K'_{t-1} = opening capital as measured at t.

On that basis, the same figures would result for opening and closing capital and cash flow and the ex post income would still be £803.

The difference between ex ante and ex post income arises when expectations change. These lead to changes in the valuations of capital, which are called 'windfall' gains and losses. The choice between ex ante and ex post income will affect the timing of the recognition of those windfall gains and losses.

For example, at time t_2 the company changed its expectations concerning cash flows due in t_3 to t_4 to £8000.

If the expected earnings had remained constant then both ex ante and ex post earnings for the period t_1 to t_2 would have been £790.[1]

Under ex ante, the expected cash flows would be unchanged for the purposes of determining capital as at t_1 and t_2. The opening and closing capital figures would be valued as at the information available at time t_2. Under ex post the realised cash flows were £2500, the opening capital was

$$\frac{2500}{1.07} + \frac{3700}{1.07^2} + \frac{8000}{1.07^3} = 12\,098$$

and the closing capital was

$$\frac{3700}{1.07} + \frac{8000}{1.07^2} = 10\,445$$

so income $= £2500 + (£10\,455 - £12\,098) = £847$. In addition, the value of capital changed at time t_2. Previously it had been valued at £11 282, but now it is known to be worth £12 098. The increase of £12 098 − £11 282 = £816 is a windfall gain. Thus, the total wealth arising during the period t_1 to t_2 was £847 + £816 = £1663.

The windfall gain will still be recognised under ex ante, but the timing of recognition will change. The revised cash flow will affect the values of capital looking forward to the period from t_2 to t_3 under ex ante and so the windfall gain will arise in that period, one year later than under ex post.

Before moving on to look at some further arguments concerning income and value, it is important to note that this discussion of ex ante versus ex post is not as abstract as it may appear. Accounting standard-setters have to decide when gains and profits should be recognised. There are issues arising from that decision. Forward-looking financial statements may be a better basis for decisions, but the information may be less reliable because of the greater reliance upon forecasting. Recognising a gain in the financial statements may trigger a demand for tax. Choices have to be made when deciding when and how to recognise income and changes in value, and those choices can have a significant impact on the quality of the resulting information.

Entry Value versus Exit Value Accounting

The previous section discussed the concept of capital from an economic point of view. In an ideal world, all companies would report their profits using some variation of the Hicks definition because that requires the net assets to be valued at their net present value. Doing so would mean that the statement of financial position was valued in terms of the shareholders' wealth and changes in wealth would be reflected by income and windfall gains and losses. The most basic concept in finance theory is that a company exists to create wealth for its owners and so these figures would be entirely consistent with the shareholders' best interests. Improving performance in these terms would bring a direct benefit to the shareholders. There would be no dysfunctional behaviour arising from managers making decisions that increased reported earnings but damaged the company in the process.

Unfortunately, there is no realistic prospect of net present value ever being the basis for the measurement of all of the figures in the financial statements. It may be the basis for some figures that have reasonably predictable cash flows, such as some financial instruments, but there can be little prospect of net present values being used routinely for all figures.

Over the years there have been several attempts to establish a viable basis for the preparation of financial statements. The challenge has been to prepare figures that are useful to the users of the financial statements and that can be prepared at a realistic cost and with reasonable reliability.

Entry values are essentially costs associated with obtaining a particular asset. It will be shown that there is more than one basis for the determination of costs and it can be argued that notional costs of replacing an asset are more relevant than the actual costs incurred in the asset's original acquisition. Entry values can be based upon historical costs, replacement costs or historical costs with an adjustment for inflation.

Exit values are the values associated with exploiting or disposing of an asset. Net present value would be an example of an exit value because it is associated with generating cash from using an asset for the remainder of its useful life. Some of the alternatives will be discussed. Exit values can be based upon net realisable value.

The key to understanding each of these methods is to understand how 'capital' is defined. Once that has been established the next step is to appreciate how performance is determined. It can often help to establish what it would mean if the business were to 'break even' over the course of the period, in other words to operate without making either a profit or a loss.

Demo – Figures for Illustration

We will use the following information to illustrate the application of our different models.

On 1 January 20X4 the shareholders of Demo established a company by investing $20 000. The opening statement of financial position, as at that date, was as follows:

Demo:
Statement of financial position as at 1 January 20X4

	$
Land	5 000
Equipment	5 000
Cash	10 000
	20 000
Share capital	20 000

The equipment has a five-year life, with no salvage value.

These opening figures were clearly at replacement cost because Demo purchased the land and equipment for the amounts stated on the reporting date.

The following transactions, all for cash, took place during the years ended 31 December 20X4 and 20X5:

Inventory purchases at cost			
20X4	1 February	100 units @ $25/unit	$2500
20X5	30 June	100 units @ $40/unit	$4000
	30 September	40 units @ $45/unit	$1800

Sales			
20X4	31 August	80 units @ $50/unit	$4000
20X5	31 August	110 units @ $70/unit	$7700

Relevant replacement costs were as follows:

	Inventory	**Equipment (new)**	**Land**
31 August 20X4	$30/unit	Not applicable	Not applicable
31 December 20X4	$36/unit	$5500	$6300
31 August 20X5	$41/unit	Not applicable	Not applicable
31 December 20X5	$48/unit	$6100	$7200

The purchasing power of Demo's unit of currency can be tracked using the following index:

1 January 20X4	100
1 February 20X4	103
31 August 20X4	115
31 December 20X4	120
30 June 20X5	124
31 August 20X5	126
30 September 20X5	127
31 December 20X5	130

This index indicates that prices have risen by an average of 30% from 1 January 20X4 to 31 December 20X5.

Historical Cost Accounting

Under pure historical cost,[2] all assets are valued at their original cost to the business, with no adjustment for changing prices. So, a piece of land that cost $500 000 in

1980 will still be valued at that. If the business owns another piece of land that cost $2 000 000 in 2010 then the total cost of land will be shown at the total of $500 000 + $2 000 000 = $2 500 000.

Historical cost accounting ignores the phenomenon of changing prices. Prices can change in two ways. Firstly, prices have tended to rise over time in virtually all economies. This process is called inflation and it means that the purchasing power of a unit of currency will tend to decline with the passage of time. In the novel Jane Eyre, which was published in 1847, the heroine becomes a wealthy woman when she inherits the sum of £20 000. By the 1970s, £20 000 would buy a relatively modest house. By 2010, £20 000 would be the cost of a reasonable car.

Price changes can also be specific. Changes in technology or other factors can affect the prices of particular goods or commodities over and above the impact of inflation. For example, DVD players were luxury items when they were first introduced. Over time their cost has fallen to the point where supermarkets often sell them as an impulse buy.

Pure historical cost accounting would mean that assets were shown at their original historical costs, possibly adjusted to reflect a depreciation charge that was itself based upon historical cost. The advantage of historical cost accounting is that the results are relatively objective. Determining the original cost of an asset is largely a matter of having an organised system for the storage of paperwork. Objectivity is an important characteristic because the preparers and auditors of financial statements are often accused of negligence or even outright dishonesty in the aftermath of an accounting scandal. Choosing an objective valuation basis makes it far easier to defend the published results.

Drawbacks of Historical Cost

Historical cost accounting also has a number of major disadvantages:

- Inconsistent figures are combined to produce meaningless totals, such as our $2 500 000 total for land.
- Historical cost accounting ignores unrealised income. The older piece of land in our example may have a historical cost of $500 000 but be worth many times that amount because of movements in the property market.
- Historical cost accounting overstates profit. Depreciation is based on historical costs that are years out of date and are generally understated relative to the revenues from sales. When prices are increasing rapidly then even the cost of sales may be understated when an item of inventory that was purchased in February is sold in April. February costs are being subtracted from April selling prices and the net effect is to overstate operating profit.

• Historical costs are unlikely to have any value for decision-making purposes unless they are a reasonable approximation to a more relevant valuation. If an item of inventory cost €1.00 yesterday then it will probably cost €1.00 to replace today. If the opportunity to sell it for €1.40 arises then the company will be better off if it makes the sale. If the inventory had been purchased for €1.00 six months ago and would cost significantly more than that to replace, then it may be unclear whether it should be sold for €1.40. Certainly, if it is sold and then replaced at a cost of €1.60 then the business will be €0.20 worse off, even though historical cost accounting would still show a profit of €1.40 − €1.00 = €0.40 on the transaction.

Historical cost accounting defines capital as the original historical cost of the entity's net assets. A profit will be recognised if the entity can generate revenues that are greater than the historical cost of the assets consumed in the process. The entity will break even if the revenues are identical to costs when measured on that basis.

It is difficult to provide a clear and meaningful interpretation of the relevance of historical cost financial statements produced during times of changing prices.

Demo's Historical Cost Figures

It is often easier to understand the statement of financial position rather than the statement of profit or loss, so we will start by looking at Demo's net assets.

At 31 December 20X4, Demo had land that had a historical cost of $5000. That land remains Demo's property and it has not been depreciated or consumed in any way. Demo also owned equipment that had originally cost $5000 but that is expected to last for only five years, so one-fifth of its life has gone so far.

Demo also owns 20 units of inventory (it purchased 100 units in February and sold 80 units in August) and these cost $25 each, so inventory has a historical cost of $500. The company made cash sales of $4000 and a cash purchase of $2500, so the bank balance has increased by $4000 − $2500 = $1500 to $11 500.

Using the same logic for 31 December 20X5, we have the same land. The equipment has been depreciated for two-fifths of its life so far. If we use the first in, first out (FIFO) assumption for inventory, then there are 50 units left in inventory, of which 10 units cost $40 each and the remaining 40 units cost $45 each. The bank balance has changed because of the further purchases and sales.

We can produce the company's statement of financial position for both year ends:

Demo:
Historical cost
Statement of financial position as at 31 December

	20X4	20X5
	$	$
Land	5 000	5 000
Equipment	4 000	3 000
Inventory	500	2 200
Bank	11 500	13 400
	21 000	23 600
Share capital	20 000	20 000
Retained profit	1 000	3 600
	21 000	23 600

Balancing figures have been inserted for retained profit. We will have to prepare historical cost statements of profit or loss in order to show that these figures are correct.

This statement highlights some of the problems with historical cost accounting. The valuation of land ignores the changes that have occurred to market value since the land was purchased. Equipment is valued on an increasingly meaningless basis. On 31 December 20X5, the $3000 shown does not tell us anything that is particularly useful. The inventory figure for 31 December 20X5 combines two different purchases, made at different times, when prices were different, and states a single total. That total is again not necessarily very relevant for decision-making. For example, if the inventory was insured for $2200, that sum would not be sufficient to replace it if it was stolen or damaged.

The statements of profit or loss for the two years are as follows:

Demo:
Historical cost
Statement of profit or loss for the year ended 31 December

	20X4	20X5
	$	$
Revenue	4000	7700
Opening inventory	nil	500
Purchases	2500	5800
Closing inventory	(500)	(2200)

	2000	4100
Depreciation	1000	1000
Total operating costs	3000	5100
Profit	1000	2600

Total retained earnings were $1000 at 31 December 20X4. There were no dividends, so total retained earnings were $1000 + $2600 = $3600 by 31 December 20X5.

Our statement of profit or loss shows that historical cost tends to overstate profits. The cost of inventory is based upon historical costs throughout, but the business always replaces the inventory that it sells. The goods sold on 31 August 20X4 were priced at their historical cost of $25 each, but their replacement cost had increased to $30 per unit by the time they were sold. The depreciation charge is also based on historical costs that are two years out of date by the year ended 31 December 20X5.

Replacement Cost Accounting

Under replacement cost accounting, 'capital' is defined in terms of operating capacity. For example, a manufacturing company has operating capacity in the form of factory buildings, equipment and materials. Costs associated with running that factory will be measured in terms of the wear and tear on the property, plant and equipment with a view to the replacement of the items in question. The cost of parts and materials will be determined in terms of the cost of their replacement, regardless of their original cost.

Demo's Replacement Cost Statement of Financial Position

We can recycle some of the calculation from the historical cost workings. For example, we have established that there were 20 units in inventory at 31 December 20X4 and 50 units at 31 December 20X5. Their replacement costs were $36 per unit at 31 December 20X4 ($36 × 20 = $720) and $48 per unit at 31 December 20X5 ($48 × 50 = $2400).

The replacement cost of the land has been established by looking at market prices.

Equipment poses a major problem. The equipment was one year old at 31 December 20X4 and two years old at 31 December 20X5. Ideally, we would like to use the costs of buying identical equipment of those ages at each of our two year ends. That can be difficult to establish because there is rarely an observable market price for, say, a two-year-old shop fitting. We have been forced to estimate a replacement cost by multiplying the replacement cost of a new item by the proportion of its remaining useful life. That gives $5500 × 4/5 = $4400 at 31 December 20X4 and $6100 × 3/5 = $3660 at 31 December 20X5. We do not necessarily claim that a two-year-old asset would cost $3660 at that date, but it is the most accurate estimate we can make using the information that is readily available.

The replacement cost statement of financial position is as follows:

Demo:
Replacement cost
Statement of financial position as at 31 December

	20X4	20X5
	$	$
Land	6 300	7 200
Equipment	4 400	3 660
Inventory	720	2 400
Bank	11 500	13 400
	22 920	26 660
Share capital	20 000	20 000
Reserves	2 920	6 660
	22 920	26 660

Again, the reserves figure is a balancing figure that we will have to prove by preparing a statement of profit or loss and undertaking some further calculations.

These figures are immediately more relevant to many decisions. At the end of 20X4, the business had property, plant and equipment that would have cost a total of $6300 + $4400 = $10 700 to replace and inventory worth $720 on the same basis. Under replacement cost accounting, the business can only been deemed to have made a profit if the cost of replacing any of those assets has been taken into account in the figures for the year ended 31 December 20X5.

Put crudely, if a business is a biscuit factory that could manufacture 100 000 biscuits every day on the first day of the year then replacement cost accounting is intended to ensure that it can still manufacture 100 000 biscuits by the year end. If selling prices are insufficient to cover the costs of inventory being replaced and wear and tear of productive assets then replacement cost accounting will show a loss.

The figures in this statement do have some value for decision-making purposes. If the opportunity arises to sell the inventory for $2250 on 31 December 20X5 then historical cost accounting will suggest that the entity will make a profit of $50 from doing so. Replacement cost accounting will show that the cost of replacing the inventory is actually $2400 and so the entity will be $150 worse off if it accepts the offer to buy.

The two statements of financial position are not necessarily directly comparable because we have not adjusted for the effects of inflation. The 20X4 statement is expressed in 31 December 20X4 dollars and the 20X5 in 31 December 20X5 dollars.

Replacement Cost Statement of Profit or Loss

The basic principle in preparing the statement of profit or loss is to compare the revenues generated throughout the period with the cost of replacing the resources consumed *as at the date of consumption*. That is not a particularly difficult concept in itself, but it does have the capacity to affect the bookkeeping arrangements.

Holding gains arise because of changes in the specific prices that affect the entity under consideration. A holding gain is the difference between the replacement cost that is recorded when the asset is consumed and the book value of that resource. For example, on 31 August 20X4, Demo sold 80 units of inventory that had cost $25 at a time when the replacement cost was $30 per unit. In that case there was a holding gain of $5 per unit = $400 on those items.

Holding gains should not be taken into account when calculating replacement cost operating profit. That is mainly because holding gains are an inevitable consequence of changing prices. They need to be taken into account in order to ensure that the statement of financial position balances, so they are a necessary bookkeeping adjustment. They should not, however, be taken into account when evaluating management's performance. If they were, then the directors could simply buy large quantities of non-perishable inventory and hold it while its replacement cost rises.

Holding gains are realised when they arise from the use or sale of inventory or other assets, for example, the holding gain on the 80 units sold on 31 August 20X4.

Unrealised holding gains arise when the assets remain in the entity and there is a change in their replacement costs. It is the difference between the year end replacement cost and the value at which they were introduced or brought forward.

Demo's Replacement Cost Statement of Profit or Loss

The figures for revenue are unchanged by the switch to replacement cost accounting.

Operating expenses must be stated in terms of the replacement costs of the assets consumed at the dates of their consumption.

Demo made one sale in 20X4: 80 units were sold at a time when their replacement cost was $30 per unit, so their total replacement cost was 80 × $30 = $2400. There was one sale in 20X5: 110 units were sold when their replacement cost was $41 per unit. So their replacement cost was $4510.

Demo's replacement cost depreciation was $5500/5 = $1100 for the year ended 31 December 20X4 and $6100/5 = $1220 for the year ended 31 December 20X5.

Holding gains arise because of differences between the expenses that have been recognised and the book values of the assets consumed. Holding gains are generally easy to calculate for the first year of operation, but become a little more complicated in the second and subsequent years because it becomes necessary to separate gains that have already been recognised from those that arose during the year.

The historical cost of inventory consumed during the year ended 31 December 20X4 was $2400 − $2000 = $400 less than its replacement cost. So the realised holding gain on inventory for the year ended 31 December 20X4 is $400.

At the start of the year ended 31 December 20X5, Demo held inventory valued at a replacement cost of $720. That is $220 greater than the historical cost, so an unrealised gain of $220 was recognised during the year ended 31 December 20X4. The difference between the cost of inventory consumed under both historical cost and replacement cost was $4510 − $4100 = $410. That gain includes the $220 brought forward from the previous period so the gain arising during the year on inventory sold is $410 − $220 = $190.

Realised holding gains on depreciation can be determined by comparing historical cost and replacement cost figures to give $1100 − $1000 = $100 for the year ended 31 December 20X4 and $1220 − $1000 = $220 for the year ended 31 December 20X5.

	Realised gain for the year
Inventory	$400
Equipment	$100
Total for the year ended 31 December 20X4	$500

Inventory	$190
Equipment	$220
Total for the year ended 31 December 20X5	$410

The unrealised holding gain on inventory for the year ended 31 December 20X4 is a simple matter of comparing the replacement cost valuation as at the end of the year with the inventory's historical cost. That gives an unrealised gain of $720 − $500 = $220 for the year ended 31 December 20X4. The same logic gives a figure of $2400 − $2200 = $200 for the year ended 31 December 20X5. We do not need to adjust the $200 for previous years because all of the inventory was purchased during the year ended 31 December 20X5 and so all of the unrecognised gain arose during the year.

The unrealised gain on the land for the year ended 31 December 20X4 is the increase in value from $5000 to $6300 = $1300. All of that gain arose during the year. By 31 December 20X5 the value had increased to $7200, giving a cumulative gain to date of $7200 − $5000 = $2200. That includes $1300 that arose prior to the year ended 31 December 20X5, so an unrealised gain of $2200 − $1300 = $900 arose during that year.

Depreciation complicates the calculation of unrealised gains on non-current assets. Apart from the first year of ownership, untangling realised gains and losses from unrealised gains and losses can become complicated.

Comparing the historical cost of equipment with its replacement cost as at 31 December 20X4 shows an unrealised gain of $4400 − $4000 = $400.

If we could somehow have protected that equipment from the effects of depreciation then its replacement cost would have increased to $6100 less one fifth (for the depreciation in the year ended 31 December 20X4) to give $4880 as at 31 December 20X5. Comparing that with the closing value of the equipment at the previous year end of $4400 suggests that a total gain of $4880 − $4400 = $480 has arisen during the year. The replacement cost statement of profit or loss shows a realised gain of $220 on equipment, so $480 − $220 = $260 must be the unrealised gain for the year:

	Unrealised gain for the year
Inventory	$220
Land	$1300
Equipment	$400
Total for the year ended 31 December 20X4	$1920

Inventory – as at 31 December 20X5	$200
Land	$900
Equipment	$260
Total for the year ended 31 December 20X4	$1360

Pulling these figures together gives:

Demo:
Replacement cost
Statement of profit or loss for the year ended 31 December

	20X4	20X5
	$	$
Revenue	4000	7700
Cost of inventory	2400	4510
Depreciation	1100	1220
Total operating costs	3500	5730
Replacement cost operating profit	500	1970
Realised holding gains	500	410
Unrealised holding gains	1920	1360
Replacement cost profit	2920	3740

There were no dividends paid, so the total retained replacement cost profit was $2920 + $3740 = $6660. Thus, the figures from the statement of profit or loss agree to the balancing figure that was inserted into the statement of financial position.

Making Sense of the Figures

The most important thing to note is that Demo made an operating profit. That means that the revenues generated from the transactions during the year were sufficient to cover the cost of replacing the resources used up. That is not a trivial concern because prices tend to increase over time and so traditional historical costs, which are generally the costs recorded by the bookkeeping system, can be out of date by the time the assets are consumed. Historical cost profit tends to overstate the true 'economic' effects of trading when prices are rising.

The best way to explain this is to imagine a naïve business that based all decisions on historical cost profit. It buys inventory on credit for $5 and sells it for $6 at a time when the replacement cost is $8. It has no other assets or liabilities. The historical cost financial statements show that the entity made a profit of $1 on this cycle of transactions. Before the sale the entity had one unit of inventory and a bank overdraft of $5. Afterwards it had an identical unit of inventory and a bank overdraft of $7. The entity is clearly undermining its capacity to continue by selling goods at a replacement cost loss.

The holding gains generally ensure that the financial statements articulate. In other words, the statement of financial position would not balance if the holding gains were not recognised. Clearly, management may feel that some holding gains arise because of astute buying and deliberate speculation. In that case there could be an argument for rewarding the ability to generate holding gains. They are, however, an inevitable outcome of holding physical assets during periods of rising prices.

Determining Replacement Costs

One of the biggest challenges in implementing replacement cost accounting is the estimation of replacement costs.

In an ideal world, each asset would be valued individually when relevant. In the case of inventory, that would involve checking the replacement cost of each unit sold at the date of sale. In the case of property, plant and equipment, that would involve looking at the replacement cost at the year end.

This ideal would be difficult to implement for a real business. A shop that purchased two months' worth of tinned vegetables for resale could not realistically contact the supplier to ask about the replacement cost every time a can was sold.

One alternative would be to obtain specific price indices. There are government agencies and commercial organisations that prepare detailed surveys of economic information. They can often provide indices. For example, there could be a specific price index for a particular category of equipment. If an asset in that category was purchased at a time when the index was 210 and the index had increased to 240 then the price has increased $240/210 = 1.14$ times. The replacement cost of the asset could be estimated by multiplying its historical cost by 1.14.

If index numbers are used to determine the replacement cost of inventory consumed during the period, then it is important to remember that the objective is to restate the cost of each unit sold during the year to the average unit price for the year. For example, suppose that the average index for the year was 370. Suppose also that the opening inventory was purchased at a time when the index was 340 and the closing inventory when it was 385. Purchases were spread throughout the year. So, we can establish the cost of inventory consumed on a replacement cost basis by multiplying the historical cost of opening inventory by $370/340$, adding that to the historical cost of purchases – which are already stated at the average unit price because they were spread through the year – and subtracting the historical cost of closing inventory multiplied by $370/385$.

Index numbers will never be as accurate as specific valuations, but they are likely to be far more cost effective. They also make it easier to deal with specific assets that might be difficult to value, perhaps because there is no observable market.

There are other problems with replacement costs. One of the biggest is in deciding what to do about assets that would not be replaced with an identical asset. For example, a sales force might be equipped with notebook computers to process customer orders. It may be that these computers are expected to be used for at least the next two years because they are still fit for purpose. If they have to be replaced immediately, however, the sales manager might buy tablet computers instead. In that case it is not always clear whether the replacement costs should be based upon the cost of notebooks or tablets.

Year One and Subsequent Years

The purpose of this chapter is to show that there are different ways to determine the value of assets and to calculate income. The calculation of income is generally easiest when we look at the first year of a business. The calculation of income during the second and subsequent years is generally affected by the gains that have already been recognised. That was shown in the Demo example, which was actually the simplest possible case. For example, there is a phenomenon called 'backlog depreciation' that can lead to the need to adjust retained earnings brought forward when the replacement cost depreciation charges will be inadequate to write off the cost of assets before the end of their useful lives.

The tutorial questions at the end of this chapter will focus on the first year, which is the simplest possible case. That should be sufficient to demonstrate the issues arising from the different bases that will be introduced in this chapter. The discussion of Demo's second year of business was intended to create some awareness of the issues arising from gains being carried forward.

Current Purchasing Power Accounting

Current purchasing power accounting eliminates the effects of inflation from the financial statements. Inflation is a general tendency for prices to increase over time. In general, the purchasing power of a unit of currency will decline because of that.

Replacement cost accounting adjusts for *specific* price changes. The specific prices of particular goods and commodities may have different implications for different entities. For example, the price per tonne of iron ore may increase and decrease because of factors that have very little to do with the economy in general. A 10% increase in the cost per tonne will have a significant effect on the business of a steel maker, a significant effect on a business that buys steel (such as a car manufacturer) and little or no effect on many other businesses (the cost of food manufacturers' company cars might increase a little).

The good news is that current purchasing power figures are far simpler to prepare than their replacement cost equivalents. Unfortunately, the resulting figures become far less relevant to management for decision-making.

The essence of current purchasing power accounting is to restate all figures to consistent monetary units. A 31 December 2012 dollar is likely to buy less than a 31 December 1982 dollar. If your grandparents tell you that they purchased their large house in 1970 for £6000, they would have to enable you to restate that sum in terms of the current purchasing power of £1 for it to make any meaningful sense.

Governments generally keep careful track of the rate of inflation, which is the basis for current purchasing power adjustments. General price levels are calculated on a frequent basis, usually monthly, and published as a key economic indicator. If, for example, the index has increased from 320 to 350, then prices have increased by $(350 - 320)/320 = 9.4\%$ in that time.

Demo Revisited

The key to preparing the current purchasing power statement of financial position is to restate figures to a consistent monetary unit. Doing so requires the use of the table showing the purchasing power of Demo's unit of currency from earlier in this chapter. In principle, we could work to monetary units as at any date, but it would be fairly common to use the year end in the first instance.

In the case of Demo, the historical costs of property, plant and equipment were expressed in terms of 1 January 20X4 $ units. Converting those to 31 December 20X4 $ units is a matter of multiplying by 120/100. For 31 December 20X5, 130/100 is used instead. Applying those rates to land gives $6000 and $6500 respectively. Equipment is $4800 and $3900.

Inventory held at 31 December 20X4 was purchased on 1 February 20X4. Converting those $ units to 31 December 20X4 gives $500 × 120/103 = $583. Inventory at 31 December 20X5 was 10 units purchased at $40 = $400 on 30 June 20X5 and 40 units at $45 = $1800 on 30 September 20X5. That gives ($400 × 130/124) + ($1800 × 130/127) = $2262.

The cash invested by the shareholders was in 1 January 20X4 $ and these are converted using 120/100 and 130/100 to get to 31 December 20X4 and 20X5 $, to give $24 000 and $26 000 respectively.

The only remaining figure is bank, which is automatically stated in terms of year end $. Indeed, any balances that are expressed in purely monetary terms that are not linked to any physical asset are stated at their current purchasing power. That includes trade receivables and payables and also any loans or other liabilities.

Inserting these figures into the current purchasing power statement of financial position gives us:

Demo: Current purchasing power
Statement of financial position as at 31 December

	20X4	20X5
	$	$
Land	6 000	6 500
Equipment	4 800	3 900
Inventory	583	2 262
Bank	11 500	13 400
	22 883	26 062
Share capital	24 000	26 000
Retained profit	(1 117)	62
	22 883	26 062

The retained profit figures are balancing figures for the moment.

Note that these two sets of figures are not directly comparable because those for 31 December 20X4 are in 31 December 20X4 $ and those for 31 December 20X5 are in 31 December 20X5 $. We could easily convert all of the figures as at 31 December 20X4 to 31 December 20X5 $ by multiplying everything by 130/120.

The figures in the current purchasing power statement of financial position are of limited value for most decision-making purposes. The reason for that is that there is very little reason to expect specific prices to move in line with the general rate of inflation. We could link the replacement cost financial statements to management decisions, but that is more difficult in the case of current purchasing power.

Current purchasing power accounting treats the entity as a financial investment made by its shareholders. If the entity makes a profit in current purchasing power terms then the financial investment has more than kept up with losses arising due to inflation. The fact that a loss has been incurred in 20X4 means that the shareholders are worse off in purchasing power terms than they were at the beginning of the period. In a sense, the loss has been incurred by the shareholders rather than by the entity itself.

The figures in the statement of profit or loss are all expressed in a variety of $ units. We can convert those to year end $ by looking at the dates when the transactions occurred. For example, the only sale that took place during the year ended 31 December 20X4 was on 31 August 20X4. Converting that to 31 December 20X4 $ requires us to multiply $4000 × 120/115 = $4174. Similarly, the only purchase was on 1 February 20X4 and so it was worth $2500 × 120/103 = $2913 in 31 December 20X4 $. Depreciation is based on historical cost × 120/100.

The same logic is applied to the figures for the year ended 31 December 20X5.

If there had been many sales and purchases throughout the year, then the historical cost totals would have been stated at the average monetary unit for the year. They would have been converted to year end units by multiplying by the year end index and dividing by the average index for the year.

There is one adjustment relating to the statement of profit or loss that is not particularly intuitive. Most entities have monetary assets and liabilities whose values are exposed to the decline in purchasing power caused by inflation. Basically, the entity loses on any monetary assets and gains on any monetary liabilities. The figure is determined by calculating the net monetary assets as at the beginning of the year and converting that sum to year end monetary units. All transactions that would affect that total, such as sales and purchases and other receipts and payments of cash, are converted to year end units and added. The result is compared to the closing net monetary assets figure, which is automatically stated in year end monetary units, and any difference is the gain or loss on monetary assets.

For example, Demo had a loss on net monetary assets during the year ended 31 December 20X4:

	31 December 20X4
	$
Net monetary assets on 1 January 20X4 = $10 000 × 120/100	12 000
Revenue	4 174
Purchases	(2 913)
'Expected' closing net monetary assets	13 261
Actual closing net monetary assets	11 500
Loss	1 761

Similarly, for the year ended 31 December 20X5:

	31 December 20X5
	$
Net monetary assets on 1 January 20X5 = $11 500 × 130/120	12 458
Revenue	7 944
Purchases	(6 036)
'Expected' closing net monetary assets	14 366
Actual closing net monetary assets	13 400
Loss (rounded down to avoid a rounding difference)	965

A loss on net monetary assets suggests that the entity had a positive cash balance for most of the period. There would have been a gain if the entity had, say, borrowed and had a net monetary liability throughout the year.

Putting these figures together we get the following statements:

Demo:
Current purchasing power
Statement of profit or loss for the year ended 31 December

	20X4	20X5
	$	$
Revenue	4 174	7 944
Opening inventory	nil	632
Purchases	2 913	6 036
Closing inventory	(583)	(2262)
	2 330	4 406
Depreciation	1 200	1 300
Total operating costs	644	2 238
Loss on net monetary assets	(1 761)	(965)
Profit	(1 117)	1 273

The cumulative profit as at the end of 20X5 was ($1117 × 130/120) + $1273 = $62, so the figures in the statement of financial position agree. Note that the opening balance on retained earnings had to be restated from 31 December 20X4 $ to 31 December 20X5 $ before they could be combined.

The Usefulness of Current Purchasing Power

Most of the criticisms that can be directed at historical cost accounting also apply to current purchasing power. Both ignore unrealised gains. Both have limited value for decision-making.

Current purchasing power does offer some advantages over historical cost:

- It allows for inflation.
- Figures can be restated to make them easy to compare over time.
- The reported figures are objective because they are based on verifiable historical costs and official government indices.
- The figures are relatively cheap and easy to prepare.

Current purchasing power may also be desirable to the shareholders because the figures are adjusted for the effects of inflation. If the entity makes a profit in current purchasing power terms, then the shareholders' equity should be keeping pace with declines in the value of money.

Net Realisable Value Accounting

So far, we have looked at a variety of bases that use entry values. Net realisable value accounting uses an exit value.

You should already be familiar with the concept of net realisable value. It is price at which an asset could be sold in an orderly market.

Net realisable value accounting was proposed in a discussion paper published by the Institute of Chartered Accountants of Scotland (McMonnies, 1988). The argument put forward in support was that adding the total net realisable value of all assets together gave a useful piece of information. That total was effectively the opportunity cost of remaining in business. Publishing that information would both challenge the directors to justify this ongoing investment and provide the shareholders with an indication of the alternatives open to them.

Demo and Net Realisable Value

We will focus on the year ended 31 December 20X4 only for the sake of simplicity.

Demo's inventory had a selling price of $47 per unit at 31 December 20X4. That gives a valuation of 20 units at $47 = $940.

The land could have been sold for $5500 and the equipment for $4200.

The statement of financial position shows all assets at their net realisable value:

Demo:
Net realisable value
Statement of financial position as at 31 December 20X4

	$
Land	5 500
Equipment	4 200
Inventory	940
Bank	11 500
	22 140
Share capital	20 000
Retained profit	2 140
	22 140

As usual, the retained profit figure is inserted as a balancing figure.

Valuing all of the figures in the statement of profit or loss at their net realisable value could prove confusing because the cost of sales would, by definition, equal the sales figure and so there would always be a loss after other expenses were taken into account.

The cost of inventory consumed can be taken as the historical cost figure of $2000. The difference between that and its selling price can be taken as a realised holding gain or as added value arising from the trading activities.

Depreciation can be calculated on the basis of movements in net realisable value from the beginning of the year to the end. So the depreciation of equipment for the year ended 31 December 20X4 = $5000 − $4200 = $800.

A holding gain of $5500 − $5000 = $500 has arisen on land and a gain of $940 − $500 = $440 has arisen on closing inventory. Total holding gains = $500 + $440 = $940.

We can derive the following statement of profit or loss from these figures:

Demo:
Net realisable value
Statement of profit or loss for the year ended 31 December 20X4

	$
Revenue	4 000
Cost of inventory	2 000
Depreciation	800
Total operating costs	2 800
Net realisable value operating profit	1 200
Holding gains	940
Replacement profit	2 140

Advantages of Net Realisable Value

A number of advantages have been claimed for net realisable value accounting. The Institute of Chartered Accountants of Scotland (McMonnies, 1988) argued that:

• Net realisable values can be readily observed in the market place.
• Net realisable value is easily understood by users.
• Net realisable value eliminates allocation problems associated with, say, depreciation. The charge is simply the movement from one period to the next.

- The numbers in the financial statements are 'additive' and 'real'. The value of equity reflects the amount that would be expected if the entity was wound up and all assets liquidated and used to settle liabilities.
- Figures are reasonably objective and can be compared between entities.

Even if the above points are accepted, it can also be argued that net realisable values are not relevant to the shareholders of a continuing business. The resulting values might be unrealistic. For example, a highly specialised asset could have very little net realisable value but could be extremely valuable to the entity.

Real Terms Accounting

In 1989, the Institute of Chartered Accountants of England and Wales published a discussion paper by David Solomons that was intended to set out a coherent basis for financial reporting. Solomons (1989) proposed a valuation basis that effectively combined elements of replacement cost, in a modified form, with current purchasing power. He called this 'real terms accounting'.

Solomons proposed that assets should be valued at their value to the business or their deprival value. Deprival value can be calculated as shown in Figure 7.1.

This diagram is best interpreted by asking what would happen if an entity was deprived of a particular asset. If the asset was worth replacing then the cost of that deprival would be its replacement cost. If the asset was not worth replacing then its deprival value depends on whether the asset was worth keeping. If it was, the entity will lose the net present value of any cash flows that the asset would have yielded. If it was not worth keeping, then the loss would be the net realisable value that would have been obtained when it was sold.

In practice, most assets would be replaced and so deprival value is basically the same as replacement cost. Using deprival value deals with the possibility that replacement costs are not always relevant.

Solomons (1989) also proposed that there should be an adjustment to reflect the gains and losses on net monetary assets to reflect the impact of inflation on monetary assets and liabilities.

We can apply this logic to prepare a set of real terms financial statements for Demo. The fact that the system combines much of the logic of replacement cost and current purchasing power accounting means that we can use many of the workings from earlier in the chapter.

The statement of financial position will essentially be the same as that for replacement cost accounting, except that we restate the owners' share capital to restate the figure in terms of year end \$. That gives \$20 000 $\times$ 120/100 = \$24 000. The other figures would only differ if deprival values were lower than replacement costs, which does not apply to Demo.

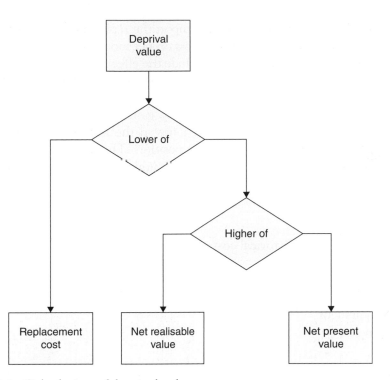

Figure 7.1 Calculation of deprival value
Source: Solomons (1989)

Demo:
Real terms
Statement of financial position as at 31 December 20X4

	$
Land	6 300
Equipment	4 400
Inventory	720
Bank	11 500
	22 920
Share capital	24 000
Reserves	(1 080)
	22 920

The statement of profit or loss is based upon the replacement cost statement of profit or loss, but we include the gain or loss on net monetary assets and we restate the replacement cost holding gains to exclude the effects of general inflation. That means that the holding gains and losses are 'real' gains – in other words, they are gains that exceed the rate of inflation.

We can determine the unrealised holding gains due to general inflation by comparing the figures for non-monetary items in the historical cost and current purchasing power statements of financial position. The unrealised holding gains come from comparing the operating profits under historical cost and current purchasing power.

Applying this logic to Demo gives us the following adjustments:

	Historical cost	Current purchasing power	Gain due to inflation
	$	$	$
Land	5 000	6 000	1 000
Equipment	4 000	4 800	800
Inventory	500	583	83
			1 883

The historical cost operating profit was $1000 and the current purchasing power operating profit was $644, which suggests a loss of $356.

Real holding gains for the period were $500 + $1920 − $1883 − $356 = $181.

Pulling these figures together gives:

Demo:
Real terms
Statement of profit or loss for the year ended 31 December 20X4

	$
Revenue	4 000
Cost of inventory	2 400
Depreciation	1 100
Total operating costs	3 500
Replacement cost operating profit	500
Real holding gains	181
Loss on net monetary assets	(1 761)
Real terms profit	(1 080)

This is a useful performance measure that combines the advantages of both replacement cost and current purchasing power. The shareholders can see that Demo made a replacement cost profit of $500, which indicates that it is maintaining its productive capacity. The real holding gains show that gains on the values of non-monetary items are more than just an illusion due to inflation. However, the significant loss on net monetary assets suggests that Demo has a cash surplus whose value is being eroded by the effects of rising prices.

Income and Valuation in Practice

So far, this chapter has discussed several conceptual approaches to the preparation of financial statements without making a great deal of reference to the real world. There is surprisingly little in the accounting standards about the selection of a basis for financial reporting.

The IASB's (2013) *Conceptual Framework for Financial Reporting* lists four measurement bases:

- historical cost;
- current cost (which is described in a manner that is broadly similar to our discussion of replacement cost);
- realisable value;
- present value (that is, net present value).

The description is followed by a brief paragraph that states that the measurement basis that is most commonly adopted is historical cost, albeit combined with other bases for particular figures. For example, inventory is generally valued at the lower of (historical) cost and net realisable value. The liabilities associated with pension plans are generally shown at net present value.

This brief discussion then leads on to an overview of the relevance of different bases to different stakeholders. Basically, some models measure and maintain financial capital whereas others focus on physical capital. These ideas were distinguished when we discussed replacement cost, which maintains physical capital, and compared it to current purchasing power, which focuses on financial capital.

The Conceptual Framework implies that this is an important distinction that requires a difficult but important choice to be made. The document does not, however, indicate which model should be adopted.

Hyperinflationary Economies

The only formal requirement to apply a model other than historical cost accounting is to be found in IAS 29 *Financial Reporting in Hyperinflationary Economies*, which was first issued in 1989.

Hyperinflation is an economic condition that is only rarely encountered. This is where prices rise so rapidly that the local currency starts to become almost irrelevant. One element of the definition is that the cumulative inflation rate over three years is 100% or more.

Under conditions of hyperinflation, the IAS requires that historical costs be restated to year end units of current purchasing power using a general price index.

Some Milestones in the Rise and Fall of the Debate about Alternatives to Historical Cost

There have been a number of attempts to replace historical cost accounting with a more relevant and credible basis for financial reporting. Those attempts have tended to prove unsuccessful because of political concerns of some description.

Inflation is regarded as an important measure of a government's ability to manage the economy. High levels of inflation are associated with falling currency values and other forms of economic unrest. For example, people are unwilling to save when the purchasing power of their savings is being eroded by inflation. Employees are prone to seek wage rises that exceed the rate of inflation so that they can protect their standard of living. It follows that any accounting system that enables users to see the impact of inflation may well be highly unpopular with governments. Current purchasing power is a relatively cheap and simple means of adjusting for inflation, but its use was phased out very quickly after its introduction in the UK in the 1970s (Accounting Standards Steering Committee, 1974). At that time, UK inflation was running at a rate of 20% or more per annum and it was viewed as a serious social and economic threat.

A less cynical explanation for government's lack of enthusiasm for the use of current purchasing power accounting is that it may be viewed as a tacit acceptance that inflation is an inevitable aspect of economic management. Historically, all major countries have seen prices rise over time, but low levels of inflation have very little impact from one year to the next and so adjustments are not particularly important. The German government was strongly opposed to the introduction of any form of inflation accounting because it intended to eradicate inflation, thereby rendering inflation adjustments unnecessary. (There is a chapter on different countries' attitudes to inflation accounting in Tweedie and Whittington, 1984.)

Current purchasing power gave way to a variation on replacement cost accounting in SSAP 16 (Accounting Standards Committee, 1980).[3] That proved a highly controversial standard from the outset. Preparers found that the figures were difficult and expensive to calculate and audit, and the overall effect of the resulting adjustments was to massively reduce profits when compared with the historical cost statements that were used as the starting point. Indeed, it was common for companies that had reported historical cost profits to report losses when the figures were restated in terms of replacement costs. Annual reports frequently included comments from the chief executive or chairman to the effect that the SSAP 16 figures were provided for the sake of complying with the standard and that shareholders should disregard them on the grounds that the numbers were confusing.

The history of SSAP 16 and the events surrounding its withdrawal are discussed in a paper by Pong and Whittington (1996). This places the story in a wider context and indicates the implications for the standard-setting process that arise from the need to withdraw the standard in the face of opposition from preparers. By the time the standard was withdrawn, a number of major companies had simply refused to comply with its requirement. That led to their auditors reporting that the company was in breach of the requirements of SSAP 16, which appeared to have relatively little impact.

To an extent, the need to adjust for changing prices depends upon the rate at which prices actually change. It could be argued that many large companies show their property, plant and equipment at a market value, which is adjusted as necessary for impairment. That could be viewed as being very close to the values that would be obtained using the deprival value method in real terms accounting. Inventory is generally valued at the lower of cost and net realisable value, but historical cost will not differ significantly from replacement cost provided the holding period is short and prices are not increasing rapidly. It could be argued that the IASB has successfully introduced a number of the elements of replacement cost accounting by the gradual replacement of historical costs with fair values on a figure-by-figure basis.

'Stealth' Adjustments

It is possible to make an argument that a number of the changes that are implied by the use of the models discussed in this chapter have already occurred.

Most non-current assets are shown at their fair values, which are clearly related to their replacement costs at a point in time and are, therefore, also stated in terms of current purchasing power. The requirement to review assets regularly for impairment has the effect of restating these replacement costs in terms of deprival value.

Expressing performance in terms of total comprehensive income has the effect of adding recognised gains to the operating profit for the year. That adds a further dimension that echoes the calculation of total profit under replacement cost accounting.

Replacement cost accounting proved unacceptable when it was introduced by means of a single standard that required the publication of a historical cost profit figure that was then adjusted for the effects of price changes. The present standard-setting regime could be accused of having achieved the same effect by a gradual process of changing individual standards so that assets are valued in a more meaningful way and profit figures are more relevant.

Summary

Developing a model for the determination of income and capital is a complex process. A number of alternatives have been proposed, some of which have been discussed in this chapter.

Ideally, the accounting system in place should enable users of financial statements to make realistic and informed decisions about company performance. That suggests that the figures should relate to meaningful economic decisions. That requires a choice to be made because different bases inform different decisions. For example, valuing assets and costs in terms of replacement costs will help the shareholders to tell whether the entity will remain a viable business in production terms. That matters if the shareholders are keen to ensure that the business can continue to produce tyres or chocolate bars or whatever else it manufactures. The use of current purchasing power means that the shareholders can view the entity as a purely financial investment and tell whether it is capable of maintaining the spending power of the cash that they have invested in it. Both sets of numbers are useful, but in different ways.

Finding an acceptable alternative to historical cost is difficult because preparers like the simplicity and objectivity associated with historical costs. They may also be attracted by the fact that historical cost profits tend to be higher than the other bases and so the entity looks more profitable. There is also a problem in getting government to agree to an alternative basis because changing prices are associated with inflation, which is an economic problem that tends to undermine a government's credibility.

Tutorial Questions

Question 1

Alpha Ltd sells electrical appliances. Purchases and sales occur steadily during the year.

According to the historical cost profit statement, the cost of goods sold for the year ended 31 December 20X5 was as follows:

	£000
Opening inventory	400
Purchases	5 200
Closing inventory	(470)
	5 130

Opening and closing inventories were, on average, two months old at the beginning and end of the year respectively.

The relevant stock indices were:

31 October 20X4	247
Average for year ended 31 December 20X5	270
31 October 20X5	273

Calculate the replacement cost of goods sold for the year ended 31 December 20X5.

Note: if purchases occurred evenly throughout the year then the historical cost figure is effectively already shown at its current purchasing power average.

Question 2

Bravo Ltd purchased a vehicle for £17 000 on 1 January 20X6. The company's cost of capital is 10%.

At that date, the directors of the company could have sold the vehicle for £14 500.

The vehicle was expected to generate savings of £4000 per annum for each of the next five years. At the end of year five, it is expected that it will be sold for £5 000.

At the end of year one, it was discovered that the annual savings would only be £3000 per annum. The anticipated residual value at the end of year five was likely to be only £2500.

The vehicle would have cost £15 000 to replace at the end of year one. It could have been sold for £9000.

Calculate the deprival value of the van at the time of its purchase and also at the end of year one.

Question 3

(a) Calculate the deprival value (value to the business) of each of the following assets (assume a 10% cost of capital throughout):
  • A vehicle that would cost £16 000 to replace. It could be sold for £14 000. It is expected to yield net cash flows of £5000 at the end of each of the next three years with a final inflow (including proceeds of disposal) of £6000 at the end of year four.
  • A piece of equipment that would cost £10 000 to replace. This could be sold for £9000. It is expected to yield net cash flows of £4500 at the end of each of the next two years.

(b) Explain what these deprival values represent.

Question 4

On 1 January 20X7, Gill established a company with share capital of €40 000. These funds were applied as follows:

	€	Estimated useful life
Premises	10 000	almost all land
Equipment	10 000	5 years
Car	8 000	4 years
Bank	12 000	

The following sales and purchases occurred during the year ended 31 December 20X7:

Purchases		€
30 January 20X7	1500 units @ €10	15 000
30 June 20X7	2000 units @ €12	24 000

Cash sales		
20 February 20X7	1000 units @ €11	11 000
20 September 20X7	1500 units @ €13	19 500

Gill obtains a copy of his supplier's price list every month. During the month of February, each unit of inventory would have cost €11.50, during September €14.00 and in December €16.00.

On 31 December 20X7, Gill visited a local car dealership and found a car identical to the one he had purchased (same model, age, mileage and general condition) on sale for €5000.

The premises were valued at €14 000 on 31 December 20X7.

The cost of new equipment similar to that used by Gill increases by 20% during the year.

Purchasing power, as expressed by the retail price index, was:

1 January 20X7	100
30 January 20X7	102
20 February 20X7	103
30 June 20X7	107
20 September 20X7	111
31 December 20X7	115

(a) Prepare Gill's statement of profit or loss and statement of financial position using:
  • historical cost accounting
  • replacement cost accounting
  • current purchasing power accounting
  • real terms accounting.
(b) Discuss the practical difficulties that you would expect to arise in the preparation of each set of figures.
(c) Discuss the relevance of each set of figures.

Questions with Answers

Question 1

D started a business on 1 March 20X4, with an investment of $30 000 in cash. The business made the following payments on 1 March 20X4:

	$
Deposit on premises	15 000
Equipment	9 000
Inventory	6 000
	30 000

The premises cost $55 000. They were purchased with the assistance of a $40 000 mortgage on the property. The loan, together with interest thereon, was to be repaid with half yearly instalments of $3500, payable on 31 August and 28 February. The company was to be charged interest of 6% per half year on the outstanding balance.

The following historical cost figures have been prepared for the year ended 28 February 20X5:

D

Historical cost statement of profit or loss for the year ended 28 February 20X5

	$	$
Sales (all cash)		124 000
Opening inventory	6 000	
Purchases	80 000	
Closing inventory	6 667	
Cost of inventory consumed	79 333	
Wages	11 000	
Depreciation – premises	1 100	
Depreciation – equipment	1 800	
Interest	4 734	
Total expenses		97 967
Profit for year		26 033

D

Historical cost statement of financial position as at 28 February 20X5

	$	$
Property plant and equipment		
Premises		53 900
Equipment		7 200
		61 100

Current assets
    Inventory   6 667
    Bank   20 000
                                26 667
                                87 767

Equity
    Share capital   30 000
    Retained earnings   12 033
                                42 033

Non-current liabilities
    Mortgage on premises   37 734
Current liabilities
    Trade payables   8 000
                                87 767

A $14 000 dividend was paid on 28 February 20X5.
The following indices are available:

	Premises	Equipment	Materials	Retail price index
At 1 March 20X4	120	180	150	200
At 31 August 20X4	124	200	164	212
When closing inventory purchased	127	219	177	223
At 28 February 20X5	127	223	179	225
Average for year ended 28 February 20X5	124	201	164	212

Recalculate D's financial statements using:

• replacement cost accounting
• current purchasing power accounting
• real terms accounting.

Endnotes

1. Opening capital would have been $(2500/1.07 + 3700/1.07^2 + 7000/1.07^3) =$ £11 282. Closing capital would have been $(3700/1.07 + 7000/1.07^2) = $£9572. Cash flow would have been £2500. Income $= 2500 + (9572 - 11\,282) = $£790.
2. Just a minor point about grammar. 'Historical cost' is the correct term for this system of accounting. There is no such thing as 'historic cost' accounting.
3. This standard defined 'current cost' in terms of deprival value. This was not a pure deprival value system. For example, if the company had significant borrowings then a 'gearing adjustment' was applied, which went some way to recognising a gain on the monetary liabilities that were declining in value because of inflation

References

Accounting Standards Committee (1980) *Statement of Standard Accounting Practice 16, Current Cost Accounting*.

Accounting Standards Steering Committee (1974) *Provisional Statement of Standard Accounting Practice 7, Accounting for Changes in the Purchasing Power of Money*.

IASB (2001) IAS 29 *Financial Reporting in Hyperinflationary Economies*.

IASB (2013) *The Conceptual Framework for Financial Reporting*. London: IFRS Foundation/IASB.

McMonnies, P.N. (1988) *Making Corporate Reports Valuable*. The Institute of Chartered Accountants of Scotland/Kogan Page.

Pong, C.K.M. & Whittington, G. (1996) The withdrawal of current cost accounting in the United Kingdom: A study of the Accounting Standards Committee. *Abacus* **32**(1) pp. 30–53.

Solomons, D. (1989) *Guidelines for Financial Reporting Standards*. Institute of Chartered Accountants in England and Wales.

Tweedie, D. & Whittington, G. (1984) *The Debate on Inflation Accounting*. Cambridge: Cambridge University Press.

FINANCIAL INSTRUMENTS

Contents

Learning Objectives

After studying this chapter, you should be able to:

- explain the accounting issues associated with financial instruments;
- account for financial liabilities and financial assets;
- explain hedge accounting (in outline);
- discuss the implications of the 2007 Credit Crunch and the extent to which accounting may have been implicated.

Introduction

The accounting treatment of financial instruments is complicated because the underlying issues are complicated. Financial instruments have been developed in order to meet the needs of a vast range of users. Many of these users have perfectly benign and responsible needs. For example, it is possible that a farmer will wish to buy a financial instrument that gives the right to sell a crop that has not yet been harvested at a known and agreed price. The farmer will, therefore, be protected from the risks associated with a declining market price if there is a glut of that product and unit prices fall.

The same instruments can also be used in highly speculative ways. For example, a commodity speculator might not grow crops, but could buy a financial instrument that grants the right to sell at a fixed price in the future (exactly the same instrument as was used by our farmer). If the price falls then the speculator can buy an instrument that grants the right to buy the same quantity on the same settlement date but at a lower price, and can close out the position. The difference between the prices will be profit. The position will still have to be closed out even if the price remains constant or rises, in which case the speculator will suffer a loss. This speculative motive complicates the valuation of financial instruments because the markets start to consider factors that might affect the demand and supply of the instruments themselves rather than just the underlying supply and demand of the agricultural crop.

These financial instruments can also make it possible to take a position in a particular market that would not otherwise be possible. It is possible, for example, to purchase an instrument that will pay out in the event of a default on, say, Greek sovereign debt, without actually owning any of that debt. These speculative practices have been discredited to an extent because of economic problems, most noticeably the 2007 Credit Crunch.

Financial instruments can also be used to mislead. For example, a variety of funding instruments have been developed to enable borrowers to classify their liabilities as equity. Doing so understates gearing and therefore makes the borrower look less risky.

For all of these reasons, the regulation of accounting for financial instruments has been contested. At the time of writing there were five standards in issue:

- IAS 32 *Financial Instruments: Presentation*
- IAS 39 *Financial Instruments: Recognition and Measurement*
- IFRS 7 *Financial Instruments: Disclosures*
- IFRS 9 *Financial Instruments*
- IFRS 13 *Fair Value Measurement*

IFRS 9 *Financial Instruments* (IASB, 2010c) is essentially a replacement for IAS 39 *Financial Instruments: Recognition and Measurement* (IASB, 2010a), but the changes that are being introduced are being phased in gradually and so sections of IAS 39 are being withdrawn and replaced with updated equivalents in IFRS 9.

'Financial' Assets and Liabilities versus the Rest

IAS 32 *Financial Instruments: Presentation* (IASB, 2008) distinguishes financial instruments by defining financial assets and financial liabilities.

A financial instrument is defined by IAS 32 as 'any contract that gives rise to a financial asset of one entity and a financial liability or equity instrument of another entity'.

A financial asset can take a number of forms:

- cash;
- equity instruments of other companies;
- contractual rights to receive financial assets or to exchange a financial asset or liability under conditions that are favourable (e.g. holding an option to buy an equity instrument for less than its market value).

The definition of financial assets is not particularly controversial, although some of the arrangements that have to be accounted for can be quite complicated. We will discuss those in some detail later in this chapter.

Similarly, financial liabilities are quite clearly defined by IAS 32 as 'any liability that is . . . a contractual obligation . . . to deliver cash or another financial asset to another entity; or . . . to exchange financial assets or financial liabilities with another entity under conditions that are potentially unfavourable to the entity'.

The definitions of both financial assets and financial liabilities have been abbreviated slightly to exclude balances arising from arrangements that are outwith the scope of this text.

These definitions restrict the application of these standards to specific forms of assets and liabilities. For example, a warranty would impose a duty to repair or replace a defective item but that duty is not a financial liability. Similarly, a tax liability arises from statutory rather than contractual obligations and so these standards will not apply.

An equity instrument is defined as being any contract that evidences a residual interest in the assets of an entity after deducting all of its liabilities.

Financial assets and liabilities can create a number of complications that do not arise with their non-financial counterparts. For example, derivatives often create contractual rights or obligations without there being any transaction other than the signature of a contract. A Belgian company could sign a forward contract that obliges it to sell an agreed quantity of US dollars at some future date for an agreed quantity of euros. It could be argued that the signature created no net asset or liability at the date of signature, although that situation might change as time passes and exchange rates change. By the settlement date of the contract, there could be a net liability on the Belgian company because the agreed quantity of US dollars is worth more in euros than the rate implied by the forward contract.

Accounting for Instruments Issued as Debt or Equity

Almost all entities raise finance by issuing financial instruments that have to be accounted for as either debt or equity. Deciding which category an instrument should appear within can be complicated because of the gearing ratio, which has been discussed from time to time in other chapters.

In an ideal world, the directors would wish to have the lowest possible gearing ratio. That would make the accounts look less risky. Ideally, they would also wish to pay the least amount of tax. Interest paid on debt is an expense for tax purposes, but any dividend paid on equity is not.

These motives have led to the creation of what amounts to an industry in 'financial engineering'. Commercial banks and other providers of finance have put a great deal of time and effort into creating financial instruments that achieve the following aims:

- The instrument looks like debt to the buyer but can be accounted for as equity.
- The instrument looks like debt for tax purposes.

Making debt look like equity will reduce the gearing ratio. Making dividends look like interest payments will reduce the tax charge.

In this context, 'looks like' is the operative phrase. The bank that designs the instrument is aware that the economic substance of the instrument is very different from the treatment in the financial statements or the tax calculations. That makes it possible to charge a premium rate for the advice. That could create a situation in which the shareholders are being misled about the risks associated with their investments and are bearing an additional cost because of this because a traditional loan would have been cheaper than a complicated financial instrument that has been used instead.

The Duck Test

IAS 32 is based on the logical assumption that if something looks like a duck and quacks like a duck then it is a duck. It does not matter what that thing is called or how the reporting entity wishes to account for it.

Table 8.1 Examples for classification

Debenture stock	A debenture instrument has been issued that grants the holder the right to annual interest payments and the repayment of the principal sum at a specified date.
Equity shares	The entity has a large number of equity shares in issue. The shareholders have become used to a steady stream of dividends and the shareholders are unlikely to tolerate any deviation.
Preference shares	The entity has a cumulative preference share in issue. Shareholders will receive a fixed preference dividend unless the directors decide to suspend the payment. Unpaid dividends accumulate and will be paid at a date to be determined by the directors. No dividend can be paid on equity shares while there is an unpaid preference dividend outstanding.
Redeemable preference shares	The entity also has a redeemable preference share in issue. It carries a cumulative preference dividend. The preference shareholders will be repaid the nominal value of the shares at a specified date in the future.

The examples in Table 8.1 have been analysed in terms of the definition of financial liabilities and equity instruments. The answers may be obvious in some cases, but we must still go through the process because the history in this area has been driven by misleading descriptions and titles.

The debenture stock is a financial liability because there is an obligation to make interest payments and to repay the amount borrowed. The same argument applies to the redeemable preference shares because their face value must be repaid at the specified date.

The equity shares and preference shares both grant management a degree of discretion over the payments. The fact that it would be undesirable to suspend or reduce either the equity dividend or the preference dividend does not mean that there is a contractual obligation to make these payments. Thus, these shares are equity instruments.

The redeemable preference shares are a relatively simple example of the ways in which companies once used to indulge in financial engineering. Before the introduction of IAS 32, the issuing entity would construct a redeemable preference share that gave the buyer virtually the same rights as would exist in a loan agreement. The fact that the buyer had virtually the same rights and security meant that the entity had made the same commitment as it would have had if it had borrowed the same amount. The instruments would then have been classified as shares and so would have been accounted for as equity. The result was misleading because the holders of that entity's ordinary shares were exposed to the same risks as if the company had borrowed. They would also have suffered a financial cost because the entity would have missed the opportunity to claim tax relief on interest if the funds had been raised by borrowing.

In practice, users of financial statements will take a great deal of care over the equity section of the statement of financial position. Even if the shares are classified as equity under IAS 32's definitions, there may be a case for treating any preference shares as debt for the purpose of calculating the gearing ratio and for treating preference dividends as interest for the purpose of calculating the interest cover.

Compound Instruments

Some instruments combine elements of liabilities and equity. For example, a debt instrument may carry the right to convert the value of the loan into equity shares at favourable terms at a specified date in the future. There can be a valid commercial reason for issuing such instruments. For example, a young business might find it easier to sell convertible loan stock than to issue shares to third parties because of the lack of an established track record. During the initial phase of the instrument's life, the holder has all of the security of being a lender. The entity should have been able to prove itself by the time of conversion and the basis of conversion is normally attractive to the bondholder. Thus, the bondholder has the opportunity to make a sizeable capital gain when converting the bonds into shares.

From the issuer's point of view, convertibles can be cheaper than debt because the possibility of a capital gain makes it possible to offer a lower rate of interest. Furthermore, the fact that the loans may effectively convert themselves into equity means that there is no need to raise further finance in order to repay the bondholder.

For example, a $10m bond was issued at par.[1] This pays an interest rate of 7% for four years, with interest paid annually in arrears. At the end of the four-year period the bondholders have the right to convert their holdings at the rate of one fully-paid $0.50 share for every $1.00 of the bond. If they do not take up their conversion rights then the bond will be redeemed at par on that date.

A four-year bond issued by a similar company would normally carry an interest rate of 12%.

IAS 32 requires that we analyse this bond to establish exactly what it is that the company is offering. One argument is that the bondholder has purchased a debt instrument at a premium to what it is actually worth because it also carries an element of equity investment (based on the argument that a rational investor would have invested elsewhere if nothing was being offered in return for the reduced interest on offer).

If the bond had been issued at the interest rate of 12% demanded by the market, then the net present value of the cash flows would have been determined as follows:

			Discount factor	Present value
End of year 1	Interest $10m @ 7%	$0.7m	$1/(1.12)^1$	$0.63m
End of year 2	Interest $10m @ 7%	$0.7m	$1/(1.12)^2$	$0.56m
End of year 3	Interest $10m @ 7%	$0.7m	$1/(1.12)^3$	$0.50m
End of year 4	Interest $10m @ 7%	$0.7m	$1/(1.12)^4$	$0.44m
	Principal repaid	$10.0m	$1/(1.12)^4$	$6.36m
Total				$8.49m

So, the cash flows are based on the actual cash payments that the bondholders will receive, based upon the coupon rate of the bond and its nominal value. These cash flows are discounted at a rate that is appropriate to the risks that the bondholder is taking and the end result is that the cash flows are worth $8.49m. Assuming that the bondholders are rational, there must be a reason for paying $10m for a series of cash flows worth only $8.49m and the logic underlying IAS 32 is that the bondholders were effectively acquiring an equity stake worth $10m − $8.49m = $1.51m.

When the bond is first issued it will be treated as a loan of $8.49m with an interest rate of 12%. A further $1.51m will be credited to equity.

During the life of the bond, the entity will account for the loan using the starting assumption that it is a 12% loan issued for $8.49m:

	Interest at 12%	Cash paid	Balance
Opening balance			$8.49m
Year 1	$1.02m	$0.7m	$8.81m
Year 2	$1.06m	$0.7m	$9.17m
Year 3	$1.09m	$0.7m	$9.56m
Year 4	$1.14m	$0.7m	$10.00m

The interest charges for years 3 and 4 have been adjusted slightly to avoid a confusing rounding error. The annual interest charge is the previous year's closing balance multiplied by 12%.

If all of the bondholders elect to convert their bondholding to shares at that date, the entity will have issued 10m $0.50 shares with a nominal value of $5m. The book value of the liability and equity converted will be $10.00m + $1.51m = $11.51m. So $11.51m − $5m = $6.51m will be added to share premium.

If none of the bondholders took up their conversion rights then the loan would be repaid with $10m of cash and the $1.51m would remain in equity.

Clearly, it is possible that there will be a partial take-up, but that would simply mean recording the partial repayment at par before applying the remainder of the balance to the issue of shares. If, say, 60% of the bondholders elected for repayment then the $6m would be paid out in cash and the remaining $4m would be added to the $1.51m equity so that $5.51m is deemed to have been received for shares with a nominal value of $2m. In that case, the $3.51m added to share premium would involve a transfer from the equity balance that was created when the bonds were first issued.

IAS 32 does not provide any specific guidance for the accounting treatment of the equity element. Arguably, the resulting reserve is not distributable and so it should be shown separately. For example, Continental AG's 2011 annual report includes the following accounting policy note:

Hybrid Financial Instruments

Financial instruments that have both a debt and an equity component are classified and measured separately by those components. Instruments under this heading primarily include bonds with warrants and convertible bonds. In the case of convertible bonds, the fair value of the share conversion rights is recognized separately in capital reserves at the date the bond is issued and therefore deducted from the liability incurred by the bond. Fair values of conversion rights from bonds with below-market interest rates are calculated based on the present value of the difference between the coupon rate and the market rate of interest. The interest expense for the debt component is calculated over the term of the bond based on the market interest rate at the date of issue for a comparable bond without conversion rights. The difference between the deemed interest and the coupon rate increases the carrying amount of the bond indebtedness. In the event of maturity or conversion, the equity component previously recognized in capital reserves at the date of issue is offset against the accumulated retained earnings in accordance with the option permitted by IAS 32.

By treating the balance as a capital reserve the company is stressing that the balance is not distributable.

Interest and Finance Charges

IAS 32 requires that the finance charge should be classified according to the treatment of the associated financial instrument. So a dividend paid on a preference share that is classified as a liability should be treated as an expense in the statement of profit or loss, and a dividend paid on any instrument that is classified as equity should be treated as a distribution of profit and shown as a dividend in the statement of changes in equity.

IFRS 9 requires that all financial liabilities should be recorded at their fair value when first issued, with any transaction costs being subtracted from the amount recognised. This requirement reflects some of the complicated instruments that have been issued in order to exploit the confusion associated with their correct accounting treatment.

For example, a 'deep discounted bond' involves issuing an instrument at a substantial discount to its par value. For example, a borrower could sell a bond with a face value of $1m and a coupon rate of 0%. In order to attract a buyer, the instrument could be issued at a significant discount so that the bondholder's return is provided by the difference between the purchase price and the eventual redemption at a much higher amount.

Before the issue of standards in this area, one reason for issuing such instruments was to exploit the fact that there was nothing to prevent this transaction being recorded as an initial liability of $1m with no subsequent interest until the time of repayment. That would have made the statement of financial position look highly geared, but reported profit would have been enhanced by the fact that the statement of profit or loss would not show any interest charges.

Again, the rules in force require the commercial reality to be shown in the financial statements. For example, an entity issues a bond with a par value of $2m. Professional fees and other costs amount to $30 000. The coupon rate is 2% paid annually in arrears with repayment due at the end of year five. The gross proceeds of sale, before allowing for the fees, were $1.42m.

IFRS 9 requires that we treat this as a liability of $1.39m (that is, we subtract the issue costs in order to determine the net sum raised from the loan).

The next step is to determine the interest rate implicit in this liability. The bondholders will receive two elements of return every year. One is the coupon rate of 2% based on the par value of the bond and the other is the effect of the time value of money 'unwinding' to increase the principal outstanding year by year until it reaches $2m by the end of year five. Offsetting the issue costs has the effect of including them in the finance charges over the life of the liability, so the accruals principle is observed.

The easiest way to determine the effective annual rate of interest is to list the cash flows and input those into a spreadsheet. The internal rate of return (IRR) function can then be used to determine the interest rate:

Time 0 – Gross cash received Issue costs	**$1.42m** **($0.03m)**
End of year 1 – interest paid (coupon rate × par value)	($0.04m)
End of year 2 – interest paid	($0.04m)
End of year 3 – interest paid	($0.04m)
End of year 4 – interest paid	($0.04m)
End of year 5 – interest paid	($0.04m)
Redemption of bond	($2.00m)

The IRR function of a spreadsheet indicates that these cash flows have an effective interest rate of 10%.

Thus, this instrument will be accounted for on the basis that it is an initial borrowing of $1.39m at a rate of 10% for five years. As each year passes, the annual coupon payments will be insufficient to cover the interest being charged and so the liability will increase to $2m by the end of year five, at which time the bonds will be redeemed. The amount outstanding at any given time is a notional amount known as the 'amortised cost'.

The following amounts will appear in the financial statements:

	Interest at 10%	Cash paid	Balance
Opening balance			$1.39m
Year 1	$0.14m	$0.04m	$1.49m
Year 2	$0.15m	$0.04m	$1.60m
Year 3	$0.16m	$0.04m	$1.72m
Year 4	$0.17m	$0.04m	$1.85m
Year 5	$0.19m	$2.04m	Nil

So, for example, the statement of profit or loss for year three will include finance charges of $160 000 and these will be shown in exactly the same way as any other interest or finance charge. The statement of financial position as at the end of year three will show a liability of $1.72m. All of that will be a non-current liability because the cash payment due in year four will amount to only a partial payment of year four's finance charge.

Two Classes of Financial Liability

In general, financial liabilities will be valued at their amortised cost, but there is a category of financial liability that is classified as 'financial liabilities at fair value through profit or loss'.

Financial liabilities classified at fair value through profit or loss will be recognised at their fair value and any subsequent adjustment to reflect changes in fair value will go through the statement of profit or loss. The rules that must be satisfied before this classification can be used are very similar to those relating to financial assets at fair value through profit or loss, and are discussed in the next section.

Accounting for Financial Instruments held as Assets

Accounting for financial instruments as assets has been complicated because they are often used to manage risk. That means that their values can change in line with market movements. Furthermore, the whole point of owning such an asset may be to prevent volatility in the underlying earnings. That has led to the need to accept the recognition of unrealised gains in the statement of profit or loss, if only to show the gains and losses on the instrument being offset against the corresponding losses and gains that the instrument is intended to remedy.

Initial Recognition

Normally, an entity shall recognise a financial asset or a financial liability in its statement of financial position when, and only when, the entity becomes party to the contractual provisions of the instrument. This requirement is imposed by IFRS 9.

The standard permits one area of choice in the case of 'regular way' purchases or sales. These occur when either regulations or custom and practice dictate the timeframe for the delivery of the asset. For example, it may be common practice to agree a price for a sale and for the instrument itself to be delivered three days later with payment occurring on the same date. That raises the question of whether the asset should be recognised at its cost on the date the sale was made (the trade date) or the date when the asset was transferred (the settlement date). Under trade date accounting, the asset (and the corresponding liability for the as yet unpaid purchase consideration) would be recorded in the books immediately. Under settlement date accounting, the asset would not appear until the transaction is completed.

In practice, the main difference between trade date and settlement date accounting is in the recognition of the purchase in the statement of financial position if the trade date and settlement date straddle the year end. Under trade date accounting, there will be an asset and a corresponding liability in the financial statements.

Companies must be consistent in their application of either trade date or settlement date accounting.

Classification of Financial Assets

Accounting for financial assets has become a major issue in the regulation of financial reporting because it has been alleged that the shortcomings in the rules in this area encouraged dysfunctional lending behaviour by banks in the run up to the 2007 Credit Crunch and failed to alert users of financial statements that the banks were seriously exposed to risks associated with those assets.

The basic issues associated with accounting for financial assets are their valuation, the timing of recognition of gains and losses, and the derecognition of assets (that is, their removal from the financial statements).

The accounting treatment of financial assets is determined by both IAS 39 and IFRS 9. Elements of IAS 39 have been replaced by IFRS 9.

Financial assets are defined in fairly broad terms that include cash, an equity instrument in another entity, contractual rights to receive cash or other financial assets, and contractual rights to exchange financial instruments under conditions that are potentially favourable.

IFRS 9 distinguishes between two types of financial asset:

1. **Financial assets measured at amortised cost:** Held with the objective of collecting contractual cash flows; carry contractual terms that give rise to cash flows on specified dates that are solely payments of principal and interest on the principal amount outstanding.
2. **Financial assets measured at fair value:** Financial assets other than those measured at amortised cost.

The titles of the two types of instrument indicate broadly how they should be accounted for:

• Financial assets measured at amortised cost are accounted for on the basis that they will be held until they mature. The expectation is that the instrument's value will reach its maturity value immediately before it is repaid. Until then, it could be argued that there is no need to recognise market fluctuations in its fair value because they are irrelevant to the bondholder.

• Financial assets at fair value are recognised initially at their cost, which should also be their fair value. Subsequent changes to fair value are taken through the statement of profit or loss, as are any receipts from interest or dividends received.

An asset will only be shown at amortised cost if there are fixed cash flows that will make it possible to see the book value unwinding towards the maturity value. Furthermore, the holder will have to have acquired the assets with a view to holding them until maturity. Investors can choose to speculate using fixed interest securities. For example, if interest rates are expected to fall then the value of fixed interest bonds will tend to rise. An investor who believed that a fall in interest rates was likely could buy bonds with a view to holding them for a short period before selling them at a profit.

Even if a bond is to be held to maturity, it need not always be accounted for at amortised cost. The holder can designate an asset that would otherwise be eligible for classification as measured at amortised cost as a financial asset measured at fair value, provided this is done in order to eliminate an 'accounting mismatch'.

An accounting mismatch could occur in circumstances in which there is a link between a financial asset and a financial liability. For example, an investment business pays its depositors a return that is based on the returns that it earns on the financial assets that were purchased using the depositors' funds. In that case it would be more realistic to take the income from those financial assets straight to the statement of profit or loss, where it can be offset against the cost of the finance charges paid to the depositors. If income was measured on the basis of the unwinding of the amortised cost then the amount paid to depositors could exceed the income recognised, even though that could never really happen with this arrangement.

Fair Values

IFRS 9 deals with the determination of fair value at the date of acquisition. There is an entire IFRS (IFRS 13 *Fair Value Measurement*; IASB, 2011) devoted to the issues associated with the determination of fair values at subsequent reporting dates.

IFRS 9 states that financial assets should be recognised at their fair value at their acquisition date. Logically, both parties would have to agree on an acceptable price and so it is difficult to imagine either accepting anything other than the fair value.

It is normally only acceptable to recognise the acquisition at a value other than the transaction price if the fair value is determined by reference to a quoted price in an active market. In that case, it would be acceptable to recognise the market value, with the difference between that and the transaction price being treated as a gain or loss.

Assets Measured at Amortised Cost

If a financial asset is to be classified as measured at amortised cost, then the initial recognition is to take the transaction price as the fair value at the date of acquisition and then to show the asset's value unwinding towards the redemption price at subsequent period ends.

In many ways, an asset measured at amortised cost is treated in the same basic way as a liability. Transaction costs can be taken into account in determining the initial cost and they will, therefore, be taken into account in determining the income recognised.

For example, a buyer paid $148 000 for a 5% bond that will be redeemed at its par value of $200 000 in five years' time. The transaction costs associated with this acquisition were $1500. The owner of this asset will receive an annual coupon payment of $10 000 for five years and the par value of the instrument at the end of year five. This equates to a return of 12% on the investment, which is determined using the IRR function of a spreadsheet. The following figures will be recognised:

	Asset at start of period ($)	Income at 12% – to statement of profit or loss ($)	Coupon payment ($)	Amortised cost at end – to statement of financial position ($)
Year 1	149 500	17 940	(10 000)	157 440
Year 2	157 440	18 893	(10 000)	166 333
Year 3	166 333	19 960	(10 000)	176 293
Year 4	176 293	21 155	(10 000)	187 448
Year 5	187 448	22 494	(10 000)	200 000

The additions have been distorted slightly to eliminate a rounding error.

Amortised costs do not necessarily bear any relation to fair values because of the effects of interest rates during the asset's life. If interest rates increase across the economy by the end of year one, then the market value of the bond will decrease in response. That need not matter to the bondholder because the intention is to hold the bond until its maturity. By the end of year five, the bond will be worth the $200 000 that is paid on maturity and so any gains and losses that occur along the way will be cancelled in time.

Assets Measured at Fair Value

IFRS 13 defines fair value as 'the price that would be received to sell an asset or paid to transfer a liability in an orderly transaction between market participants at the measurement date'.

Fair values do not include transaction costs. The example relating to an asset measured at amortised cost did take transaction costs into account on the acquisition of the asset, but that was in the context of an asset that is expressly measured on a basis other than fair value.

The IFRS recognises that fair value may be not be observable and so fair value may have to be determined using a valuation technique that is 'appropriate in the circumstances'. In other words, if the asset is not traded on an open and observable market that permits participants to observe market prices, then a model must be developed and appropriate facts and figures input into that model.

In some cases, there will be a reasonably robust model that can be used to produce a valuation. For example, when we measured the debt component of a convertible financial instrument earlier in this chapter we started with known cash flows from the debt element of the bond and calculated a net present value using interest rates paid on simple bonds with the same duration that had been issued by similar businesses. In that case, there is unlikely to be a great deal of concern about the relevance of the valuation.

In other cases, the valuer may have to use more than one valuation technique in order to establish a range of possible values. Ideally, the different models and different assumptions will produce some consensus as to the likely value, and a point can be chosen within the range of possible outcomes that can be defended as a realistic valuation.

For example, if the financial asset comprises shares in an unquoted company then it might be possible to use a variety of techniques for determining a fair value. There are dividend valuation models that set a value based on the most recent dividend and the expected rate of growth on future dividends. Earnings can be valued by calculating earnings per share and multiplying by the price/ earnings ratio of quoted companies in the same industry. There are many alternative models, each of which is likely to offer a different value, and the best that can be hoped for is that they will tend to agree in terms of orders of magnitude. More complex financial instruments, such as derivatives, can be valued using extremely complex models that are well beyond the scope of this text.

All valuation models require inputs in the form of observations and assumptions. IFRS 13 requires that the greatest possible use is made of observable inputs. Ideally, there would be no scope for subjectivity in the valuation process, but it is highly unlikely that subjectivity can ever be eliminated.

Table 8.2 IFRS 13's three categories of input

Level 1	Quoted prices in active markets for identical assets that can be observed at the measurement date. These will normally be unadjusted, although adjustments may be considered necessary if, for example, a significant event occurred after the market closed but before the measurement took place.

Level 2	Observable inputs other than Level 1.
	    This includes such observations as prices for similar (but not identical) assets or prices quoted on markets that are not active.
	    Level 2 inputs can also include rates and other observable factors that can be used in valuation models.

Level 3	Unobservable inputs. These should reflect the assumptions that market participants would make in pricing the asset. In other words, the objective is to estimate the market price rather than attach the entity's valuation to the asset.

IFRS 13 offers a hierarchy of three categories of inputs that can be drawn upon, with the greatest priority to be given to the level 1 inputs and the least to level 3 (Table 8.2).

Quoted market prices are generally the most reliable method of valuation because they are determined by the laws of supply and demand. Buyers are unlikely to pay more than the economic value of an asset and sellers are unlikely to accept less. IFRS 13 allows for the possibility that the market is not particularly active. In other words, if transactions are few and far between, then there may not be the same confidence that the most recent transaction price reflects the latest information. Furthermore, the markets may infer some information from the next trade. If someone wishes to sell, then the market price may decrease in response, just as a wish to purchase may lead to an increase.

IFRS 13 requires detailed disclosures concerning the extent to which the financial statements include fair values and the basis upon which they have been determined. These disclosures include classifications on the basis of the hierarchy of inputs that have been employed.

It is important to appreciate that financial assets can be extremely complex and that makes their values both potentially very volatile and difficult to determine. For example, a call option gives the right, but not the obligation, to buy an underlying asset at an agreed price at a future date. For example, an option holder may be entitled to buy a quantity of shares for $2 in three months' time. The cost of buying such an option can be relatively small. If the share price is less than $2 when the option expires then the holder will obtain no benefit and the options will lapse worthless. If the price exceeds $2 then the profit may be significant in comparison to the initial investment. That can make the market values of options fluctuate substantially in response to news concerning the underlying share price.

Gains and Losses on Assets Measured at Fair Value

Generally, gains and losses on financial assets are recognised in the statement of profit or loss. There are exceptions to this if hedge accounting, which is discussed later, applies. This may mean that gains and losses on financial assets are recognised in a manner that is inconsistent with gains and losses on non-financial assets. The problem with recognising a gain is that the gain may never be realised and so the gain recognised in one accounting period may have to be reversed if the fair value declines before the end of the next accounting period or if the asset is subsequently sold at a lower price.

It is possible to make an election that leads to gains and losses being taken to other comprehensive income rather than to the statement of profit or loss. That election is available when the investment is an equity instrument that is not held for trading. A financial asset is held for trading when the following applies:

- the asset was acquired principally for the purpose of selling it in the near term;
- on initial recognition it is part of a portfolio of financial instruments that are managed together and for which there is a pattern of short-term profit-taking; or
- the asset is a derivative.

In other words, gains and losses must go through the statement of profit or loss in the situations shown in Table 8.3.

Even if the company elects to take gains and losses to other comprehensive income, the treatment is still inconsistent with normal accounting practice. Gains

Table 8.3 Situations in which gains and losses must go through the statement of profit or loss

The entity acquired a financial asset with the intention of reselling it (hopefully) at a profit in the short term.	The financial asset is a derivative.	The financial asset is not an equity instrument.
None of the above apply, but the company does not elect to have gains and losses treated as other comprehensive income.		

on property, plant and equipment are recognised as other comprehensive income, but losses tend to go to the statement of profit or loss. If the election is available on a financial asset and is taken, then the company is still going to take losses straight to equity.

Impairment

IAS 39 requires that all financial assets measured at amortised cost be subject to an impairment review at every reporting date. There is no need to review assets measured at fair value because any impairment will automatically be reflected in their book values.

Impairment must be determined in terms of objective evidence that future cash flows have been affected by some event. The event itself must have occurred. For example, the possibility that a borrower *may* default is not sufficient to justify impairment. The borrower would have to have failed to make scheduled repayments or been downgraded by an independent credit rating agency.[2]

It is important to note that impairment is the result of changing expectations concerning future cash flows. Some assets may change in value because of economic changes, but that will not necessarily imply any impairment in terms of IAS 39. For example, if interest rates increase across the economy then the net present value of a fixed interest bond will decrease, not because of any concerns about the credit rating of the borrower but simply because the cash flows will have a smaller net present value when discounted at the higher prevailing rates. In that case, the market value of the asset will decline, but that does not lead to the asset being impaired.

The recoverable amount is calculated by taking the best estimate of the future cash flows and working out their net present value based on the original effective interest rate of the asset. The result is subtracted from the asset's carrying amount and the difference is recognised as an impairment loss in the statement of profit or loss.

Derecognition

The apparent disposal of financial assets or apparent settlement of financial liabilities can sometimes prove illusory. This is because there can be situations in which an asset is sold, but there are associated undertakings that leave the 'seller' in full possession of the risks and rewards of ownership. One example would be where the buyer has both the right and the obligation to return the asset at a price that is likely to reflect the original value of the transaction plus a realistic amount of interest for the 'loan' of the asset in the meantime. Under those circumstances, the risks and rewards associated with the asset will remain with the seller throughout because the assets will be returned without any compensation for a gain or loss that occurs while it is legally somebody else's property.

IFRS 9 sets out the requirements associated with the derecognition of all financial assets:

- **Risk and rewards approach:** Have the risks and rewards of ownership been retained, or have they been transferred?
- **Control approach:** Has control over the transferred asset been retained?

If an entity retains substantially all of the risks and rewards associated with ownership, then IFRS 9 requires that it continue to be recognised in the entity's financial statements. No gain or loss is recognised in the light of the transfer. This would be the case in our earlier example where the asset will be returned at a fixed price at a designated date.

If the entity transfers substantially all of the risks and rewards of ownership then the asset should be derecognised in its entirety: for example, the seller makes an outright sale of the asset to a buyer and there are no further conditions; or the seller retains the right to repurchase, but at the fair value of the asset as at the repurchase date. In that case, there will be a gain or loss in the statement of profit or loss reflecting the difference between the carrying amount and the proceeds from the sale.

The risks and rewards approach is applicable in the clear-cut circumstances where either substantially none of the risks and rewards have been transferred or substantially all have been transferred. The control approach is used in the intermediate position where there has been a partial transfer of risks and rewards. In that case, the question of derecognition hinges on whether the entity retains control of the transferred financial asset. The entity is deemed to have lost control if the third party on the other end of the transaction has the ability to sell the asset in its entirety to a third party without any restriction.

If the entity has lost control, then the financial asset is derecognised in its entirety.

If the entity retains control, then the asset continues to be recognised to the extent that it retains an exposure to the risks and rewards of ownership. This could be complicated in practice and will not be discussed further.

Hedging

Hedging is a method of managing risk. It involves identifying risks and countering them so that the effects of any adverse changes are cancelled or at least reduced. For example, if an entity has a foreign currency deposit that will decline in value if the foreign currency is devalued, the entity might take out a loan in that same currency. In that case, the decline in the deposit will be matched by a decline in the value of the loan and so there will be no net loss (or the loss will be limited to the net amount if the loan is smaller than the deposit).

Hedging can take many forms and can involve the use of complicated derivative instruments, all of which would be beyond the scope of this text. Hedge accounting is used in specific cases where the entity has designated a 'hedging instrument' as having been acquired in order to offset changes in either the fair value of or the cash flows from a particular hedged item. The fact that an entity has to designate the hedging instrument in this manner means that hedge accounting is effectively voluntary.

Generally, the hedging instrument must be a derivative before hedge accounting can be applied. That does not mean that hedging strategies must always involve derivatives, but they will not necessarily be accounted for under hedge accounting when they do not. A derivative has three characteristics:

• Its value changes in response to the change in a specified interest rate, financial instrument price, commodity price, foreign exchange rate, or whatever. In other words, the value of a derivative is derived from the value of some underlying asset, liability or other variable. For example, a currency future gives the right to buy or sell a specific quantity of one currency for a specific quantity of another. The currency future itself will change in value as exchange rates move against one another. If the currency future gives the holder a significantly better exchange rate than that offered on the spot markets, then the instrument will be worth more than if the rate is only slightly in the holder's favour. If the currency future offers a poorer rate, then it will be difficult to find a buyer unless there is some reason to believe that the currency rates will change significantly.

• It requires no initial net investment, or requires an initial net investment that is smaller than would be required for other types of contracts that would be expected to have a similar response to changes in market factors. In the case of a currency future, the main payment between the parties takes place when the future matures. Prior to that, the parties have to place a relatively small amount on deposit as a margin to protect the counterparties against default. If a speculator believed that the market prices for, say, the US dollar against the euro were out of line and that the euro was going to strengthen, then it would be possible to invest in euros while the price was weak in the hope of a speculative gain. It would be possible to get the same gain by entering into currency futures. There would be no need to make any actual investment in the financial instrument itself at that point. Even the margin payment would be very small in comparison. A real gambler would enter into currency futures rather than the actual currency itself, using all available funds for the margin. The returns will be massive if the predicted strengthening occurs, although there could also be a major loss if the euro weakens instead.

 • It is settled at a future date. A currency future must be settled on an agreed date.

Derivatives can take many forms. For example, an option is a derivative because it gives the right to buy or sell an asset, such as equity shares or currency, at a specified price on a particular date. On a day-to-day basis, the value of the option is affected by changes in the underlying asset or liability. The premium paid to purchase an option will generally be far smaller than the cost of taking a direct position in that asset or liability. So all three criteria are satisfied.

It is possible to designate a non-derivative financial asset or liability as a hedging instrument, but only for the hedge of a foreign currency risk.

IAS 39 recognises three situations in which hedge accounting can be applied:

 • **Fair value** hedging arises when the function of the hedge is to protect the entity against changes in the value of an asset or a liability. Any gains or losses on the hedging instrument will be recognised in the statement of profit or loss at the same time as the corresponding losses or gains on the hedged item, thereby reducing or even cancelling the movement.
 • **Cash flow** hedging arises when the function of the hedge is to protect the entity against variability in the future cash flows associated with the hedged item. Changes in the fair value of the hedging instrument are recognised as part of other comprehensive income, and lodged in equity. They are released to the statement of profit or loss when the hedged item affects profit or loss.
 • A **net investment in a foreign operation** is similar to a cash flow hedge. It will not be discussed further in this text.

Hedge accounting is permissible only when four criteria have been met:

1. When the hedge is first established it must be formally documented within the entity, and the specific relationship between the hedging instrument and the hedged item must be noted.
2. The hedge must be expected to be highly effective.
3. It must be possible to measure the effectiveness of the hedge. That will require knowledge of the fair values or cash flows for both the hedged item and the hedging instrument.
4. The hedge must be assessed on an ongoing basis and be found to be highly effective. Effectiveness is measured in terms of offsetting changes in fair values or cash flows. Actual effectiveness must be within a range of 85% to 125%.

Hedge accounting can be used to hedge a wide variety of qualifying items:

- recognised assets or liabilities
- unrecognised firm commitments
- highly probable forecast transactions
- net investments in foreign operations.

Fair Value Hedges

A fair value hedge arises when the entity has a fixed rate asset or liability whose fair value will increase or decrease in line with movements in market interest rates. It can also be useful when the entity has entered into a binding contract to buy or sell a non-financial item at a fixed price. For example, a shipping company could have agreed to buy a tanker priced at a price that is fixed in a foreign currency; or a manufacturer could have contracted to buy a specific quantity of electricity over a five-year period for a fixed price.

There is a variety of derivative instrument whose values will move in the opposite direction to those of the fair values of the asset or liability that is to be hedged, so our shipping company could purchase a derivative whose value will increase whenever the foreign currency liability to the shipbuilder increases and will decline when the liability decreases.

The gain or loss from re-measuring the hedging instrument is recognised immediately in the statement of profit or loss.

The gain or loss on the hedged item that is attributable to the hedged risk is taken to the statement of profit or loss, even if gains and losses on such an item are normally taken to equity via other comprehensive income.

For example, on 1 October 20X4, a Swedish company enters into a contract to buy a production line from a Dutch supplier for €9m. The agreed sum is to be payable on 31 March 20X5. The spot rate on the date that the contract was signed is €1 = SKR8.5. The production line is recognised as an asset under construction and the agreed price was recognised as a liability of €9m × 8.5 = SKR76.5m.

On the date that the contract is signed, the Swedish company protects its liability by buying a currency future to exchange SKR76.68m for €9m, an exchange rate of €1 = SKR8.52. The fair value of the future is nil on that date (because both parties are paying a fair price, which implies that neither is expected to make a gain or a loss on the future).

The liability due to the equipment manufacturer is designated as a hedged item and the currency future as a hedging instrument. The currency future is expected to be highly effective in dealing with any fluctuations in the fair value of the liability.

At 31 December 20X4, the exchange rate is €1 = SKR8.8. The Swedish company shows a loss of SKR76.5m − (€9m × 8.8) = SKR2.7m.

The market value of the currency future has increased because it may make it possible to exchange SKR for euros at a favourable rate. The futures held by the Swedish company now have a fair value of SKR76.68m − (8.8 × €9m) = SKR2.52m, all of which is a gain from the initial fair value of zero. That gain is equal to 93% of the loss on the liability, so the hedging relationship is highly effective. The currency loss of SKR2.7m and the gain of SKR2.52m on the financial asset will both be taken to the statement of profit or loss.

Cash Flow Hedges

A cash flow hedge is useful when cash flows to or from the hedged item are variable and could affect profit or loss. For example, a variable rate loan leaves the entity exposed to the risk that interest rates will rise. That can be countered using an arrangement called a swap.[3]

Cash flow hedge accounting is only permissible when the transaction affecting cash flow risk is highly probable and will ultimately affect profit. In the example of the Swedish company discussed above, the fact that a contract has been signed for the purchase of the production line makes the cash flows highly probable and any change in exchange rates will affect profit.

The portion of the gain or loss on the hedging instrument that is determined to be an effective hedge is recognised in other comprehensive income. Any further gain or loss is recognised immediately in the statement of profit or loss.

For example, our Swedish company signed a contract with a Portuguese supplier on 1 October 20X4 to buy raw materials for €5m, with delivery due on 28 February 20X5. Nothing will be recognised in the bookkeeping records before delivery, but the company has decided to protect itself against any fluctuation in the exchange rates by entering into a forward contract.[4] The forward contract means that the €5m will cost SKR42.75m. The forward contract had a zero value when it was signed and no cash exchanged hands at that date.

This arrangement was designated as a cash flow hedge.

On 31 December 20X4 the cost of the materials would have been SKR44.0m, but the forward contract ensures that the cost is fixed at SKR42.75m. The hedge is 100% effective and so it has a value to the Swedish company of SKR44.0 m − SKR42.75 m = SKR1.25 m. The gain from zero to SKR1.25m will be recognised in other comprehensive income for the year ended 31 December 20X4. The statement of financial position will show the forward contract as an asset worth SKR1.25m and there will be an equity balance called cash flow hedge reserve (or similar) of the same amount.

When the company takes delivery of the materials, then the purchase will be recorded in terms of the exchange rate in force at that time. If, for the sake of argument, the SKR value of the purchase was SKR44.3m, then the value of the forward contract will have increased by a further SKR0.3m since the beginning of the year. The transaction will be recorded as:

Debit Purchases	SKR44.3m	
Credit Bank		SKR42.75m
Credit Forward contract		SKR1.55m

The balance of $SKR1.25m + SKR0.3m = SKR1.55m$ on the cash flow hedge reserve will then be offset against the cost of the inventory.

Disclosure

IFRS 7 *Financial Instruments: Disclosures* (IASB, 2010b) deals with the disclosures required in connection with financial instruments.

Statement of Financial Position

Entities are required to disclose information that enables users of their financial statements to evaluate the significance of financial instruments for financial position and performance.

The carrying amounts of each of the main categories of financial assets and liabilities must be disclosed, either in the statement of financial position or in the notes:

- financial assets/liabilities at fair value through profit or loss, distinguishing those held for trading from those designated as such upon initial recognition
- held-to-maturity investments
- loans and receivables
- available-for-sale financial assets
- financial liabilities measured at amortised cost.

These disclosures must be supplemented with detailed information concerning matters such as derecognition.

Statement of Comprehensive Income

The following should be shown in the statement of comprehensive income or the notes:

- net gains or net losses on:
  - ◦ financial assets or financial liabilities at fair value through profit or loss, distinguishing those held for trading from those designated as such upon initial recognition
  - ◦ available-for-sale financial assets, showing separately the amount of gain or loss recognised in other comprehensive income during the period and the amount reclassified from equity to profit or loss for the period
  - ◦ held-to-maturity investments
  - ◦ loans and receivables
  - ◦ financial liabilities measured at amortised cost
- total interest income and total interest expense for financial assets or financial liabilities that are not at fair value through profit or loss
- fee income and expense arising from financial assets or financial liabilities that are not at fair value through profit or loss
- interest income on impaired financial assets
- the amount of any impairment loss for each class of financial asset.

Hedge Accounting

Separate disclosures are required for fair value hedges, cash flow hedges, and hedges of net investments in foreign operations:

- a description of each type of hedge, a description of the financial instruments designated as hedging instruments and their fair values at the end of the reporting period, and the nature of the risks being hedged
- for cash flow hedges:
  - ◦ the periods when the cash flows are expected to occur and when they are expected to affect profit or loss
  - ◦ a description of any forecast transaction for which hedge accounting had previously been used, but which is no longer expected to occur
  - ◦ the amount that was recognised in other comprehensive income during the period
  - ◦ the amount that was reclassified from equity to profit or loss for the period
  - ◦ the ineffectiveness recognised in profit or loss that arises from cash flow hedges (and also from hedges of net investments in foreign operations).

Risks Arising from Financial Instruments

Users must be able to evaluate the nature and extent of risks arising from financial instruments to which the entity is exposed. These risks typically include, but are not limited to, credit risk, liquidity risk and market risk.

The disclosures must include a *qualitative analysis* of: the exposures to risk and how they arise; the entity's objectives, policies and processes for managing the risk; and the methods used to measure the risk and any changes in either of the exposures or responses since the previous period.

Entities are also required to provide summary *quantitative data* about their exposure to risk at the end of the reporting period. This disclosure shall be based on the information provided internally to key management personnel of the entity. If the information as at that date is not representative, then that analysis must be supplemented with further information that is representative.

The disclosures must also cover specific matters relating to:

- **Credit risk:** Essentially, the risk of default by a borrower (for example, details of collateral, impairment and overdue balances)
- **Liquidity risk:** Essentially, the impact on the entity's cash flows (for example, the maturity of the financial liabilities so that users know when funds will be required for settlement)
- **Market risk:** Essentially, the volatility of asset values (for example, historical information about the movements in asset values).

The 2007 Credit Crunch

The 2007 Credit Crunch was a major economic crisis that almost brought down the banking system in many countries and that led to a downturn that had still not been remedied more than five years later. While accounting was not directly to blame for the Credit Crunch, it has certainly been argued that accounting had a role to play in it.

One of the basic functions of banks is to provide individuals with mortgages so that they can buy their homes. The traditional banking model was that savers deposited their funds with the bank in return for interest. The banks used those funds to finance loans at a higher rate of interest. This yielded a modest profit. Banking regulations published by the Basel Committee on Banking Supervision (the Basel Accord), which have been agreed by the central banks of the leading economies, required that banks maintain a minimum level of liquidity. Mortgage loans on homes were not liquid assets and so the Basel accord required the banks to place sums on deposit in relation to the amounts tied up in mortgage loans. Those deposits had to be in low risk and highly liquid accounts or instruments, such as low yield bonds. This further eroded the profitability of traditional mortgage lending.

The banks responded by changing their business model. They continued to make mortgage loans, but started to sell the mortgages on to third parties (often other banks). They could then earn a fee from the sale and release the funds that would otherwise have been tied up in the mortgage loans, with the associated need to place additional funds on deposit for liquidity purposes.

The mortgages tended to be securitised before they were sold. In other words, the bank would package a bundle of mortgages together and split the cash flows from these into separate tranches. These tranches were then sold at prices that were commensurate with the risk profile of the cash receipts. For example, the right to receive the first 30% of the cash from the package of mortgages was probably fairly secure because that first tranche would be the least affected by any default by the mortgage borrowers. Conversely, the riskiest tranches were quite heavily exposed, but even there the fact that the cash flows came from a portfolio of mortgages meant that the cash flows were reasonably predictable and the price reflected the risks being taken.

This led to a circular effect on the markets. The banks could make profits from selling mortgages and were keen to lend as widely as possible. That stimulated demand for houses and so individuals were keen to buy property. The banks started to make 'liar loans' – in other words, potential mortgage borrowers were not required to furnish any documentary evidence to support their claims to be in secure employment. Many mortgages were made to NINJA (No Income, No Job, No Assets) borrowers, with loans being made to unemployed or poorly paid borrowers who wished to purchase low quality homes. The banks themselves were not too concerned because they intended to resell the mortgages and even the buyers of the collateralized debt obligations (CDOs) were happy because these bundles of mortgages offered high returns.

The CDOs were carried in their owners' financial statements at their fair values. The gains and losses on those instruments were reported in the statement of profit or loss. For a while, those assets were increasing in value because of the demand that was being stimulated, in part, by the reported profits. Unfortunately, the market prices for both the CDOs and the underlying real property were not sustainable. A crisis of confidence destroyed the value of the financial assets, and in many countries the property market slumped. Many banks had invested heavily in CDOs, meaning that they were very heavily exposed to those losses, and so many governments had to step in to rescue their banking industries.

It could be argued that accounting was implicated in these events because the recognition of gains in income boosted reported profits (and so boosted profit-related bonuses paid to directors of banks who held appreciating CDOs). The assets were carried in the statement of financial position at those market-based fair values. When the downturn started, the reporting of losses on fair values stimulated the downward spiral of prices and that may have made the economic disaster even more pronounced.

The IASB and FASB established the Financial Crisis Advisory Group (FCAG) to consider accounting issues emerging from the global crisis.[5] The FCAG concluded that the Credit Crunch exposed weaknesses in accounting standards and their application and that those weaknesses contributed to the general loss of confidence in the financial system. However, the FCAG did not believe that accounting standards were the root cause of the crisis.

Perhaps part of the problem is that unrealistic expectations are placed on accounting. Certainly, when assets are shown at their market values there is a possibility that the financial statements will be a fair presentation of the financial position at a point in time, but that position could change very quickly and so the figures may be out of date soon after they are produced.

The Credit Crunch has been the subject of considerable academic scrutiny, with mixed messages from authors. Barth and Landsman (2010) concluded that fair value accounting played little or no role in the Credit Crunch, although there may well have been insufficient transparency concerning the values of CDOs.

Conversely, a special edition of *Accounting, Organizations and Society* in 2009 presented a range of papers that were generally critical of the accountancy profession. An editorial by Hopwood (2009) argued that there was a need for accounting research to be more challenging of practice. There is a tendency for research to operate within the parameters set by practice. The papers in this special edition developed arguments that alleged shortcomings of the accounting regulators and auditors.

There is probably no real answer to the question of whether accountancy was to blame for the Credit Crunch. It can certainly be argued that the fundamental problem was the manner in which banks were monitored and supervised. If the banks had not taken positions in risky investments then there would not have been a crisis. That does not necessarily absolve the accountancy profession of all responsibility because it could be argued that the bank regulators and others responsible for preventing and managing the crisis could have been better informed by accounting statements.

Summary

The accounting treatment of financial instruments is complicated because of the ingenuity and imagination that has gone into the development of instruments that are designed to suit specific purposes. Some of those instruments are intended to manage risks in a particular way so that buyers and sellers can enter into mutually profitable arrangements. Others are intended to present a potentially misleading impression in the financial statements, although that is becoming increasingly difficult to achieve because of developments in IFRS.

Accounting standards have had to ensure that financial instruments used to raise finance are correctly classified as either debt or equity. There have been attempts in the past to classify carefully designed preference shares as equity despite the fact that the financial commitments were effectively debt. There have also been attempts to distort reported earnings by issuing debt instruments at a discount and exploiting the ambiguities created over the subsequent treatment of those balances. These problems have been addressed to ensure that gearing ratios and reported profits cannot be distorted by such practices.

Financial instruments have also created difficulties from the asset holder's point of view. There have been problems with valuations and the recognition of gains and losses at the end of accounting periods. These problems culminated in the Credit Crunch, which will forever be associated with press accounts of banks making massive loans to unemployed homebuyers who invested the banks' money in worthless property. Those banks sold financial instruments backed by those mortgages to other banks around the world and brought the financial system to the brink of a global collapse in the process.

Tutorial Questions

Question 1

Download a quoted company's annual report from the Internet and study the disclosures relating to financial assets and financial liabilities.

Summarise the information and be prepared to discuss the usefulness of the notes.

Question 2

B issued £17m of 14% redeemable preference shares on 1 January 20X1 at par. The preference dividend is payable at the directors' discretion, although any unpaid dividend will accumulate and B cannot pay any dividend to its equity shareholders while an unpaid preference dividend is outstanding. The redeemable preference shareholders have the right to redeem the par value of their shares on 31 December 20X4. If they choose not to redeem their shares on that date then the shares will become irredeemable, with future dividend rights continuing as described. The dividend for the year ended 31 December 20X1 was paid at the year end.

Required
Explain how these shares should be classified in B's financial statements and calculate the figures that will appear in B's financial statements for the year ended 31 December 20X1.

Question 3

T issued a $20m, five-year convertible bond at par with a coupon rate of 8%. At the end of year five, the bondholders can elect to receive repayment at par or they can exchange their bonds for equity on the basis of $4 of bond for every $1 equity share, fully paid.

A similar entity issued a five-year bond that had no conversion rights that carried an effective rate of 11%.

At the end of the five-year period, 70% of the bond was converted to shares and the remainder was redeemed for cash.

Required

Show how the bond will be accounted for in years one to five, up to and including the conversion.

Question 4

U purchased a 1% holding in a quoted company for $10m. At the end of the first year, the shares were revalued at $12m. At the end of the second year, they were revalued at $13m. During the third year, they were sold for $15m.

Required

Show how the shares would be accounted for by U, assuming that U made the election to recognise gains and losses in comprehensive income.

Question 5

A farmer grows wheat and anticipates a crop of 6000 tonnes. The farmer is concerned that the selling prices of wheat in seven months may be depressed by a world slump in the selling price of wheat. The farmer is considering the purchase of a wheat future that would fix the selling price of the 6000 tonnes.

Required

Discuss the accounting issues that would arise from the purchase of the commodity future by the farmer.

Question 6

Discuss the implications of the Credit Crunch for the accountancy profession's reputation.

Questions with Answers

Question 1

Baxter issued 10 million 5% convertible £1 bonds on 1 January 20X1. The bonds give the holder the right to convert them to equity on the basis of a fully-paid £1 share for every £1 of bond held on 31 December 20X5.

The proceeds of £10 million were credited to non-current liabilities and debited to bank. The 5% interest paid has been charged to finance costs in the year to 31 December 20X1.

The market rate of interest for a similar bond with a five-year term but no conversion terms is 7%.

Required

Explain how this convertible instrument should have been accounted for at the date of issue and calculate the figures that should appear with respect to the bond in the financial statements for the year ended 31 December 20X1.

Question 2

Baxter also issued 5 million £1 6% cumulative redeemable preference shares on 1 January 20X1. The proceeds of the issue were £7.7 million and issue costs amounted to £53 000. The shares are redeemable on 31 December 20X5 at a premium of £0.80 per share.

The directors have treated this issue as equity, but have stated that a bond offering similar cash flows would offer bondholders a 7% return.

Required

Explain how the preference shares should have been accounted for at the date of issue and calculate the figures that should appear with respect to the shares in the financial statements for the year ended 31 December 20X1.

Question 3

S issued a $5m bond, redeemable at the end of four years with an annual coupon rate of 3% with interest paid annually in arrears. The bond was issued for $3.8m. Issue costs were $170 000. The effective interest rate was 12%.

Required

Show how this bond will be accounted for in years one to four of its life.

Endnotes

1. Just a quick word about terminology. A financial instrument has a nominal value or face value (for example, an ordinary share may have a face value of $1). The market value of that instrument will be determined by market forces and so the initial issue can be 'at par' (which means that it was sold at its face value of $1), 'at a discount' (which means that it was sold for less than $1) or 'at a premium' (in which case it was sold for more than $1).
2. There are commercial organisations that sell credit ratings of various entities' bonds and debt instruments and those ratings can affect the market price of the bonds themselves. An AAA bond will be worth more than an AAB bond that has the same coupon and maturity.
3. Discussion of swaps is well beyond the scope of this text, but the essence of a swap is that a borrower with a variable rate loan can arrange a mutually convenient agreement with a borrower who has fixed rate debt to exchange cash flows. That can be cheaper and/or more convenient for both parties.
4. A currency future is a standardised instrument that can be bought and sold on the open market. A forward contract is a direct agreement between two counterparties. They both have the effect of guaranteeing the exchange rate on a given date, but they will be valued in different ways.
5. The FCAG's final report can be downloaded from the FASB website (www.fasb .org).

References

Barth, M. & Landsman, W. (2010) How did financial reporting contribute to the financial crisis? *European Accounting Review* **19**(3) pp. 399–423.

Hopwood, A.G. (2009) The economic crisis and accounting: Implications for the research community. *Accounting, Organizations and Society* **34**(6–7) pp. 797–802.

IASB (2008) IAS 32 *Financial Instruments: Presentation.*

IASB (2010a) IAS 39 *Financial Instruments: Recognition and Measurement.*

IASB (2010b) IFRS 7 *Financial Instruments: Disclosures.*

IASB (2010c) IFRS 9 *Financial Instruments.*

IASB (2011) IFRS 13 *Fair Value Measurement.*

GROUP ACCOUNTS

Contents

Learning Objectives

After studying this chapter, you should be able to:

- explain why businesses are organised as groups;
- explain why consolidated financial statements are necessary;
- explain the basic approach to preparing consolidated financial statements;
- outline the legal background to the publication of consolidated financial statements.

Introduction

Accounting for groups of companies has been one of the most controversial areas in accounting over the years. Broadly speaking, the boundaries that have been established round groups for accounting purposes have been difficult to define and that has made it possible to exclude some very significant information from the resulting consolidated financial statements.

This chapter will discuss the importance of group financial statements and will also deal with the mechanics of preparing consolidated financial statements.

Groups of Companies

Unless a business is very small, it will almost certainly be organised as a group of companies. In much of the world, that means that there will be a *parent company*, which normally owns a controlling interest in each of the other companies in the group, and various *subsidiaries*, which are united by virtue of the fact that they are all under the common control of the parent company.

There are several reasons why it is better to operate in this way, rather than having one large company:

• Sometimes the easiest way to expand is by buying other companies. It would be possible to transfer all of the purchased companies' assets and staff after it has been taken over, but that would be expensive (because of the need to transfer titles to assets and employment contracts). It would also lead to the loss of business names that could have some value on the market. Therefore, it is usually simpler and cheaper to let the existing companies continue as before, albeit under new ownership.

• In future years, it might be desirable to sell off part of the business that is a distraction from the core activities or that is not generating sufficient profit. It will be much easier to sell a company because it will be possible to show purchasers audited financial statements for the business that they are buying. It will also be much easier to identify the assets and liabilities belonging to a company that is being sold off than it would be to identify the boundaries of a division that was part of a larger company.

• In desperate situations, a company that runs into difficulty can be allowed to fail. The parent company need not have any legal responsibility for the debts of a failing subsidiary. It might create bad publicity to leave a subsidiary to collapse while it has unpaid bills, but that is a matter for the parent company's senior management to decide. If all of the companies had been merged into one large company, then one failing segment could pull the whole business down.

If you obtain the published accounts of almost any business, even a relatively small one, you will almost certainly find that it is either the parent company of a group or a subsidiary. If it is listed on a stock exchange, then it is more or less bound to be a parent company.

Why Do We Need Consolidated Financial Statements?

Imagine a world with no group accounts. Picture the following situation. Mega plc is a major quoted company that prospects, extracts, and refines oil all over the world. Surprisingly, it has a very simple statement of financial position:

Mega plc:
Statement of financial position as at ????

	£m
Non-current asset investments	
Mega Drilling Ltd	2000
Mega Shipping Ltd	2300
Mega Refining Ltd	1900
Mega Retail Ltd	1300
Mega Management Ltd	120
	7620
Current assets	
Bank	90
	7710
Share capital	5000
Retained profits	2710
	7710

Mega plc owns all of the shares of each of the five companies listed under the heading of non-current asset investments. The first four companies listed operate in many different parts of the world, finding, extracting, and processing oil and natural gas and selling the resulting products. Mega Management Ltd employs the board of directors who manage Mega plc, and owns and operates the head office and employs all of the staff who work there (see Figure 9.1).

Mega plc has a bank account but rarely has much cash in it. From time to time, the companies that it owns pay dividends. Sometimes the cash is used to invest in other companies and sometimes it is used to pay dividends to Mega plc's shareholders.

You might have noticed that the statement of financial position is undated. That is because the figures themselves will never change much, unless Mega plc decides to buy another company or sell one of its existing holdings. There might be some fluctuation in the bank balance while it receives dividends and passes those on to its

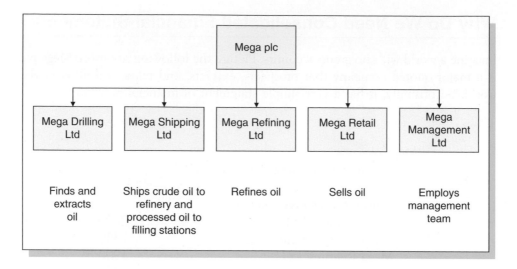

Figure 9.1 Mega plc

own shareholders, but the statement of financial position will otherwise remain as it is.

We could have shown Mega plc's statement of profit or loss, but that would have been just as unrevealing as its statement of financial position. Its only income would be dividends received. It would have no expenses.

You would not find these financial statements terribly helpful if you were a shareholder in Mega plc. It would be impossible to tell whether the companies that it owns are doing well or badly. Provided the companies continue to pay their dividends (which they might do even if they make losses), everything will appear to be in order regardless of the true position.

Imagine . . .

The solution to this problem sounds simple, although it has proved to be one of the biggest sources of problems for accounting regulators over the years. Rather than telling the shareholders about their *legal* rights with respect to the company, we could tell them about their *economic* rights. In terms of strict, legalistic theory, the shareholders of Mega plc own shares in a 'parent company' that enters into very few transactions and merely acts as a vehicle for owning all the shares of a series of other companies known as 'subsidiaries'. There is, however, an economic reality, which is that the shareholders in Mega Ltd see themselves as owning shares in an enterprise that extracts, refines, and sells oil (Figure 9.2).

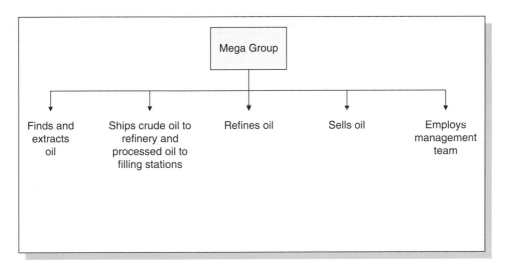

Figure 9.2 Mega Group

Consolidated financial statements are intended to bridge the gap between the *legal form* and the *economic substance* of the relationship between the group companies.

Suppose our statement of financial position actually relates to 31 December 20X8. The following schedule relates to Mega plc and its subsidiary companies:

Statements of Financial Position as at 31 December 20X8	Mega plc £m	Mega Drilling Ltd £m	Mega Shipping Ltd £m	Mega Refining Ltd £m	Mega Retail Ltd £m	Mega Management Ltd £m	Total £m
Property, plant and equipment							
Land and buildings		200	100	300	700	100	1 400
Plant and equipment		1 600	1 900	1 500	400	10	5 410
	–	1 800	2 000	1 800	1 100	110	6 810
Fixed asset investments							
Mega Drilling Ltd	2 000						2 000
Mega Shipping Ltd	2 300						2 300
Mega Refining Ltd	1 900						1 900
Mega Retail Ltd	1 300						1 300
Mega Management Ltd	120						120
	7 620	–	–	–	–	–	7 620
Current assets							
Inventory		8	5	25	50		88
Trade receivables		6	13	10	30		59
Due from group members		10	14	38	–	6	68

Bank	90	7	9	7	8	5	126
	90	31	41	80	88	11	341
	7 710	1 831	2 041	1 880	1 188	121	14 771
Share capital	5 000	1 600	1 800	1 500	1 000	60	10 960
Retained profits	2 710	215	212	347	128	58	3 670
	7 710	1 815	2 012	1 847	1 128	118	14 630
Current liabilities							
Trade payables		14	21	15	20	3	73
Due to group members		2	8	18	40		68
	–	16	29	33	60	3	141
	7 710	1 831	2 041	1 880	1 188	121	14 771

This is a complicated table, but take a few minutes to study it closely.

Firstly, we can see that the directors of Mega plc can control 'real', tangible assets worth a total of £6.81 billion. They can manage current assets worth approximately £341 million. They can make these assets work together in an efficient manner. If, for example, Mega Retail Ltd requires a short-term loan, they could tell the directors of Mega Refining Ltd to transfer cash or to wait for payment for supplies.

While this table is a massive improvement on the statement of financial position of Mega plc on its own, it is still complicated because it still retains the artificial distinctions between each of the companies in this 'group'. As far as the shareholders in Mega plc are concerned, this is just one large business that produces and sells oil. The assets and liabilities of the separate companies are of little importance to them.

Making Things Clearer

One way around this would be to publish just the total column from the extreme right-hand edge of the table. That would simplify the document, but it would not be entirely satisfactory in presenting the economic reality. The reason for that is that the individual statements of financial position contain a host of *internal* relationships *between* companies. The most obvious of these are the current assets of balances due from group members and the liabilities of balances due to group members. These are valid entries in the financial statements of the group members themselves, but they are quite misleading when we try to present the companies collectively, as a single economic entity. The solution to this is to cancel these offsetting amounts against one another.

There are some less obvious internal relationships between the group members. Mega plc's statement of financial position shows a variety of investments in other companies. Those companies have corresponding equity balances that reflect the share capital and reserves purchased at the time of Mega plc's investment. Again, the secret is to cancel these. That process is slightly more complex than the process used on the intercompany balances, and so we will return to it in Chapter 10.

Once all of the cancellations have been made and the statement tidied up, we are left with the following statement of financial position:

Mega plc:
Consolidated statement of financial position
as at 31 December 20X8

	£m
Property, plant and equipment	
Land and buildings	1400
Plant and equipment	5410
	6810
Current assets	
Inventory	74
Trade receivables	59
Bank	126
	259
	7069
Share capital	5000
Retained profits	1996
	6996
Current liabilities	
Trade payables	73
	7069

Many of the figures are simply the totals of the separate statements. Inventory is slightly more complicated because of the complications of buying and selling between group members at slightly artificial prices. The inventory figure stated in the consolidated statement of financial position represents the cost to the group, ignoring any internal transfers. We will return to the calculation of inventory in Chapter 13. There is insufficient information in the case for you to derive the amount shown above.

The most complex figure of all to derive is that for retained profits. Again, there is insufficient information to derive this figure in the case, and, again, we will have to return to the topic in Chapter 13. Calculating the figure for retained profits is complicated because some of the balances on the subsidiaries' retained earnings will have to be cancelled against the parent company's investment in them.

The Mega Group statement of financial position illustrates the point of preparing consolidated financial statements. We can tell at a glance what resources were available to the directors of Mega plc. This makes them far more accountable to their shareholders. We can also see what the overall liquidity of the group is, what liabilities it owes, and how it has changed since last year. We can prepare a consolidated statement of profit or loss that will enable us to see exactly how profitable the group has been. Even though this is a very simple example, it illustrates why we need group financial statements.

A Few Words of Warning

The title of the statement of financial position sheet makes it very clear that this is a *consolidated* statement relating to a *group* of companies. This is important because the statement is intended to show an *economic* entity in a realistic manner. It is not, however, a *legal* entity. There are, therefore, a number of areas in which you have to take care when reading consolidated financial statements:

• A group of companies has no legal identity of its own. You can enter into a contract with any of the companies in the group, but not with the group itself. In an extreme case, the group might not choose to support a company that has got into difficulties. The group statement of financial position might leave you with a false sense of security. It is possible, however, to benefit from the fact that a subsidiary is part of a larger group. The secret is to ask for a formal, written guarantee from the parent company or from other group companies. That means that you could make a loan to, say, Mega Management Ltd, that was guaranteed by Mega plc. If Mega Management Ltd defaulted on the loan, you could use the guarantee to demand settlement from the parent company.

• The directors of the parent company can normally control all of the activities of the subsidiaries, but there can be extreme situations where that is not so. For example, if one of the subsidiaries was based overseas in a country that had 'exchange controls' in force, it would be necessary to seek government approval before sending cash home. There is no guarantee, therefore, that Mega Group can call on all of the £126 million in cash in its statement of financial position. Everything depends on the location of those subsidiaries.

• Some subsidiaries may be only part owned. That can sometimes constrain the actions of the parent company because the 'minority' shareholders of the subsidiary might have rights if they feel that their welfare has been compromised. For example, the parent company might ask the subsidiary to make an interest-free loan to a fellow group member. In certain circumstances, minority shareholders in the lending company might be able to bar such an action.

The difficulties outlined above are unlikely to arise in practice, but they are sufficiently important for us to ensure that we make the nature of the statements clear by always including the words 'group' and 'consolidated' in their titles.

What Is a Subsidiary?

The parent company/subsidiary company relationship is not expressed in terms of ownership because our interest is in the exercise of economic control. It is possible to control another company without owning all of the shares or even more than half of the voting shares. For example, a parent company could have total control if it owned, say, 40% of the shares and a third (otherwise independent) party owns another 40% and has agreed to support any decision made by the parent.

IFRS 10 *Consolidated Financial Statements* (IASB, 2011) defines a subsidiary as 'an entity that is controlled by another entity'. IFRS defines a parent as 'an entity that controls one or more entities'.

Control requires three elements:

- the parent must have power over the subsidiary;
- the parent must have exposure, or rights, to variable returns from its involvement with the subsidiary;
- the parent must have the ability to use its power over the investee to affect the return from its involvement.

The most obvious way in which such power could be achieved would be by owning more than half of the shares that carry voting rights. However, it is not necessary to own any shares in order to have control. For example, the parent could have control through a contractual right to set financial and operating policies or through a contractual right to appoint or remove the majority of the board of directors.

If a subsidiary company has a subsidiary of its own, then the 'sub-subsidiary' will be subject to the dominant influence of the subsidiary's parent company and so all three companies will be part of the group.

If You've Got It, Why Not Flaunt It?

The definition of a subsidiary might appear to be unnecessarily complicated, but there are good historical reasons for that. There have been problems in the past with parent companies deliberately creating 'controlled non-subsidiaries' or quasi-subsidiaries that were excluded from the formal definitions that existed at the time. There were various reasons for doing this:

- A 'non-subsidiary' could be used to borrow money from third parties and then make it available to group companies. For example, it might use the money raised to purchase assets and then make a series of very short-term operating leases to subsidiaries. The fact that the liabilities were excluded from the consolidated statement of financial position means that the group's gearing ratio would be very much lower because of this.

• If the group owned assets that made little or no return, then they could be sold to a non-subsidiary and, again, made available to the group using short-term operating leases. This would have the effect of increasing the group's return on capital employed. This was one of the techniques used by Enron to bolster its profitability in the late 1990s and early 2000s.

• If the group had business interests that might appear to be socially or morally unacceptable, then these could be transferred to a 'non-subsidiary' so that it might continue without the associated bad publicity.

These motives have led to a number of scandals involving misleading consolidated statements of financial position that excluded 'actual' subsidiaries that were effectively part of the group but that were excluded from the formal definitions of subsidiaries. This has led to the development of wider definitions of the parent company/subsidiary company relationship, so that it is far more difficult to exclude anything from it. Previously, the definition was based largely on ownership. In general, owning more than 50% of the voting rights was sufficient to create a subsidiary. This was where the abuse tended to come in, because it was relatively common for parent companies to structure their relationships with certain sensitive subsidiaries so that the formal definitions did not come into effect. For example, merchant banks might be given sufficient cash to acquire a controlling interest. They would be paid a fee and given guarantees against any losses from holding the shares. In return, they would use their control to manage the company exactly as the parent company wished.

IFRS 10's definition is based on control because that reflects the economic reality that the standard-setters are trying to capture. If one company controls another, then the other company is a subsidiary, even if no shares are owned. Thus, control through a contractual agreement with a bank, as described in the previous paragraph, would create a subsidiary.

Reporting Requirements

IFRS 10 requires all parent companies to publish consolidated financial statements. There are some exceptions to this. The main ones arise when the parent/subsidiary relationship arises within a group:

• If the parent is itself a wholly owned subsidiary, then it is exempt.
• If the parent is a partially owned subsidiary of another entity, then it can be exempt provided its other owners have been informed that it will not prepare group accounts and they agree to this.

For example, consider the companies in the A Group.

A is required to publish consolidated financial statements that will include subsidiaries B, C, D and E (unless A fulfils one of the other conditions for exemptions that are discussed below).

B is C's parent, but it is exempt from the requirement to prepare group accounts because it is a 100% subsidiary of A.

D is E's parent, but may be exempt provided the shareholders who hold the other 20% of D's share capital have been informed that the company does not wish to publish group financial statements and they agree to this.

IFRS 10 also grants exemptions to parent companies whose debt or equity are not traded in any public markets or who have not filed financial statements with a view to issuing debt or equity securities in a public market. Thus, A might be exempt if none of its securities is publicly traded.

Finally, a parent company is exempt if its ultimate or any intermediate parent company publishes consolidated financial statements that comply with IFRS. Thus, D could be exempt on the basis that A will publish group financial statements that comply with IFRS.

Thus, if a parent company is quoted on any stock exchange, then it must publish consolidated financial statements unless it is itself the subsidiary of another company. Providing an exemption for parent companies that are subsidiaries is quite logical because subgroups such as the D Group in Figure 9.3 are not independent economic

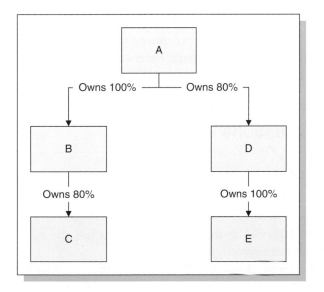

Figure 9.3 Companies in the A Group

entities. The directors of D are subject to A's control, and so there is no real point in preparing financial statements that consolidate the financial statements of D and E.

The exemption for parent companies that are unquoted is less easy to justify, although there may be an argument that the shareholders of an unquoted parent company could simply require their directors to prepare consolidated financial statements if they so wished.

Summary

Most businesses of any great size are organised as groups of companies. There are several practical and legal reasons why it is convenient to do so.

Unfortunately, the financial statements of a company that owns shares in other businesses would tell its shareholders very little in the way of useful information. Group financial statements overcome this problem by portraying the group as an economic entity, even though it is actually organised as a series of independent legal entities.

The key to preparing group financial statements is to identify offsetting balances and totals between the individual companies' accounts, cancel these, and then add the remainder together. While that sounds simple, it can require several adjustments, and these will be discussed in detail in later chapters.

Parent companies are required to publish a consolidated profit and loss account and a consolidated statement of financial position. These statements must include each and every subsidiary, defined in terms of the parent company's ability to exercise control. There are very few exceptions to the requirement to prepare group accounts or to include every subsidiary. Parent companies that are wholly owned subsidiaries are, however, exempt.

Tutorial Questions

Question 1

A owns 52% of B.

B Ltd owns 51% of C.

A plc owns 10% of the shares in D, but also has the right to appoint a majority of the voting members of D's board.

Identify the members of the A Group, explaining why each should be included.

Question 2 ✓

The following statements of financial position have been prepared for G and its two wholly owned subsidiaries, H and K, as at 31 March 20X4:

	G £000	H £000	K £000
Property, plant and equipment	26	9	8
Investment in H Ltd	15		
Investment in K Ltd	10		
Current assets	2	4	3
	53	13	11
Share capital	34	7	7
Retained earnings	19	6	4
	53	13	11

None of the companies owned any inventory.

Prepare a consolidated statement of financial position and explain what each figure in the statement means. (*Hint: Assets equals capital (liabilities).*)

Question 3 ✓

M plc owns 60% of the share capital of N plc. Explain whether the M Group consolidated statement of financial position should include 60% or 100% of the balances in N plc's financial statements. (*Hint: Think about the purpose of consolidated financial statements.*)

Question 4 ✓

You have been asked to make a loan to Aitch, a wholly owned subsidiary of the Aitch Worldwide Group. The directors of Aitch have shown you their company's statement of financial position, which is not impressive, and a copy of their parent company's group statement of financial position, which is. Explain why you should be careful about relying on the group financial statements before making a loan to a member of the Aitch Worldwide Group.

Question 5 ✓

The directors of Y have asked for your advice. Their group of companies manufactures clothing and sells much of this through its own shops. One group company brews vinegar and sells this to supermarkets that are not part of the Y Group. The directors are concerned that it is misleading to include the figures from the vinegar company in the group accounts and have asked for your advice.

Explain whether it is logical to include the vinegar company in the group accounts. Explain whether it is likely that the directors would be permitted to exclude the company.

Questions with Answers

Question 1

One of your friends owns shares in Parent plc and has asked you a number of questions about the company's annual report. She has access to the financial statements of the individual group members and is concerned about the following points:

- She cannot reconcile the total sales of the individual group members to the figure according to the consolidated statement of profit or loss in Parent plc's annual report. She is concerned that there has been some fraudulent understatement.
- The total figure for the retained profits of all of the group members is far short of the retained profits according to the consolidated statement of financial position. Again, this appears to suggest fraud or error in the preparation of the group accounts.

Advise your friend.

Question 2

Explain why the identification of subsidiary companies has been such a difficult area in accounting regulation.

Question 3

Discuss the difficulties of reading and understanding a set of consolidated financial statements.

Reference

IASB (2011) IFRS 10 *Consolidated Financial Statements*.

The Mechanics of Consolidation

Contents

Learning Objectives

After studying this chapter, you should be able to:

- prepare simple group statements of financial position, dealing with adjustments for pre-acquisition retained earnings, goodwill on acquisition, and non-controlling interests;

- account for the effects of recognising fair values in the calculation of goodwill on acquisition and non-controlling interest;
- reconcile and cancel intercompany balances;
- prepare a consolidated statement of profit or loss and summarised statement of changes in equity.

Introduction

In many respects, the identification of the group members is the difficult part of consolidation. Once that has been accomplished, the actual process of consolidating the figures can be viewed as almost mechanical. The process of preparing group financial statements involves identifying relationships between group members and cancelling those so that the resulting financial statements reflect the group as an economic entity in its own right. That process of cancellation and adjustment can be complicated and it is a constant source of exam questions. It is, therefore, important to understand it.

There is one minor controversy about presenting workings in these questions and that is whether to lay these out as journal entries, drawing upon double entry bookkeeping principles, or to start with the figures according to the group members' financial statements and to add and subtract the adjustments required to arrive at the figure according to the group accounts. Each approach has its advantages and disadvantages and both will be demonstrated so that readers can choose between them.

Consolidated Statement of Financial Position

The starting point is the preparation of a set of financial statements for each group member, accompanied with some additional information. The following example deals with the simplest possible case.

H acquired 100% of the shares in S on 31 December 20X8. The statements of financial position of the two companies at that date were as follows:

	H £000	S £000
Property, plant and equipment	8	6
Investment in S	10	
Current assets	12	10
	30	16

Share capital	20	10
Current liabilities	10	6
	30	16

In order to prepare a consolidated statement, we need to look for internal relationships that exist only between group members. In this case, the only relationship is H's £10 000 asset of Investment in S, which can be offset against the £10 000 equity balance that S shows as due to its shareholders.

This gives us a choice of approach to the preparation of a consolidated statement:

• The first approach would be to use double entry bookkeeping to reduce the asset of investment and also the equity balance of share capital:

Debit share capital	10 000	
Credit Investment in S		10 000

• Alternatively, we could simply state that the asset of Investment in S exists only in terms of a relationship between the two members of the H Group and so it should be eliminated. In the same vein, the equity balance of Share capital in S's figures is also an obligation that exists only between group members and so ought to be eliminated.

Regardless of the manner in which the adjustments have been presented, all that remains is to add the remaining figures together:

H Group
Consolidated statement of financial position
as at 31 December 20X8

	£000
Property, plant and equipment	14
Current assets	22
	36
Share capital	20
Current liabilities	16
	36

This illustrates the purpose of consolidated financial statements. The directors of H control property, plant and equipment with a book value of £14 000 and current assets valued at £22 000. We can see how those assets have been financed using the group's equity and borrowings.

More about Equity Balances

The parent company's investment is best understood as the amount paid for the subsidiary's equity as at the time control was acquired. That means that any and all equity in the subsidiary's statement of financial position must be offset against the investment.

For example, P acquired 100% of the shares issued by Q on 31 December 20X3. The companies' statements of financial position as at that date were as follows:

	P £000	Q £000
Property, plant and equipment	25	10
Investment in Q	13	
Current assets	8	7
	46	17
Share capital	20	10
Retained earnings	20	3
Total equity	40	13
Current liabilities	6	4
	46	17

The parent has paid £13 000 for equity worth a total of £13 000 and both amounts have to be cancelled before the consolidated statements can be prepared:

Debit Share capital	10 000	
Debit Retained earnings	3 000	
Credit Investment in S		13 000

This gives us the following consolidated statement of financial position:

P Group
Consolidated statement of financial position
as at 31 December 20X3

	£000
Property, plant and equipment	35
Current assets	15
	50
Share capital	20
Retained earnings	20
Total equity	40
Current liabilities	10
	50

Post-Acquisition Retained Earnings

The parent's investment in its controlling interest in the subsidiary will always be cancelled against the equity that was acquired as at that date. That has the effect of forcing us to distinguish between pre- and post-acquisition reserves. Any equity balances acquired when the parent took control are *pre-acquisition* and must be cancelled against the parent's investment. Any equity balances that arise after that date are *post-acquisition* and may be included in the consolidated equity balances (although only to the extent to which they are attributable to the group – more on that later in this chapter).

Returning to the P Group example, but four years later, the statements of financial position of the same two group members were as follows:

Statement of financial position as at 31 December 20X7	P	Q
	£000	£000
Property, plant and equipment	34	19
Investment in Q	13	
Current assets	15	10
	62	29

Share capital	20	10
Retained earnings	30	13
Total equity	50	23
Current liabilities	12	6
	62	29

The same adjustment is required to cancel the parent company's investment against the obligation according to the subsidiary company's equity. The holding company's £13 000 is still offset against equity valued at £13 000. The journal that we need to cancel this relationship remains:

Debit Share capital	10 000	
Debit Retained earnings	3 000	
Credit Investment in S		13 000

Alternatively, it would be just as valid to calculate group retained earnings as follows:

P – per statement of financial position	30 000
Q – per statement of financial position	13 000
Less – pre-acquisition profits in Q	(3 000)
	40 000

Regardless of how the figures are arrived at, the consolidated statement of financial position is as follows:

P Group
Consolidated statement of financial position
as at 31 December 20X7

	£000
Property, plant and equipment	53
Current assets	25
	78

Share capital	20
Retained earnings	40
Total equity	60
Current liabilities	18
	78

Goodwill on Acquisition – Ignoring Fair Values

So far, our examples have been somewhat artificial in that the amount paid by the holding company has been equal to the book value of the equity acquired according to the subsidiary's financial statements. In practice, the cost of acquiring a company is very unlikely to be the same as the book value of its equity.

If the cost of the investment is different from the book value of the equity then the consolidated statement of financial position will not balance if the two figures are cancelled against one another. To avoid that, a balancing figure called 'goodwill on acquisition' is inserted to ensure that the consolidated statement balances.

For example, T acquired all of the share capital in V on 31 December 20X3. At that date the two companies' statements of financial position were as follows:

	T £000	V £000
Property, plant and equipment	8	6
Investment in V	15	
Current assets	2	4
	25	10
Share capital	22	8
Retained earnings	3	2
Total equity	25	10

We have already seen that T's asset of £15 000 must be offset against V's equity of £8000 + £2000 = £10 000. The problem is that the amounts being cancelled differ by £5000.

Goodwill can be calculated using the following calculation:

Investment in V	£15 000
Share capital acquired	(£8 000)
Retained earnings acquired	(£2 000)
Goodwill on acquisition	£5 000

Alternatively, the figure can be determined using a ledger account called 'cost of control'. That would involve transferring the cost of the investment and the associated equity acquired into the account and the remaining balance would be the goodwill figure:

Cost of control

Investment in V	15	Share capital	8
		Retained earnings	2
		Goodwill c/d	5
	15		15
Goodwill b/d	5		

Using ledger accounts and journal entries means that debits and credits have to agree, and so the resulting figures should be guaranteed to produce a square consolidated statement of financial position. For example, the credit to cost of control will have a corresponding debit to the retained earnings account:

Retained earnings

Cost of control	2	Balance b/d	3
Balance c/d	3	Balance b/d	2
	5		5
		Balance b/d	3

The consolidated statement of financial position will show the goodwill as a non-current asset:

T Group
Consolidated statement of financial position
as at 31 December 20X3

	£000
Property, plant and equipment	14
Goodwill	5
Total non-current assets	19
Current assets	6
	25
Share capital	22
Retained earnings	3
Total equity	25

Bargain Purchases

It is possible for goodwill to be negative, although that is unlikely because businesses are normally worth more than the combined value of their individual net assets. That makes it unlikely that the seller will be prepared to accept a discount against the book values when selling the shares.

IFRS 3 *Business Combinations* (IASB, 2010a) goes to the extent of stating that the figures should be checked to ensure that all liabilities have been taken into account and that asset values are realistic before recognising a gain.

If the goodwill figure is negative despite a thorough check of the figures, then it should be added to the parent's retained earnings.

Understanding Goodwill

It is important to realise exactly what the goodwill figure actually means. It is really just a balancing figure that has to be inserted into the consolidated statement of financial position in order to make it square after cancelling the cost of investment against the equity that was purchased at the date of acquisition. The same adjustments are made, without any alteration of the numbers, every year into the indefinite future and so any relevance that the goodwill figure may have had when the controlling interest was first acquired will diminish very rapidly.

Goodwill is reviewed annually for impairment; otherwise the figure is left unadjusted. That may appear illogical but the reasons are largely historical. In the past, goodwill on acquisition had to be eliminated against retained earnings, which drove up gearing ratios, or amortised over an estimated useful life, which drove down profit. Both treatments were unpopular with preparers and so creative accounting schemes were developed in order to minimise the adjustments. Carrying the original goodwill forward indefinitely, unless it has been impaired, does not affect either gearing or profit and so reduces the temptation to find loopholes in the rules.

We will return to the calculation of goodwill once we have introduced the concept of non-controlling interests. There is a further complication that can arise as a result of fair value adjustments as at the date of acquisition.

Non-Controlling Interests

The parent need not acquire all of the subsidiary's equity in order to have control. If the initial investment is for less than 100% then the portion of the subsidiary's equity that is left in the hand of outside shareholders is called a 'non-controlling interest'.

In the simplest possible case it is very easy to calculate non-controlling interest. If book values are in line with fair values as at the date of acquisition then there is no need to distinguish between pre- and post-acquisition equity balances. In the next section, we will see that adjustments associated with fair values can complicate matters.

For example, Q acquired 75% of R's equity on 31 December 20X4. R's retained earnings at that date were £8000:

Statements of financial position as at 31 December 20X7

	Q £000	R £000
Property, plant and equipment	33	28
Investment in R	25	
Total non-current assets	58	28
Current assets	11	9
	69	37
Equity		
Share capital	40	20
Retained earnings	22	12
Total equity	62	32
Current liabilities	7	5
	69	37

As questions get more complicated, it makes sense to work through the figures in a systematic way. It is usually a good idea to start with the calculation of goodwill because that requires a clear understanding of the structure of the group and of what was purchased and when. In this case, the parent paid £25 000 for 75% of the equity, which comprised share capital of £20 000 and retained earnings of £8000; 75% of those figures comes to £15 000 and £6000 respectively:

Cost of control			
Investment in R	25	Share capital	15
		Retained earnings	6
		Goodwill c/d	4
	25		25
Goodwill b/d	4		

Alternatively:

Investment in R	25 000
Share capital acquired	(15 000)
Group share of *pre-acquisition* profits	(6 000)
Goodwill	4 000

In either case, goodwill was £4000 as at the date of acquisition and it will remain so at 31 December 20X7 unless it has suffered an impairment.

The minority shareholders are entitled to 25% of the equity in the subsidiary's statement of financial position:

Non-controlling interest			
		Share capital	5
Balance c/d	8	Retained earnings	3
	8		8
		Balance b/d	8

Thus, the minority shareholders are entitled to £8000 of equity:

Non-controlling interest in share capital	5 000
Non-controlling interest in retained earnings	3 000
	8 000

The following section will develop the discussion of the calculation of non-controlling interest. There can be situations in which the calculation is complicated by the need to make adjustments for fair values in the subsidiary's net assets as at the date of acquisition.

Finally, the account for retained earnings is as follows:

Retained earnings			
Cost of control	6	Balance b/d	22
Non-controlling interest	3	Balance b/d	12
Balance c/d	25		
	34		34
		Balance b/d	25

Retained earnings is the most complicated figure to determine and leaving it until last makes it easier to recycle figures from the other workings. The T account shown above simply completes the double entry adjustments made in the cost of control and minority interest figures. Alternatively, the working can be laid out as:

Retained earnings – Q	22 000
Retained earnings – R	12 000
Group share of pre-acquisition profit	(6 000)
Non-controlling interest	(3 000)
	25 000

Now that we have completed the workings, we can prepare the statement:

Q Group
Consolidated statement of financial position
as at 31 December 20X7

	£000
Property, plant and equipment	61
Goodwill	4
Total non-current assets	65
Current assets	20
	85

Share capital	40
Retained earnings	25
	65
Non-controlling interests	8
Total equity	73
Current liabilities	12
	85

Note the treatment of non-controlling interests in the statement of financial position. IFRS 10 *Consolidated Financial Statements* (IASB, 2011) requires that the non-controlling interests are presented in the consolidated statement of financial position within equity, but separately from the equity of the owners of the parent. That is probably the most sensible compromise because the parent company's shareholders would not regard the non-controlling interest as having the same rights and interests as they have in the group's equity, and yet the non-controlling interest is not a liability.

Presenting Workings

By now, you should have decided whether you prefer to work with T accounts or to calculate the figures directly. The advantage of T accounts is that consolidation exercises in the real world use that approach (at least in the sense that entries and adjustments are set out as journal entries). They also make it far easier to ensure that all of the adjustments are made consistently in double entry terms so that the consolidated statement of financial position balances. On the other hand, calculating the figures individually using working notes requires some thought about what the resulting numbers actually mean and so that might encourage a better understanding.

The remaining examples in this chapter will alternate between the two approaches.

Fair Values and Consolidation

Fair values may have an impact on the consolidation process in several ways, each of which is dealt with by IFRS 3:

- the fair value of the consideration
- the fair value of the identifiable assets acquired
- the fair value of the non-controlling interest.

Fair Value of the Acquirer's Consideration

Controlling interests are only rarely purchased for cash. Very few companies or groups of companies would have sufficient cash reserves to buy control in a subsidiary for cash. In practice, the parent will issue its own shares in exchange for the shares acquired.

The shares issued by the parent should be valued at their fair value and so there will almost certainly be a share premium to be recognised in addition to the nominal value of the shares.

For example, G acquired 60% of the equity of H by issuing three new $1 shares in exchange for every two $1 shares in H. H had 2m shares in issue at the date of acquisition. At that date, the two companies' share prices were quoted at $4.00 and $4.20 respectively. In this case, the acquirer has to issue $2m \times 60\% \times 3/2 = 1.8m$ new shares. The fair value of those shares is $1.8m \times \$4.00 = \$7.2m$. Thus, G will have to record the issue of 1.8m $1 shares with an associated share premium of $\$7.2m - \$1.8m = \$5.4m$. G's statement of financial position will show an increase in the asset of investment in H of $7.2m, an increase in ordinary shares of $1.8m and an increase in share premium of $5.4m.

The market value of the shares acquired is not particularly relevant, although it is worth remembering that the cost of a controlling interest may be greater than the cost implied by the market value of a small number of shares. The acquirer is likely to have plans for the target company that make it possible to extract a higher price than the current market value. For example, there could be synergies between the two companies so that uniting them under common control will reduce costs or generate additional revenues, or the bidding company's directors may believe that they have superior management skills to those of the target company's present board – so that taking control will enable wasted potential to be put to good use.

The issuing costs associated with the new shares should not be treated as part of the cost of acquisition. The parent should account for those costs in accordance with the rules laid down by IAS 32 *Financial Instruments: Presentation* (IASB, 2008) and IFRS 9 *Financial Instruments* (IASB, 2010b) as discussed in Chapter 8 of this text.

The cost of acquisition excludes incidental costs such as professional fees associated with identifying or negotiating the purchase: for example, the legal costs associated with drawing up contracts or accountancy fees paid for 'due diligence' investigations into the affairs of the target company. All such costs should be written off as expenses when they are incurred.

There is the possibility that the parent will provide a 'contingent consideration'. For example, G's agreement with H's former shareholders could provide that an additional sum will be paid if H's reported profit exceeds $5m in any given accounting period ending during the next five years. Such an agreement might simplify negotiations between buyers and sellers because the buyer will only pay the additional consideration if the acquired company meets the targets implied by the contract and so there is less risk of overpaying for a company that might not deliver the performance that is hoped for. Conversely, the seller is protected from accepting too low a price for a company that has the potential to succeed after it has been taken over.

IFRS 3 requires that the fair value of any such contingent consideration be valued at its fair value and included in the acquirer's books as a financial instrument (either equity or liability in accordance with the rules in IAS 32).

The fair value of a contingent consideration is essentially the amount for which the liability could be discharged between knowledgeable and willing parties in an arm's length transaction. This is clearly a difficult figure to determine, but if the parties to the purchase of H by G would (hypothetically) agree to set aside the additional payment in return for an additional $6m at the date of acquisition then that sum would be the fair value of the contingent consideration and the total cost of the shares in H would be the $7.2m of equity plus the $6m to give $13.2m overall. The problem is, of course, that there is no readily observable market that would enable the value of such agreements to be determined objectively.

The treatment of changes in the fair value of any contingent consideration depends on the cause of the change. If the change arises because additional information relating to the facts or circumstances as at the date of acquisition comes to light, then the value of the contingent consideration and the related figure of goodwill on acquisition will both be adjusted retrospectively. Such corrections could occur if information that was available at the time of the acquisition was overlooked or misinterpreted.

If the change arises because of information relating to changes after the acquisition date, such as the company meeting profit targets that indicate that the contingent element of the consideration will be paid, then the change will be recognised within the parent's financial statements:

• If the contingent consideration is classified as equity then its value will be adjusted against the parent's retained earnings.
• If the contingent consideration is a liability that is classified as a financial instrument then the value will be adjusted and the provisions of IFRS 9 or IAS 39

Financial Instruments: Recognition and Measurement (IASB, 2010c) will be applied in deciding whether the resulting gain or loss goes through the statement of profit or loss or the statement of comprehensive income.

• If the consideration is a liability that is not a financial instrument then the movement will be accounted for in accordance with the provisions of IAS 37 *Provisions, Contingent Liabilities and Contingent Assets* (IASB, 2001b).

Fair Values of the Subsidiary's Identifiable Assets

IFRS 3 requires the parent to recognise the identifiable assets acquired and the liabilities assumed by the group, and also any non-controlling interest in the subsidiary on that basis. The main significance of this is that the parent may have to recognise assets and liabilities that the subsidiary had not accounted for in its statement of financial position as at the date of acquisition.

Identifiable assets are defined as being capable of being disposed of separately from the business itself or arising from contractual or other legal rights.

Furthermore, IFRS 3 also requires the assets and liabilities recognised as at the date of acquisition to be reflected at their fair values as at the date of acquisition.

These requirements can mean that the values that are taken into account when calculating the equity acquired at the date of acquisition are different from those reflected in the subsidiary's financial statements. That can happen because the valuation conducted by the buyer is more up to date or uses different criteria than the valuation according to the subsidiary's financial statements. It could also happen because the subsidiary's financial statements do not recognise contingent liabilities to which the parent has been able to attach a value for the sake of arriving at a comprehensive figure for identifiable net assets.

It would simplify the consolidation process slightly if the subsidiary restated its financial statements to recognise those adjustments at the time of acquisition, but there is no specific requirement for the subsidiary to do so. In addition, the recognition criteria applied by IFRS 3 are sometimes different from those applied by companies preparing their individual financial statements. Furthermore, the additional adjustments may be left simply to add some rigour to an exam question.

It should be borne in mind that the fair value adjustment may also require additional depreciation to be charged against the group's property, plant and equipment. Care has to be taken when reading questions to ensure that any such adjustments are made correctly.

For example, S acquired 80% of T's equity on 31 December 20X2. T's retained earnings at that date were £15 000:

Statements of financial position as at 31 December 20X6

	S £000	T £000
Property, plant and equipment	96	101
Investment in T	90	
Total non-current assets	186	101
Current assets	15	10
	201	111
Equity		
Share capital (£1 shares, fully paid)	40	30
Share premium	72	20
Retained earnings	83	52
Total equity	195	102
Current liabilities	6	9
	201	111

S exchanged three of its own shares for every four shares acquired from T's shareholders. At that time S's shares were traded at £5 each.

At the time of acquisition, T owned an item of plant whose fair value exceeded its book value by £40 000. The item of plant had an estimated remaining useful life of ten years. None of this information has been reflected in T's books.

S did not actually part with any cash in order to acquire control of T. In fact, it issued shares with a nominal value of $30\,000 \times 80\% \times 3/4 \times £1 = £18\,000$. Those shares had a fair value of $18\,000 \times £5 = £90\,000$. The share issue has already been accounted for in S's books and so there is no need for any further adjustment.

The fair value adjustment with respect to the plant effectively adds £40 000 to T's equity as at the date of acquisition. That is shared 80:20 with the non-controlling interest. That gain has been eroded by four years' additional depreciation and so the consolidated retained earnings will be charged an additional $£40\,000 \times 10\% \times 4 = £16\,000$. Again, that will be shared 80:20 with the minority shareholders.

Cost of control

Investment in T	90.0	Share capital	24.0
		Share premium	16.0
		Plant	32.0
		Retained earnings	12.0
		Goodwill c/d	6.0
	90.0		90.0
Goodwill b/d	6.0		

Note that share premium as at the date of acquisition is taken into account because it is an element of the equity that was acquired as at that date.

Property, plant and equipment

Balance b/d	96.0	Retained earnings	12.8
Balance b/d	101.0	Non-controlling interest	3.2
Cost of control	32.0		
Non-controlling interest	8.0	Balance c/d	221.0
	237.0		237.0
Balance b/d	221.0		

Non-controlling interest

Plant	3.2	Share capital	6.0
		Share premium	4.0
		Plant	8.0
Balance c/d	25.2	Retained earnings	10.4
	28.4		28.4
		Balance b/d	25.2

Retained earnings

Cost of control	12.0	Balance b/d	83.0
Non-controlling interest	10.4	Balance b/d	52.0
Plant	12.8		
Balance c/d	99.8		
	135.0		135.0
		Balance b/d	99.8

S Group
Consolidated statement of financial position
as at 31 December 20X6

	£000
Property, plant and equipment	221.0
Goodwill	6.0
Total non-current assets	227.0
Current assets	25.0
	252.0
Share capital	40.0
Share premium	72.0
Retained earnings	99.8
	211.8
Non-controlling interests	25.2
Total equity	237.0
Current liabilities	15.0
	252.0

Fair Value of Non-Controlling Interest

IFRS 3 offers two methods for the valuation of non-controlling interest at the date of acquisition.

The first method calculates non-controlling interest as a percentage of the subsidiary's identifiable net assets as at the date of acquisition. That is the simplest treatment and is consistent with the approach applied when the concept of the non-controlling interest was introduced earlier in this chapter.

The second method requires that the fair value of the non-controlling interest be determined at the date of the parent's acquisition. That fair value may be determined by market prices if the shares are publicly traded or by some other means. This is known as the 'full value' or 'fair value' method. This is likely to result in a higher value for goodwill on acquisition.

For example, refer back to the acquisition of R by Q earlier in this chapter. The answer as given in that section is already consistent with the first method. Alternatively, suppose that the market value of the 25% non-controlling interest in R was £10 000 as at the date of acquisition. In that case, goodwill would be calculated as follows:

Investment in R	£25 000
Fair value of non-controlling interest	£10 000
Fair value of net identifiable assets	(£28 000)
Goodwill	£7 000

In this case, we are assuming (in the absence of any information to the contrary) that the book value of equity as at the date of acquisition (share capital of £20 000 plus retained earnings of £8000 = £28 000) is the same as the fair value of the identifiable net assets.

If we use this approach, then non-controlling interest as at the date of consolidation will have to be calculated on the basis of the fair value as at the date of acquisition plus or minus any increases or decreases arising since then. In the case of the Q Group, that gives us:

Non-controlling interest as at acquisition date	£10 000
Non-controlling interest in post-acquisition retained earnings $= 25\% \times (12\,000 - 8000)$	£1 000
	£11 000

Intercompany Balances

All balances between group members must be cancelled. This means a thorough check through all receivables and payables to ensure that all amounts are cancelled.

The cancellation process can be complicated by the fact that timing differences can lead to disagreement between the figures according to the individual group members. For example, E's trade payables show a balance of £3000 due to F, a fellow group member. F's trade receivables include a balance of £10 000 due from E.

A typical explanation for such a disagreement could be that each party to the relationship recorded the transactions at different times. Suppose F despatched inventory worth £5000 to E. F would record that sale immediately but E would not update its records until the goods had arrived and the paperwork processed. Similarly, if E paid £2000 to F then E would record the payment while the cash was still in transit through the banking system and before it had been recorded by F.

Dealing with such timing differences is a simple matter of pretending either that the transactions were completed by both parties or that the transactions had not taken place in either company. The end result will be the same and so it does not matter which approach is taken.

Assuming that the inventory had arrived at E would increase the company's inventory and trade payables by £5000. Assuming that the cash had arrived in F's bank account would increase bank and decrease trade receivables by £2000. On that basis, E and F will both show the intercompany balance as £8000, which makes it easy to cancel the amount.

This sequence of adjustments can be shown as the following series of journal entries:

Debit Inventory	5000	
Credit Trade payables		5000
Debit Bank	2000	
Credit Trade receivables		2000
Debit Trade payables	8000	
Credit Trade receivables		8000

Consolidated Statement of Profit or Loss

The consolidated statement of profit or loss is prepared in exactly the same manner as the consolidated statement of financial position. All transactions between group members are cancelled against one another and the remaining figures are combined. Any non-controlling interest in subsidiary profits is subtracted and the result is the group profit for the year.

For example, N publishes a daily newspaper. It sells 90% of its daily print run to third parties and 10% to S. N owns 90% of S. The latest statements of profit or loss for the two companies are as follows:

Statements of profit or loss
for the year ended 31 December 20X3

	N £000	S £000
Sales to third parties	9 000	3 000
Sales to S	1 000	
	10 000	3 000
Cost of sales, excluding purchases from N	(5 200)	(800)
Purchases from N		(1 000)
Gross profit	4 800	1 200
Other charges	(2 200)	(400)
Profit before tax	2 600	800
Tax	(800)	(300)
Profit after tax	1 800	500

Combining the sales and expenses, but offsetting the transactions between group members against one another, gives:

N Group
Consolidated statement of profit or loss
for the year ended 31 December 20X3

	£000
Revenue	12 000
Cost of sales	(6 000)
Gross profit	6 000
Other charges	(2 600)
Profit before tax	3 400
Tax	(1 100)
Profit for the year, net of tax	2 300
Profit attributable to:	
Owners of the parent	2 250
Non-controlling interest	50
	2 300

IAS 1 *Presentation of Financial Statements* (IASB, 2001a) requires that the split of the group's profit between the parent's shareholders and the non-controlling interest be shown on the face of the statement of profit or loss.

If there are any additional items of comprehensive income then the other comprehensive income should also be split and the split shown in the same manner.

Closing Inventory

The example in the previous section did not have any closing inventory arising from the intercompany sales. That is significant because it is normally necessary for group members to sell goods to one another at their normal selling prices. If they did not, then the tax authorities in most countries would start to ask whether artificial prices were being used to minimise the tax burden. For example, a group member in a country with a high tax rate might sell goods to fellow group members based in a lower tax country at cost so that there is no profit at all in the country with the higher tax rate.

Selling goods within the group at normal selling prices is not a problem if those goods are resold before the end of the financial year. For example, if the parent buys an item of inventory for €10 and sells it to a subsidiary for €12 and the subsidiary resells it for €13 then the cost to the group is €10 and the selling price obtained by the group is €13. The profit of €3 will appear in the consolidated statement of profit or loss when the two sets of figures are combined.

The problem arises when the goods are not resold before the end of the year. In that case, the cost to the group is €10 but those same goods have been revalued at €12 because of the intercompany sale. In addition, a profit of €2 has been recognised even though the goods have not been sold to a third party. This must be corrected by reducing the asset of closing inventory by €2 and also increasing cost of sales by the same amount so that the unrealised gain is not recognised in the consolidated financial statements.

All such unrealised profits have to be identified as part of the consolidation process. The trick in exam questions is to read the question carefully in order to calculate the profit that has to be cancelled. Typically, questions will describe the manner in which the inventory figure has been arrived at, and it is necessary to unravel that in order to reduce the figure to its original cost. For example, if the question states that closing inventory includes $500\,000$ of inventory that had been purchased from another group member at cost plus 25%, then the original cost to the group is $500\,000 \times 100/125 = \$400\,000$.

Opening Inventory

Very few exam questions pick this point up, but the opening figure for inventory should be adjusted to deal with the consolidation adjustments that were made at the end of the previous year. Cancelling the profit on closing inventory has the effect of reducing closing inventory and thereby increasing cost of sales.

It is very easy to overlook the fact that the opening inventory is likely to have been overstated by intercompany sales. Correcting that will reduce opening inventory and thereby reduce cost of sales.

Strictly speaking, the consolidation process should net the decrease in opening inventory against the decrease in closing inventory, and only the remainder should be taken into account in determining the cost of sales.

For example, D owns 70% of E. D's opening inventory included $100 000 of inventory that been purchased from E. D's closing inventory included $140 000 of inventory that had been purchased from E. E's selling prices include a 20% markup from cost.

In this example, the opening inventory in question cost the group $100 000 $\times$ 100/120 = $83 333, and so E's statement of profit or loss would have included an unrealised profit of $100 000 − $83 333 = $16 667. That would have been split 70% to the group ($11 667) and 30% to the non-controlling interest ($5000). If the sale had been made by the parent company to the subsidiary, then the whole of the unrealised profit would have been adjusted against the group

The closing inventory cost $140 000 $\times$ 100/120 = $116 667 and the profit element was $140 000 − $116 667 = $23 333, split $16 333 to the group and $7000 to the non-controlling interest.

The opening balance on the provision for unrealised profit on inventory was $16 667 and that will be increased to $23 333 (an increase of $6666) by the following journal entry:

Debit Retained earnings	4666	
Debit Non-controlling interest	2000	
Credit Unrealised profit		6666

The debit entries are the difference between the opening and closing figures ($23 333 − $16 667 = $4666 and $7000 − $5000 = $2000).

The closing balance of $23 333 will be subtracted from group inventory in order to show the asset at its cost to the group.

Do not be surprised if an exam question does not provide any information about opening inventory. Examiners sometimes overlook this adjustment.

Dividends

Any dividend paid between group members should be eliminated because that would be a further example of a transaction that occurs only within the group.

If a dividend is paid by a partly owned subsidiary then the amount paid to the non-controlling interest will be subtracted from their balance. That reflects the fact that the payment of a dividend to the minority shareholders has the effect of reducing their stake in the group.

So, there are a number of adjustments that may be required in respect of the consolidated statement of comprehensive income.

Y acquired 60% of U in 20X2. At that date U had share capital of £2m and retained earnings of £3.0m. Goodwill on acquisition was £2.5m and that sum was written down to £1.2m in 20X4 because of impairment.

U made sales of £15m to Y during the year ended 31 December 20X6. One-third of those goods remain unsold as at the year end. U's selling prices include a 20% mark-up on top of cost.

U paid a dividend of £1m during the year ended 31 December 20X6 and Y's investment income comprises its share of that dividend.

The group members' statements of profit or loss for the year ended 31 December 20X6 were:

Statements of total comprehensive income
for the year ended 31 December 20X6

	Y £m	U £m
Revenue	50.0	28.0
Cost of sales	(12.1)	(18.3)
Gross profit	37.9	9.7
Other operating expenses	(6.2)	(2.1)
Investment income	0.6	
Profit before tax	32.3	7.6
Tax	(3.4)	(1.2)
Profit after tax	28.9	6.4
Other comprehensive income		
gains from revaluation (after tax)	5.0	4.0
Total comprehensive income	33.9	10.4

The intercompany sales of £15m will be deducted from group revenue and cost of sales.

Closing inventory includes £5m valued at cost to the group plus 20%, so the unrealised profit element $= £5m \times 20/120 = £0.8m$. That amount will be added to group cost of sales. The non-controlling interest in the profit for the year will be affected by that because the profit is shown in the subsidiary's statement of profit or loss. That will reduce non-controlling interest by $£0.8m \times 40\% = £0.3m$.

The investment income all arises from intercompany dividends and so the full amount will be eliminated.

The consolidated statement of comprehensive income will be:

Y Group
Consolidated statement of total comprehensive income
for the year ended 31 December 20X6

	£m
Revenue	63.0
Cost of sales	(16.2)
Gross profit	46.8
Other operating expenses	(8.3)
Profit before tax	38.5
Tax	(4.6)
Profit after tax	33.9
Other comprehensive income	
gains from revaluation (after tax)	9.0
Total comprehensive income	42.9

	£m
Profit attributable to:	
Equity holders of the parent	31.6
Non-controlling interest	2.3
	33.9

	£m
Total comprehensive income attributable to:	
Equity holders of the parent	39.0
Non-controlling interest	3.9
	42.9

Statement of Changes in Equity

A summarised statement of changes in equity should be provided that shows the totals of equity attributable to the parent's shareholders and to the non-controlling interest.

For example, the Y Group's members had the following summarised statements of changes in equity for the year ended 31 December 20X6:

Summarised statements of changes in equity for the year ended 31 December 20X6

	Y	U
	£m	£m
Opening equity	98.0	38.0
Total comprehensive income	33.9	10.4
Dividends	(3.0)	(1.0)
Balance at end of year	128.9	47.4

In the absence of any information to the contrary, we have to assume that non-controlling interest was based on a percentage of the value of net assets as at the date of acquisition.

The group's opening equity comprises the parent's equity, plus the group share of the subsidiary's equity that has arisen since control was acquired, less the goodwill that was written off against equity in 20X4. That gives a figure of $£98.0 + ((38.0 - 2.0 - 3.0) \times 60\%) - 1.3 = £116.5$m.

The opening balance on non-controlling interest is 40% of £38.0 = £15.2m.

That leaves us with the following:

Y Group
Consolidated summarised statement of changes in equity for the year ended 31 December 20X6

	Attributable to equity holders of the parent	Non-controlling interest	Total
	£m	£m	£m
Opening equity	116.5	15.2	131.7
Total comprehensive income	39.0	3.9	42.9
Dividends	(3.0)	(0.4)	(3.4)
Balance at end of year	152.5	18.7	171.2

Summary

Preparing the consolidated financial statements is really quite a mechanical process. In the real world, the greatest problems are associated with identifying subsidiaries. The actual mechanics of drawing up the consolidated statements themselves is really just a bookkeeping process.

The secret to preparing group accounts is to draw up a clear set of workings and keep the objectives of group accounting in mind.

Tutorial Questions

Question 1

Prepare a consolidated statement of financial position from the following information.

E acquired all of the share capital of F on 31/12/X1 when the balance on F's retained earnings was £6000:

Statements of financial position as at 31/12/X4

	E £000	F £000
Non-current assets		
Property, plant and equipment	39	29
Investment in F	38	—
Current assets	14	21
	91	50
Share capital	50	25
Retained earnings	38	23
	88	48
Current liabilities	3	2
	91	50

Question 2

Prepare a consolidated statement of financial position from the following information.

G acquired 80% of the share capital of H on 1 January 20X4.

The statements of financial position of G and H were as follows as at 31 December 20X6:

	G		H	
	£000	£000	£000	£000
Non-current assets				
Tangible				
Property		104		155
Plant and equipment		130		55
		234		210
Investment in H		300		—
		534		210
Current assets				
Inventory	80		35	
Trade receivables	150		45	
H current a/c	30		—	
Bank	10		6	
		270		86
		804		296
Share capital		400		100
Retained earnings		249		90
		649		190
Current liabilities				
Trade payables	125		72	
Tax	30		18	
G current a/c	—		16	
		155		106
		804		296

(a) H had retained earnings of £40 000 on 1 January 20X4.

(b) H made a payment of £4000 to G during December 20X6. G did not record this receipt until January 20X7.

(c) G despatched inventory with an invoiced value of £10 000 in December 20X6. This was not received until after the year end. G made a profit of £2000 on this sale.

(d) G's closing inventory at 31 December 20X6 includes goods that had been purchased from H for £15 000. The profit element included in this amount was £3000.

(e) Non-controlling interest is to be valued at its proportionate share of net assets.

Question 3

I acquired 80% of the share capital of J on 30 June 20X1.

The statements of financial position of the two companies as at 30 June 20X9 were as follows:

	I £000	J £000
Non-current assets		
Investment in J	9 000	
Property, plant and equipment	5 500	9 200
	14 500	9 200
Current assets		
Inventory	900	700
Trade receivables	750	450
Bank	420	210
	2 070	1 360
Total assets	16 570	10 560
Equity		
Share capital	5 000	6 000
Share premium	2 000	1 000
Retained earnings	9 000	3 260
	16 000	10 260
Current liabilities		
Creditors	570	300
Total equity and liabilities	16 570	10 560

(a) At the date of acquisition, J had retained earnings of £1.6m. ~~The fair value of the non-controlling interest was £1.0m.~~

(b) 20% of the goodwill on acquisition is to be written off as a result of an impairment review on 30 June 20X8.

(c) J held inventory at 30 June 20X9 that had cost the group £40 000 but was valued at £60 000 in J's books.

Prepare a consolidated statement of financial position for the I group as at 30 June 20X9.

Question 4

K purchased 90% of the share capital of L when the balance on L's retained profit was £400 000. The most recent statements of financial position for the two companies were as follows:

Statements of financial position as at 31 July 20X8

	K		L	
	£000	£000	£000	£000
Property, plant and equipment		1240		2010
Investment in L		1800		—
Inventory	400		300	
Trade receivables	500		380	
Bank current account	70		—	
		970		680
		4010		2690
Share capital		2000		850
Share premium		500		450
Retained profit		560		570
		3060		1870
Long-term loans		500		400
Trade payables	450		360	
Bank overdraft	—		60	
		450		420
		4010		2690

(a) At the date of acquisition the non-controlling interest in L was £200 000.
(b) The figure for L's property, plant and equipment includes a plot of land that is valued at its historical cost of £400 000. The land's fair value was £510 000 on the date that K acquired its interest in L.
(c) During the year, K made sales of £700 000 to L. These goods cost K £500 000. L still held 20% of these goods at the year end.
(d) An impairment review of goodwill on acquisition as at 31 July 20X7 led to a write-down of £50 000. That was the only occasion on which an impairment write-down was required.

Required:
Prepare a consolidated statement of financial position for the K Group as at 31 July 20X8.

Question 5

M purchased 60% of N's share capital on 31 December 20X0.

During the year ended 31 December 20X4, M made sales to N of £3.0m. N's closing inventory includes £500 000 purchased from M. M's profit margin is 10% of selling price.

The two companies' statements of profit or loss for the year ended 31 December 20X4 are as follows:

Statements of profit or loss for the year ended 31 December 20X4

	M £000	N £000
Revenues	19 000	11 000
Cost of sales	(11 000)	(4 600)
Gross profit	8 000	6 400
Other expenses	(2 600)	(800)
Profit before tax	5 400	5 600
Tax	(1 300)	(800)
Profit after tax	4 100	4 800

Prepare a consolidated statement of profit or loss and summarised statement of changes in equity for the M Group for the year ended 31 December 20X4.

Question 6 ✗ No solution.

P acquired 100% of Q's shares at a time when the fair value of Q's net assets was $90 000.
   The consideration paid by P comprised:

- Cash of $35 454 to be paid immediately. A further payment of $20 000 is to be paid in one year. Assume a discount rate of 10%.
- 10 000 fully paid shares in M. Each share had a nominal value of $1 and a market value of $4.
- A further $100 000 will be paid in one year if Q's profits for the year exceed $200 000. The probability of this occurring has been estimated at 40%. The fair value of this consideration can be taken as the present value of the expected payment.
- Legal fees associated with the acquisition are $18 000.

   Calculate the goodwill arising on the acquisition of Q and explain the treatment of each item that comprises P's consideration.

Questions with Answers

Question 1 ✓

R acquired 100% of the share capital of S on 31/12/X5, when the balance on S's retained earnings was £7000:

Statements of financial position as at 31/12/X9

	R £000	S £000
Property, plant and equipment	32	18
Investment in S	30	—
Current assets	4	8
	66	26
Share capital	28	14
Retained earnings	38	12
	66	26

Prepare a consolidated statement of financial position for the R Group.

T acquired 80% of U's £1 ordinary shares three years ago. The balance on U's retained profits at that date was £1 500 000 and the fair value of the non-controlling interest was £900 000. U has not issued any shares since that date. The statements of financial position for the two companies were as follows as at 31 December 20X6:

	T		U	
	£000	£000	£000	£000
Non-current assets				
Tangible		15 460		9 000
Investments		8 500		—
		23 960		9 000
Current assets				
Inventories	1 800		770	
Trade receivables	1 000		650	
Bank	450		—	
		3 250		1 420
		27 210		10 420
Equity and liabilities				
Equity				
Ordinary shares		10 000		2 500
Retained profits		15 000		4 500
		25 000		7 000
Non-current liabilities				
Loans		1 000		500
Current liabilities				
Trade payables	800		2 000	
Tax	410		520	
Overdraft	—		400	
		1 210		2 920
		27 210		10 420

(a) T's investments comprise the cost of its investment in U.

(b) U's figure for property, plant and equipment includes a piece of machinery whose fair value exceeded its net book value by £200 000 at the date of acquisition. U has not revalued the machine in its own books. The machine's estimated remaining useful life at the date of acquisition was five years.

(c) T sold goods to U for £140 000 during the year. These were transferred at a mark-up of 40% on cost. Three-quarters of these goods remained in U's closing inventory at 31 December 20X6.

Prepare the consolidated statement of financial position of the T Group as at 31 December 20X6.

Question 3

V acquired 75% of the share capital of W for £6m on 31 March 20X0.

During the year ended 31 March 20X4, V made sales of £1.9m to W. This included £400 000 of inventory that was still unsold by W at the year end. This inventory had originally cost V £250 000.

During the year ended 31 March 20X4, W made a dividend payment of £1m.

The statements of profit or loss of the two companies for the year ended 31 March 20X4 were as follows:

Statements of profit or loss for the year ended 31 December 20X4

	V	W
	£000	£000
Revenue	25 000	19 000
Cost of sales	(15 300)	(11 000)
Gross profit	9 700	8 000
Other expenses	(4 800)	(2 200)
Operating profit	4 900	5 800
Dividend income	750	—
	5 650	5 800
Tax	(900)	(600)
Profit after tax	4 750	5 200

Prepare a consolidated statement of profit or loss for the V Group for the year ended 31 March 20X4.

References

IASB (2001a) IAS 1 *Presentation of Financial Statements.*

IASB (2001b) IAS 37 *Provisions, Contingent Liabilities and Contingent Assets.*

IASB (2008) IAS 32 *Financial Instruments: Presentation.*

IASB (2010a) IFRS 3 *Business Combinations.*

IASB (2010b) IFRS 9 *Financial Instruments.*

IASB (2010c) IAS 39 *Financial Instruments: Recognition and Measurement.*

IASB (2011) IFRS 10 *Consolidated Financial Statements.*

MORE COMPLICATED GROUP STRUCTURES

Contents

Learning Objectives

After studying this chapter, you should be able to:

- prepare group financial statements for groups that include indirect shareholdings;
- account for associate companies;
- account for special purpose entities;
- account for joint arrangements.

Introduction

So far, we have assumed fairly close and direct relationships between the different group members. This chapter discusses the implications of indirect control, which can occur when a parent company is itself a subsidiary or where shares are held by more than one group member. We will also discuss the implications of share-holdings that provide influence rather than control.

The accounting issues arising from these circumstances vary. In some cases, there is simply a need to understand the mechanics of the adjustments necessary to consolidate the financial statements. In others, there are some more substantive accounting issues to consider.

Indirect Shareholding and Sub-Subsidiaries

It is possible for a parent to obtain control indirectly through its control over other group members. For example, the group in Figure 11.1 contains three members: Parent, Sub1 and Sub2.

Parent controls Sub1 by virtue of a controlling interest of 60% of Sub1's equity. Sub1 controls Sub2 and so Parent effectively controls Sub2, even though it might be argued that Parent's interest in Sub2 is only 60% × 55% = 33%. Sub2 is a subsidiary of Parent, but it may be convenient to refer to Sub2 as a sub-subsidiary from time to time, in order to distinguish indirect ownership from direct.

Sub-subsidiaries create the question of when they joined the group. That is a matter of determining when the parent acquired control.

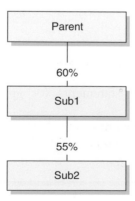

Figure 11.1 Group containing three members

Subsequent Acquisition

One possibility is that the parent acquired control of a subsidiary, which subsequently took control of another company. In that case, the parent company would acquire control on the same date as the acquisition of the sub-subsidiary by the direct subsidiary.

For example, the following information relates to B, C and D.

B acquired 60% of C's shares on 31 December 20X1 when C's retained earnings were £800 000. At that date the fair value of the shares retained by the non-controlling interest was £170 000.

C acquired 70% of D's shares on 31 December 20X2 when D's retained earnings were £230 000. At that date the fair value of the 30% of the shares retained by non-controlling shareholders in D was £150 000.

The statements of financial position of the three companies as at 31 December 20X5 were as follows:

	B £000	C £000	D £000
Property, plant and equipment	802	550	853
Investment in C	950		
Investment in D		700	
Current assets	18	16	14
	1770	1266	867
Share capital	800	300	500
Retained earnings	960	900	350
Current liabilities	10	66	17
	1770	1266	867

The adjustments relating to the investment in C are fairly straightforward:

Investment in C	950
Fair value of non-controlling interest	170
Fair value of net identifiable assets (300 + 800)	(1100)
Goodwill on acquisition of C	20

Investment in D	700
Fair value of non-controlling interest	150
Fair value of net identifiable assets (500 + 230)	(730)
Goodwill on acquisition of D	120

Total goodwill $= 20 + 120 = 140$

The calculation of the non-controlling interest is complicated by the fact that C's net assets include the investment in D. That investment will be cancelled as for any other consolidation exercise, but the non-controlling shareholders in C are entitled to their share of D's net assets. We deal with this by taking the group's effective interest in D into account when calculating the non-controlling interest. B owns 60% of C, which owns 70% of D. That gives B an interest of $60\% \times 70\% = 42\%$. The non-controlling interest is 58%.

The fact that the full value method was used to determine the non-controlling interest means that the non-controlling interest is calculated as follows:

	C	D
Non-controlling interest as at date of acquisition	170	150
Non-controlling interest in C's post-acquisition reserves (900 − 800) × 40%	40	
Non-controlling interest in D's post-acquisition reserves (350 − 230) × 58%		70
Non-controlling interest	210	220

Total non-controlling interest = 430

Retained earnings are calculated in the usual way.

The calculation of group retained earnings is straightforward:

B's retained earnings	960
Group share of C's retained earnings (900 − 800) × 60%	60
Group share of D's retained earnings (350 − 230) × 42%	50
	1070

B Group
Consolidated statement of financial position
as at 31 December 20X5

	£000
Goodwill	140
Property, plant and equipment	2205
Current assets	48
	2393
Share capital	800
Retained earnings	1070
	1870
Non-controlling interest	430
	2300
Current liabilities	93
	2393

The basic process of consolidation is unchanged, apart from the adaptation of the mechanics to deal with the difference in the parent's interest in the subsidiary.

Sub-Subsidiary in Place at Time of Acquisition

The only difference arising from the sub-subsidiary having been acquired by the subsidiary prior to the date of the subsidiary's acquisition is that the parent must base the calculation of goodwill and non-controlling interest as at the date the sub-subsidiary joined the group.

Suppose that C had acquired its 70% of D on 31 December 20X0 and at that date D's retained earnings were £160 000 and the fair value of the 30% of the shares retained by non-controlling shareholders in D was £105 000.

Suppose that D's retained earnings were £205 000 when B acquired its 60% holding on 31 December 20X1. At that date the fair value of the 30% of the shares retained by non-controlling shareholders in D was £130 000.

Assuming that the changing the date made no difference to the fair value of C's net identifiable assets, the goodwill on the acquisition of C was unchanged and remains at £20 000.

The acquisition of D is dealt with on the basis that D became a member of the B Group on 31 December 20X1. The facts and figures provided as at the date of C's acquisition of the shares are irrelevant (they were provided above in order to emphasise that fact). The goodwill calculation is, therefore:

Investment in D	700
Fair value of non-controlling interest	130
Fair value of net identifiable assets (500 + 205)	(705)
Goodwill on acquisition of D	125

Total goodwill = 20 + 125 = 145

The non-controlling interest is calculated as before, albeit with the figures changed to reflect the different date.

The fact that the full value method was used to determine the non-controlling interest means that the non-controlling interest is calculated as follows:

	C	D
Equity as at date of acquisition	170	130
Non-controlling interest in C's post-acquisition reserves (900 − 800) × 40%	40	
Non-controlling interest in D's post-acquisition reserves (350 − 205) × 58%		84
Non-controlling interest	210	214

Total non-controlling interest = 210 + 214 = 424

The calculation of group retained earnings is also as before, but reflecting the date that D joined the group:

B's retained earnings	960
Group share of C's retained earnings (900 − 800) × 60%	60
Group share of D's retained earnings (350 − 205) × 42%	61
	1081

B Group
Consolidated statement of financial position
as at 31 December 20X5

	£000
Property, plant and equipment	2205
Goodwill	145
Current assets	48
	2398

Share capital	800
Retained earnings	1081
	1881
Non-controlling interest	424
	2305
Current liabilities	93
	2398

Control Through a Mixture of Direct and Indirect Shareholdings

The parent company's control may be acquired by means of a combination of direct and indirect shareholdings (see Figure 11.2).

In this case the parent controls 25% of Sub2's equity through its control of Sub1, which gives it a controlling interest of 55% when combined with its direct shareholding in Sub2.

The treatment of this structure is virtually the same as for a group containing a sub-subsidiary. As before, the dates are important because the acquisition is deemed to take place when the parent obtains control. If each of the two shareholdings in this example was purchased in separate transactions, then Sub2 would be deemed to become a subsidiary only after the second investment.

Later in this chapter we will discuss the concept of the associate company, where there is 'influence' but not control. That could mean that Sub2 was accounted for as an associate of Parent for a time while Parent controlled either 25% or 30% of Sub2's equity and could use that to influence Sub2's management without having outright control.

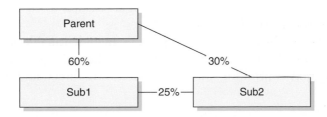

Figure 11.2 Parent company control by direct and indirect shareholdings

The concept of effective interest applies just as for sub-subsidiaries. For example, suppose that E acquired 75% of F on 31 December 20X2 and 40% of G on 31 December 20X3. F acquired 30% of G on 31 December 20X4. That would make F a subsidiary from 31 December 20X4.

E has a direct interest in G of 40% and an indirect interest via F of 75% × 30% = 22.5%, giving E a total interest of 62.5% and leaving a non-controlling interest in G of 37.5%.

Before we go any further, the figures that we require to prepare a consolidated statement of financial position are as follows:

Statements of financial position as at 31 December 20X7

	E £000	F £000	G £000
Property, plant and equipment	600	1000	1700
Investment in F	2200		
Investment in G	1100	1300	
Current assets	40	30	32
	3940	2330	1732
Share capital	1000	500	800
Retained earnings	2918	1700	895
Current liabilities	22	130	37
	3940	2330	1732

E purchased 75% of F when F's retained earnings were £1 300 000 and the fair value of F's identifiable net assets was £2 450 000. The fair value adjustments associated with the recognition of fair value related to non-depreciable assets. The fair value of the non-controlling interest in F was £700 000.

E purchased its investment in G when G's net identifiable assets were £1 200 000 and retained earnings were £500 000.

F purchased its investment in G when G's net identifiable assets were £1 400 000 and retained earnings were £600 000. At that date the fair value of the whole of the non-controlling interest in G (both direct and indirect) was £740 000.

There is nothing complicated about the calculation of goodwill on the acquisition of F:

Cost of control – F			
Investment in F	2200	Share capital	500
Non-controlling interest	700	Retained earnings	1300
		Property	650
		Goodwill c/d	450
	2900		2900
Goodwill b/d	450		

The fair value adjustment takes the book value of the net assets acquired to $500 + 1300 + 650 = 2450$. The adjustment has been debited to property on the basis that it probably relates to land.

In dealing with the acquisition of G, we have to deal with the fact that G became a subsidiary on 31 December 20X4. The parent's costs amount to the 1100 that it invested directly, plus 75% of the 1300 that is controlled indirectly through F. Thus, the cost to the group $= 1100 + (75\% \times 1300) = 2075$. In order to eliminate the whole of the 1300 asset showing in F's books, we treat the remaining 25% of the cost as if it belongs to the non-controlling interest in F and deduct it from their balance.

No adjustment was required in respect of the fair value of G's identifiable net assets as at the date of acquisition because their book value equals their fair value of 1400.

Cost of control – G			
Investment in G	2075	Share capital	800
Non-controlling interest	740	Retained earnings	600
		Goodwill c/d	1415
	2815		2815
Goodwill b/d	1415		

Total goodwill $= 450 + 1415 = 1865$.

Non-controlling interest in F is unaffected by the structure of the group:

Non-controlling interest – F			
		Fair value as at date of acquisition	700
Bal c/d	800	Retained earnings	100
	800		800
		Bal b/d	800

G's non-controlling interest is based upon the 37.5% calculated above with respect to post-acquisition retained earnings $(895 - 600) \times 37.5\% = 111$. In addition, the non-controlling interest in F's investment in G is worth 25% of $1300 = 325$:

Non-controlling interest – G			
Investment	325	Fair value as at date of acquisition	740
Bal c/d	526	Retained earnings	111
	851		851
		Bal b/d	851

Total non-controlling interest $= 800 + 526 = 1326$.

Retained earnings should now be a simple matter of ensuring that double entry is maintained:

Retained earnings			
Cost of control – F	1300	Bal b/d – E	2918
Cost of control – G	600	Bal b/d – F	1700
Non-controlling interest – F	100	Bal b/d – G	895
Non-controlling interest – G	111		
Bal c/d	3 402		
	5 513		5 513
		Bal b/d	3402

This gives us the following consolidated statement of financial position:

E Group
Consolidated statement of financial position
as at 31 December 20X7

	£000
Goodwill	1 865
Property, plant and equipment	3 950
Current assets	102
	5 917
Share capital	1 000
Retained earnings	3 402
Total equity	4 402
Non-controlling interest	1 326
	5 728
Current liabilities	189
	5 917

Accounting for Associates

The relationship between parents and subsidiaries can be summed up in terms of the fact that, by definition, the parent can *control* each of its subsidiaries. Bearing in mind that the whole point of preparing consolidated financial statements is to recognise the existence of an economic entity, there is another form of relationship that we must consider.

An associate is an entity over which another entity has 'significant influence' but which is neither a subsidiary nor a joint venture. The accounting treatment of such a relationship is dealt with by IAS 28 *Investments in Associates and Joint Ventures* (IASB, 2003).

Determining Whether Significant Influence Exists

IAS 28 spells out the circumstances in which one entity may be an associate of another. As with the parent–subsidiary relationship, the level of shareholding is a useful place to start even though holding shares is neither a necessary nor a sufficient condition to establish the existence of influence.

In the first instance, if the investor controls more than 20% of the voting power of an entity then it is presumed that the investor has significant influence. Conversely, it is presumed that control of less than 20% means that the investor does not have significant influence. Both presumptions are open to challenge, however, and the 20% threshold is only intended as a guide.

If investor A owns 20% of entity C's equity and the other 80% belongs to investor B, then it is very likely that B can exercise outright control of C and very likely that A has no real influence despite its ownership of a significant block of shares and votes. IAS 28 lists the following factors that could provide evidence of influence:

- representation on the board of directors or equivalent governing body of the investee;
- participation in policy-making processes, including participation in decisions about dividends or other distributions;
- material transactions between the investor and the investee;
- interchange of managerial personnel; or
- provision of essential technical information.

For example, imagine that an entrepreneur established a small company and sold 15% of the equity to an investor who bought those shares in return for cash but demanded a contractual right to appoint one of the new company's directors. If this appointee has a right to attend board meetings and is able to influence the board's decisions, then that will almost certainly indicate 'significant influence'. The fact that the investor holds less than 20% means that there will be a presumption that the company is not an associate, but that presumption should be rebutted because of the investor's ability to appoint a board member.

Derivatives and other complex financial instruments can create the right to acquire voting shares. IAS 28 deals with the implications of such instruments. If the investor holds options, warrants or convertible debt that can be converted into voting equity then the investor is permitted to take those *potential* voting rights into account when deciding whether significant influence exists. Such instruments can only be counted if the rights can be exercised immediately or at the investor's discretion. Rights that will only become available at some future date or after a particular event has occurred are not taken into account.

Significant influence must be kept under review. It is possible that influence could be lost because of changes in the relationship between the entities. In that case the investor will have to cease treating the investee as an associate.

Equity Accounting

Equity accounting is used to account for the relationship between an investor and an associate. The basic approach is that the group is credited with its share of the associate's earnings in the consolidated statement of profit or loss. The consolidated statement of financial position shows the investment in the associate as a single line entry that is valued at the group's share of the associate's net assets.

The logic behind accounting for associates is that it would be inappropriate to consolidate the associate's figures into the group financial statements because the associate is not under a parent's control and so it would be inappropriate to combine its figures with the group as a whole. On the other hand, the fact that the associate is subject to 'significant influence' means that it would be wrong to include nothing further than the dividends received from the associate in the group statement of profit or loss and the cost of the investment in the group statement of financial position. The equity method reflects the associate's overall performance and, to an extent, its financial position in the group financial statements, and so it is a compromise between consolidation and simply accounting for an investment.

This logic means that equity accounting is not applied to investments that are classified as held for sale, with a view to their disposal in the near future.

The Mechanics of Equity Accounting

The consolidated statement of profit or loss shows the investor's share of the associate's profit after tax as a single line entry in the statement of profit or loss 'income from associate'. The figure appears separately on the face of the statement of profit or loss.

If the associate paid a dividend during the year then that will effectively be offset against the value of the investor's investment and so the dividend will be eliminated from the group statement of profit or loss. That avoids double counting the same income because the dividend is paid out of the profits.

The consolidated statement of financial position shows the initial acquisition of the associate at cost and thereafter that balance is adjusted to reflect the investor's share of the increase or decrease in the associate's net assets. That carrying value is reviewed for impairment.

The equity method does not treat the associate as part of the group and so any transactions between group members and the associate are left uncancelled, both in the statement of profit or loss and, if there are any outstanding balances, in the statement of financial position. The only exception to that is when there is an unrealised profit arising from a transaction between the associate and a group member, in which case the group's share is eliminated.

- If the inventory is held by the investor, then the value of the group's inventory is reduced by the amount of the unrealised profit.
- If the inventory is held by the associate, then the unrealised profit is offset against the investment in the associate.

For example, H purchased 70% of I on 31 December 20X2 when I's retained earnings were $80 000. H purchased 40% of J on 31 December 20X4, when J's retained earnings were $60 000. During the year ended 31 December 20X6, J sold goods to the value of $40 000 to H at cost plus one-third. Those goods remain unsold at the year end and the associated receivable and payable are still outstanding. The companies' latest statements of financial position are as follows:

Statements of financial position as at 31 December 20X7

	H $000	I $000	J $000
Property, plant and equipment	86	162	132
Investment in I	98		
Investment in J	50		
Current assets	11	7	6
	245	169	138
Share capital	80	50	40
Retained earnings	151	110	90
Total equity	231	160	130
Current liabilities	14	9	8
	245	169	138

The workings relating to I are very straightforward:

Investment in I	98
Fair value of non-controlling interest (30% × 130)	39
Fair value of net identifiable assets (50 + 80)	(130)
Goodwill on acquisition of I	7

Equity as at date of acquisition	39
Non-controlling interest in I's post-acquisition reserves	9
(110 − 80) × 30%	
Non-controlling interest	48

The unrealised profit arising from sales between J and H is $40 \times 1/4 = 10$. The group share is 40% of $10 = 4$. That amount is deducted from inventory, so group current assets $= 11 + 7 - 4 = 14$.

The receivable and payable associated with the transactions between H and J are left in place because J is an associate, not a subsidiary.

The group's share of post-acquisition net assets = $(130 - 100) \times 40\% = 12$. So the investment in the associate is $50 + 12 = 62$.

The group retained earnings are as follows:

H's retained earnings	151
Group share of I's retained earnings $(110 - 80) \times 70\%$	21
Group share of J's retained earnings $(90 - 60) \times 40\%$	12
Less: unrealised profit	(4)
	180

H Group
Consolidated statement of financial position
as at 31 December 20X7

	£000
Property, plant and equipment	248
Goodwill	7
Investment in associate	62
Current assets	14
	331
Share capital	80
Retained earnings	180
Total equity	260
Non-controlling interest	48
	308
Current liabilities	23
	331

Joint Arrangements

The accounting treatment of joint arrangements is dealt with by IFRS 11 *Joint Arrangements* (IASB, 2011b).

A joint arrangement is one in which two or more parties have joint control. That can apply to a very simple business arrangement where, for example, two farmers agree to work together to raise a crop and split the proceeds from selling the harvest. At the other extreme, two competing car manufacturers can invest jointly in a factory that will produce body parts and other components that are suitable for both companies' product ranges. The manufacturers will continue to operate independently and to sell their respective products in opposition to one another. Their motive will be that they will both enjoy economies of scale without losing any competitive advantage.

Joint control exists when there is a contractually agreed sharing of control in which decisions about the relevant activities require the unanimous consent of the parties sharing control.

Joint arrangements can be large and complex entities in their own right. For example, in the oil industry it is quite common for two or more major companies that are otherwise independent of one another to fund an entity that will acquire and operate a major undertaking such as an oilfield. That entity will have its own management and will maintain its own records.

The existence of joint control means that the arguments concerning majority ownership and lesser investments are irrelevant. For example, owning, say, 55% of the joint venture's shares will not give outright control because the other venturer(s) must give their consent before any decisions about strategy or operations can be made. In the same way, owning less than 50% (even less than 20%) will give the right to veto any proposals by the other venturer(s) and so the holding will carry a disproportionate influence.

IFRS 11 distinguishes two types of arrangement, each of which will be accounted for differently.

Joint Arrangements not Structured through a Separate Vehicle

If a joint arrangement is not structured through a separate vehicle, such as a company, then it is a *joint operation*. In this case, the contractual arrangement between the parties establishes their respective rights and obligations with respect to assets, liabilities, revenues and expenses.

For example, one of our two farmers could provide a field for the operation and another could pay for seed. The two could maintain their own separate records of labour and work so that the total cost of wages, diesel fuel and so on could be totalled. When the crop is sold, the contract would specify the manner in which profit is to be determined and shared.

Joint operations are accounted on the basis that individual parties account for their own assets and liabilities.

In the event that a joint operation involves the joint ownership of an asset then each party will account for its share of that asset. So, our farmers could buy a field together with a view to sowing an annual crop. If the agreement is that the joint operation is split 60:40 then one farmer will include 60% of the field's value in the farm's financial statements and the other will include 40%.

If the joint arrangement is structured through a separate vehicle, such as a company, then it may still be classified as a joint operation and accounted for as above.

Joint Arrangements Structured through a Separate Vehicle

A joint arrangement that is structured through a separate vehicle will be classified as either a *joint operation* or as a *joint venture*. The classification depends upon the parties' rights and obligations arising from their interest in the vehicle.

If the parties have contractual rights and obligations with respect to the assets and liabilities of this arrangement, then it is a joint operation. For example, our venture could involve the operation of a parts factory that supplies the individual parties. If each party remains the legal owner of an agreed proportion of the factory and has a direct legal liability for a proportion of its liabilities, then the arrangement is a joint operation. It will be accounted for by each party in the manner indicated in the previous subsection.

If the arrangement's assets and liabilities belong to the arrangement itself, then it is a joint venture. For example, our car manufacturers could have established a company to own and operate a parts factory. The company owns assets and has obligations. The parties' interests are in the company rather than in the separate assets and liabilities and their contracts give them joint control of the arrangement. In that case, the arrangement is a joint venture.

The individual parties will account for their interests in joint ventures using the equity method.

Special Purpose Entities

Historically, the biggest controversies arising from the preparation of group accounts have involved the identification of group members. The biggest problem has been to ensure that all group members are included in the consolidated financial statements.

In principle, a special purpose entity (or SPE) is a business (usually a company) that is created for a very specific task, such as conducting a high-risk project. This could be a simple matter of establishing a 100% subsidiary and taking care to ensure that any contracts relating to the subsidiary's activities are with the subsidiary itself and do not directly involve the parent (as a co-signatory or a guarantor).

In practice, a special purpose entity is often established in such a way that the party who controls it in substance owns little or no equity and has no direct means of controlling it. This can be accomplished by specifying the activities that will be undertaken at the time of creation and granting full authority to an independent management company who will put these into effect.

The motivation for such an arrangement is that the SPE can be used to engage in activities with which the sponsor who brought about its creation does not wish to be directly associated. For example, the SPE might be used to raise debt that is not included in the consolidated financial statements. This might be accomplished by setting up the SPE in such a way that its activities are predetermined and placed under the control of an independent management company (an 'autopilot' arrangement). The sponsor, who was responsible for the SPE's creation, may own little or no equity and have no formal right to affect the management of its operations.

Accounting for Special Purpose Entities

Before the introduction of IFRS 10 *Consolidated Financial Statements* (IASB, 2011a), the definition of the parent–subsidiary relationship did not deal directly with this type of arrangement and so it was difficult to ensure that SPEs were consolidated. Arguably, the ambiguity about the question of control was due to the companies who created this type of SPE being keen to find ways to avoid their consolidation and so great care went into the design of these vehicles. It took an interpretation by the Standing Interpretations Committee – SIC 12, *Consolidation – Special Purpose Entities* (IASB, 1998) – to deal with this problem. The definition of control was extended to include such circumstances as:

- in substance, the activities of the SPE are being conducted on behalf of the entity according to its specific business needs;
- in substance, the entity has the decision-making powers to obtain the majority of the benefits of the activities of the SPE or, by setting up an 'autopilot' mechanism, the entity has delegated these decision-making powers;
- in substance, the entity has rights to obtain the majority of the benefits of the SPE and therefore may be exposed to risks incident to the activities of the SPE;
- in substance, the entity retains the majority of the residual or ownership risks related to the SPE or its assets in order to obtain benefits from its activities.

There is no specific accounting treatment of an SPE under IFRS. If it falls within the broader definition of control as indicated above then it must be consolidated in the same manner as any other subsidiary.

Enron

Enron is the classic example of a case involving SPEs. The company started as an energy utility company that owned and operated a number of power stations. The return on capital employed from generating electricity was not particularly rewarding and so the directors attempted to improve the appearance of their statement of financial position by creating more than 3000 SPEs. These were used to raise finance and take ownership of assets with a book value of $27 billion, almost half of Enron's total.

Enron appeared to go from strength to strength. That could be partially attributed to other forms of creative accounting that had the effect of overstating profits and that are not particularly relevant to this chapter. Much of the profit came from Enron's successful speculation in the futures markets for energy and other commodities. The use of SPEs meant that the profit was being earned by a business that appeared to be lean and healthy in terms of gearing.

The creation and funding of those SPEs required considerable assistance from many of the major commercial banks. The circumvention of accounting rules frequently requires the creation of elaborate and costly schemes.

It is debatable whether Enron could have continued to maintain this façade of success indefinitely. Many of the SPEs held Enron shares and so the continuing success of the scheme meant that Enron itself had to continue to deliver growth in profits and in its share price. That had the effect of forcing the company to make increasing use of its creative accounting schemes and there would have come a point where the company was unable to manufacture sufficient profits. The actual failure of the scheme was, however, due to an administrative error.

It was discovered that one of the SPEs had not been set up in quite the right way to be excluded from the definition of a subsidiary under US GAAP. That meant that the company had to incorporate it into the group financial statements and that required notice to be given to the stock market because the overall effect was to reduce Enron's equity by $1.2 billion. Even though that was only a fraction of the value of the funds that had been raised using SPEs it was sufficient to trigger questions that led to the collapse of the company.

The Enron case was one of the most significant corporate scandals in the early 2000s. It was one of the reasons that the Sarbanes–Oxley Act was created in the US and it even inspired a 2009 film based on the perspective of a junior manager at Enron's head office (*Crooked E: The Unshredded Truth About Enron*).

Related Parties

Technically, related parties have nothing to do with the consolidation process itself, but they do create the need to recognise relationships in the financial statements.

IAS 24 *Related Party Disclosures* (IASB, 2009) requires disclosure of transactions involving related parties. The logic behind this is that an entity's reported performance or its financial position might be affected by transactions and balances that involve third parties who are nevertheless linked in some way.

For example, suppose that Mr Smith owns two companies that are otherwise independent of one another. Suppose the first company buys goods from the second at a substantial discount that is only available because of Mr Smith's ownership of both; and suppose that the credit terms are relaxed. It would be unfortunate if a buyer purchased the first company without being aware that the apparent profitability and liquidity disappeared when it was no longer in Mr Smith's interest to have one business provide the other with preferential terms.

IAS 24 requires disclosures of related party transactions if transactions have occurred between the entity and a related party. Related parties can be persons or other entities.

A person is a related party if that person (or a close member of that person's family):

- has control or joint control over the reporting entity;
- has significant influence over the reporting entity; or
- is a member of the key management personnel of the reporting entity or of a parent of the reporting entity.

An entity is a related party if:

- the entity and the reporting entity are members of the same group;
- the entity is controlled or jointly controlled by a person who is a related party; or
- a person who is a related party has significant influence over the entity or is a member of the key management personnel of the entity (or of a parent of the entity).

There are other ways in which two entities can be defined as related parties, including associate and joint venture relationships and relationships arising from pension arrangements.

IAS 24 requires the disclosure of relationships between parents and their subsidiaries, regardless of whether there have been any transactions between them. A subsidiary must disclose the name of its immediate parent and of its ultimate parent, where the two are different.

IAS 24 also requires disclosures when there have been transactions involving related parties:

- the nature of the related party relationship;
- the amount of the transactions;

- the amount of outstanding balances, including commitments, and:
  - their terms and conditions, including whether they are secured, and the nature of the consideration to be provided in settlement; and
  - details of any guarantees given or received;
- provisions for doubtful debts related to the amount of outstanding balances; and
- the expense recognised during the period in respect of bad or doubtful debts due from related parties.

These are minimum disclosures. The basic principle is that users must be able to understand the potential effect of the relationship on the financial statements.

Summary

Group relationships can be far more complicated than the immediate control implied in the previous chapter, and the fact that there can be a relationship without there being outright control complicates matters still further.

Each of the different scenarios described in this chapter required a different approach to the bookkeeping and other adjustments but the important thing to bear in mind is that we are constantly aiming to present the group as an economic entity. Doing so may require some thought when we do not have a straightforward parent–subsidiary relationship, but it should be possible to see that principle in operation.

One constant concern that runs through the regulation of group accounts is the extent to which preparers have attempted to abuse any flexibility in the rules and regulations. The most common objective in creative accounting schemes is the exclusion of subsidiary companies in order to alter the gearing or return on capital employed ratios when calculated on the basis of reported figures. That has led to the need for care in the drafting of standards and constant updating.

Tutorial Questions

Question 1

Prepare a consolidated statement of financial position for the Q Group from the following information.

Q acquired 70% of the shares in R on 31 December 20X3 when R's retained earnings were £400 000. At that date, the value of the non-controlling interest in R was £250 000.

R acquired 70% of S's equity on 31 December 20X5, when S's retained earnings were £300 000. The fair value of the 30% of the shares that were not acquired by R was £180 000:

Statements of financial position as at 31 December 20X9

	Q £000	R £000	S £000
Non-current assets			
Property, plant and equipment	1200	985	970
Investment in R	690		
Investment in S		420	
Current assets	80	55	40
	1970	1460	1010
Share capital	1000	450	200
Retained earnings	580	720	480
	1580	1170	680
Non-current liabilities	300	240	300
Current liabilities	90	50	30
	1970	1460	1010

Question 2

Use the following information to prepare a consolidated statement of financial position for the T Group.

V acquired 80% of the share capital of W on 31 December 20X2. At that date, W's retained earnings were €400 000 and the non-controlling interest had a fair value of €800 000.

T acquired 75% of the share capital of V on 31 December 20X4. V's retained earnings were €1 200 000 and the non-controlling interest in the remaining 25% of V's equity had a fair value of €2 100 000.

On 31 December 20X4, the 20% of W's equity that was not owned by V had a fair value of €900 000 and the retained earnings were €600 000.

Statements of financial position as at 31 December 20X8

	T	V	W
	€000	€000	€000
Non-current assets			
Property, plant and equipment	6 040	2 210	1 620
Investment in V	6 000		
Investment in W		3 700	
Current assets	740	210	230
	12 780	6 120	1 850
Share capital	6 000	4 000	800
Retained earnings	6 600	1 800	900
	12 600	5 800	1 700
Current liabilities	180	320	150
	12 780	6 120	1 850

Question 3

On 1 January 20X4, D acquired 36% of the issued equity of C. At that date, C's retained earnings were £25 000.

On 1 January 20X6, E acquired 75% of D's equity. At that date D's retained earnings stood at £30 000.

On 1 January 20X7, E acquired 30% of the issued equity of C. At that date, C's retained earnings were £60 000.

The statements of financial position of the three companies at 31 December 20X8 were as follows:

	E	D	C
	£000	£000	£000
Non-current assets			
Property, plant and equipment	269	232	150
Investment in D	310		
Investments in C	52	48	
	631	280	150

Current assets			
Inventory	120	60	75
Trade receivables	210	75	92
Cash	30	25	18
	360	160	185
	991	440	335
Equity			
Share capital	500	100	80
Retained earnings	281	250	145
	781	350	225
Non-current liabilities			
Loan stock	50	20	30
Current liabilities			
Trade payables	160	70	80
	991	440	335

Prepare a consolidated statement of financial position for the E Group as at 31 December 20X8.

Question 4

L acquired 75% of the ordinary share capital of M on 1 January 20X2, when the balance on M's profit or loss account was £2.5m and the share capital was £3.0m. The fair value of the non-controlling interest at the date of acquisition was £1.5m.

On 1 January 20X3, L acquired 30% of the share capital of N. As part of this transaction, N was given the right to appoint its nominee to N's board. N had a balance of £900 000 on its retained earnings at that date and its share capital was £2m.

The latest statements of financial position of the three companies are:

Statements of financial position as at 31 December 20X4

	L £000	M £000	N £000
Property, plant and equipment			
Land and buildings	6 000	5 100	2 000
Plant and machinery	4 000	900	700
	10 000	6 000	2 700

Investments			
Investment in M	7 500		
Investment in N	1 500		
	19 000	6 000	2 700
Current assets			
Inventory	2 200	1 100	1 000
Receivables	2 400	1 200	600
Bank	200	100	90
	4 800	2 400	1 690
	23 800	8 400	4 390
Share capital	6 000	3 000	2 000
Retained earnings	15 500	4 500	1 890
	21 500	7 500	3 890
Current liabilities	2 300	900	500
	23 800	8 400	4 390

L conducted its annual impairment review of the goodwill on acquisition of M on 31 December 20X4. It was found that goodwill on acquisition had declined in value by £844.

Required:

(a) Prepare a consolidated statement of financial position for L Group as at 31 December 20X4.

(b) Associate companies are treated neither as full members of the group nor as simple investments. Critically appraise the logic behind the accounting treatment of associates as laid down by IAS 28.

Question 5

Discuss the logic associated with the parties to joint operations accounting for their respective shares of any assets that are held jointly.

Is this approach consistent with the principles of consolidation?

Question 6

Discuss the implications of Enron's use of SPEs for accounting standard-setters.

Are the changes introduced by IFRS 10 likely to be effective in preventing such misleading exclusions from the consolidated financial statements?

Questions with Answers

Question 1

I purchased 60% of the shares in J on 31 December 20X0. At that time, the balance on J's retained earnings account was €820 000.

The shares held by J's non-controlling shareholders had a fair value of €510 000 on 31 December 20X0.

J purchased 60% of the shares in N on 31 December 20X2. The balance on N's retained earnings account was €640 000 on that date.

The shares held by N's non-controlling shareholders had a fair value of €400 000.

Statements of financial position as at 31 December 20X6

	I €000	J €000	N €000
Non-current assets			
Property, plant and equipment	2 500	1 900	2 100
Investment in J	1 500		
Investment in N		850	
Current assets	200	120	90
	4 200	2 870	2 190
Share capital	2 000	900	450
Retained earnings	1 275	1 400	1 090
	3 275	2 300	1 540
Non-current liabilities	750	500	600
Current liabilities	175	70	50
	4 200	2 870	2 190

Prepare a consolidated statement of financial position for the I Group as at 31 December 20X6.

Question 2

Y acquired 75% of G's share capital on 31 December 20X2. At that date, G's retained earnings were $900 000 and the non-controlling interest had a fair value of $1 500 000.

G acquired 60% of V's share capital 31 December 20X1. At that date, V's retained earnings were $2 000 000 and the non-controlling interest had a fair value of $3 800 000. At 31 December 20X2, these figures were $2 200 000 and $3 900 000 respectively.

Statements of financial position as at 31 December 20X5

	Y $000	G $000	V $000
Non-current assets			
Property, Plant and equipment	12 200	4 600	4 000
Investment in G	12 000		
Investment in V		8 000	
Current assets	1 600	450	500
	25 800	13 050	4 500
Share capital	10 000	7 000	1 000
Retained earnings	10 460	4 350	2 700
	20 460	11 350	3 700
Non-current liabilities	5 000	1 000	600
Current liabilities	340	700	200
	25 800	13 050	4 500

Prepare a consolidated statement of financial position for the Y Group as at 31 December 20X5.

The following share acquisitions led to the creation of the T Group:

Company	Acquired	Percentage acquired	Date	Acquired company's retained earnings at that date
F	C	40%	31 December 20X5	£60 000
T	F	80%	31 December 20X7	£75 000
T	C	40%	31 December 20X8	£90 000

The statements of financial position of the three companies at 31 December 20X9 were as follows:

	T £000	F £000	C £000
Non-current assets			
Property, plant and equipment	900	160	350
Investment in F	600		
Investments in C	500	450	
	2000	610	350
Current assets			
Inventory	200	130	160
Trade receivables	400	150	190
Cash	70	50	50
	670	330	400
	2670	940	750
Equity			
Share capital	1800	520	500
Retained earnings	510	310	170
	2310	830	670
Current liabilities			
Trade payables	360	110	80
	2670	940	750

Prepare a consolidated statement of financial position for the T Group as at 31 December 20X9.

Question 4

U acquired 60% of H's share capital on 31 December 20X2, when the balance on H retained earnings was €300 000.

The fair value of H's non-controlling interest at that date was €520 000.

U acquired 40% of B's equity on 31 December 20X3, when B's retained earnings were €400 000.

U's closing inventory includes goods obtained from H for €120 000. H's selling price was cost plus 20%.

U's trade receivables include a balance of €45 000 payable by H. H's trade payables include a liability due to H of €17 000. The difference is due to a payment made by H that had not been recorded by U before the reporting date.

The companies' statements of financial position as at 31 December 20X6 are as follows:

	U €000	H €000	B €000
Property, plant and equipment	1500	950	1700
Investment in H	1200		
Investment in B	570		
	3270	950	1700
Current Assets			
Inventory	420	250	460
Trade receivables	1300	445	175
Bank	223	148	119
	1943	843	754
	5213	1793	2454
Equity			
Share capital	3000	800	400
Retained earnings	1343	710	1890
	4343	1510	2290
Current liabilities			
Trade payables	870	283	164
	5213	1793	2454

Prepare the consolidated statement of financial position for the U Group as at 31 December 20X6.

References

IASB (1998) SIC 12 *Consolidation – Special Purpose Entities*.
IASB (2003) IAS 28 *Investments in Associates and Joint Ventures*.
IASB (2009) IAS 24 *Related Party Disclosure*.
IASB (2011a) IFRS 10 *Consolidated Financial Statements*
IASB (2011b) IFRS 11 *Joint Arrangements*.

CHANGES IN GROUPS

Contents

Learning Objectives

After studying this chapter, you should be able to:

- prepare consolidated financial statements that reflect the acquisition of control through more than one transaction;
- prepare consolidated financial statements that reflect acquisition of additional shares in a subsidiary after control has been acquired;
- prepare consolidated financial statements that reflect the disposal of some or all of the parent's investment in a subsidiary.

Introduction

This is (intentionally) a short chapter. It deals with the mechanics of buying and selling shares in subsidiary companies. That is not necessarily a topic that will feature in degree courses in financial reporting, but it will arise in many professional examinations. It is offered in the spirit that it may or may not be included in the lecture programme, depending upon the syllabus that is being covered.

Some of the adjustments that are required in order to deal with these transactions are not particularly intuitive. Indeed, it could be argued that the main reason for covering this material is that goodwill may not be affected by the subsequent purchase of additional equity or the partial disposal of the equity that gave rise to the balance. That illustrates the fact that goodwill on consolidation is not intended to be a particularly relevant disclosure. Instead, it provides a means to complete the double entry associated with the initial acquisition of control.

It may be worth making a mental note that this chapter provides a (hopefully) gentle introduction to some of the more complicated accounting adjustments that can arise in professional syllabuses and so it may be worth returning to it when preparing for professional exams.

Acquisition in Stages

So far, we have assumed that the parent acquired its controlling instrument through a single transaction. It is possible, however, that the holding could be built up through a series of acquisitions.

In such cases, the treatment is very straightforward. The basic principle is that the subsidiary did not become a member of the group until the parent acquired its controlling interest. When control is obtained, the investment held prior to the final acquisition that led to control will be restated at its fair value. Any gain or loss will be accounted for according to the rules in IFRS 9 *Financial Instruments* (IASB, 2010).

Goodwill and non-controlling interest will be accounted for in the usual way.

For example, suppose K paid €50 000 for 15% of the equity of L on 1 January 20X5. On 31 December, 20X5 K paid €250 000 for a further 60% of L's equity. On that date, the fair value of K's initial investment was €62 000 and the fair value of the non-controlling interest was €82 000.

The statements of financial position of both companies as at 31 December 20X5 were as follows:

	K €000	L €000
Investment in L	312	
Property, plant and equipment	900	348
	1 212	348

Share capital	800	200
Retained earnings	412	148
	1 212	348

K's investment in L is based upon the total of the fair value of the shares held immediately prior to the acquisition of control and the investment in the controlling interest. The gain arising from the restatement of the initial holding in L has been credited to K's retained earnings.

Once the value of the investment has been determined, the calculation of goodwill and non-controlling interest are not really affected by the fact that the investment was acquired in stages:

Investment in L	312
Fair value of non-controlling interest	82
Fair value of net identifiable assets	(348)
Goodwill	46

There have been no post-acquisition profits or adjustments, so non-controlling interest remains at €82 000.

The consolidated statement of financial position is as follows:

K Group
Consolidated statement of financial position
as at 31 December 20X5

	€000
Goodwill	46
Property, plant and equipment	1 248
	1 294
Share capital	800
Retained earnings	412
	1 212
Non-controlling interest	82
Total equity	1 294

Increasing Holdings in a Company that was Previously Controlled

It is also possible that the parent company will acquire further shares after it has gained control. In that case, the best way to deal with the further acquisition is to treat it as a transaction between the parent and the non-controlling interest.

The parent's further acquisition will reduce the non-controlling interest. Comparing that reduction with the cost of the additional shares will leave a balancing figure, which will be taken to equity.

No further adjustments are required. For example, goodwill on acquisition will not be affected by the purchase of additional equity.

For example, suppose that K acquired a further 5% of L on 31 December 20X8 for €28 000. The statements of financial position for both group members as at that date are shown below:

	K €000	L €000
Investment in L	340	
Property, plant and equipment	1 112	427
	1 452	427
Share capital	900	200
Retained earnings	552	227
	1 452	427

The investment in L according to K's financial statements includes the further investment in L.

The acquisition of the additional shares will affect the non-controlling interest (NCI) in L as follows:

Fair value of NCI at acquisition	82
NCI share of post-acquisition earnings at 25% × (277 − 148)	32
	114
Fair value of NCI at acquisition	82
NCI share of post-acquisition earnings at 20% × (277 − 148)	26
	108
Decrease in NCI	6

The additional investment cost is €28 000, so the adjustment to equity will require a decrease of €22 000 on retained earnings.

The group retained earnings will now be:

Parent	552
Group share of L's post-acquisition earnings	97
(75% × 227 − 148)	
Adjustment on further acquisition	(22)
	627

Note that L was a 75% subsidiary for the period to 31 December 20X8. The group was not entitled to 80% of profits until the further acquisition on that date. From 1 January 20X9 onwards, the group will consolidate 80% of L's profits and losses.

Goodwill on acquisition will remain at €46 000.

The consolidated statement of financial position for the K Group will be as follows:

Consolidated statement of financial position as at 31 December 20X8

	€000
Goodwill	46
Property, plant and equipment	1 589
	1 635
Share capital	900
Retained earnings	627
	1 527
Non-controlling interest	108
Total equity	1 635

Disposals

The disposal of some or all of the parent's investment requires the adjustment for gains and losses that might arise from the disposal. There is also the possibility that the relationship between the parent and the subsidiary will change. This section will deal with some of the more obvious possibilities:

- a reduction in the parent's holding, but control is retained;
- total disposal;
- a trade investment is retained;
- the parent loses control, but retains significant influence.

Each of these possibilities requires a little thought about the adjustments that must be recorded in the parent's bookkeeping records and also the presentation of the consolidated financial statements.

The Parent Company

Before we start to look at the implications for the group financial statements, we have to consider the implications of a disposal for the parent company.

The parent company is unlikely to sell its investment at its carrying value and so there will be a gain or loss on the disposal. There may also be tax implications. That requires a fairly self-explanatory calculation:

	$
Sale proceeds	X
Carrying amount according to parent's statement of financial position	(X)
Gross gain on disposal	X
Tax (assuming that a taxable gain has arisen)	(X)
Net gain/loss to parent	X

The gain may be disclosed separately on the face of the parent's statement of profit or loss.

The tax charge will become part of the parent's total tax expense and so will find its way into the group tax charge.

Any questions involving disposals will have to be read carefully to determine whether the parent's accounting records have been updated to include these adjustments.

Reduction in Holding of a Subsidiary – Control Retained

If the parent reduces a controlling interest in a subsidiary, but still retains control, then the disposal is effectively treated as a transaction between the parent and the non-controlling interest.

In that case, the subsidiary continues to be consolidated as before (on the basis that it remains a subsidiary because it is still under the parent's control).

Consolidation requires some thought because the disposal could have occurred part of the way through the year. That could mean that the proportion of profits due to the NCI might change in the course of the year and so it may be necessary to calculate the NCI in the profit earned before the disposal separately from the NCI in the profit earned afterwards.

The carrying value of goodwill on the original acquisition is left unchanged. That may seem counter-intuitive, but it can be argued that goodwill on acquisition is effectively a balancing figure and so the amount shown in the statement of financial position has relatively little significance in and of itself. The figure has to be reviewed for impairment every year and so any concern that goodwill is overstated can be addressed during that review.

The group's equity is adjusted to reflect the difference between the proceeds of the disposal and the increase in NCI arising as at the time of disposal. This adjustment means that it is unnecessary to adjust the consolidated financial statements to take account of the gain or loss to the parent in the parent's individual financial statements.

Example

The following extracts are from the draft consolidated financial statements of the A Group. The A Group comprises a parent and several subsidiaries. All of the subsidiaries have been consolidated, except for B. All subsidiaries are 100% owned except for B.

Extracts from draft statements of profit or loss for the year ended 31 December 20X8

	A Group $000	B $000
Revenue	155 500	25 800
Operating costs	(97 750)	(13 900)
Profit before tax	57 750	11 900
Income tax	(25 250)	(4 300)
Profit for period	32 500	7 600

Extracts from draft statements of financial position as at 31 December 20X8

	A Group $000	B $000
Goodwill on acquisition	20 000	
Investment in B	11 000	
Other assets	63 400	24 000
	94 400	24 000
Equity and liabilities		
Share capital ($1 shares, fully paid)	30 000	10 000
Retained earnings	54 400	12 000
	84 400	22 000
Liabilities	10 000	2 000
	94 400	24 000

A originally paid $11m for 80% of B's equity in 20X4, at which time B's retained earnings were $1.4m. There has been no goodwill impairment since the date of acquisition.

The NCI of B is valued at the proportionate share of the fair value of the net assets.

A has reviewed the fair value of its investment in B since the date of acquisition but has not observed any changes in value.

A sold 1m shares in B for $1.9m on 1 October 20X8. This disposal has not yet been recorded in A's bookkeeping records.

Accounting for the Partial Disposal of Shares in B

We need to know the goodwill on the initial acquisition of the shares in B:

Goodwill on acquisition

	$000	$000
FV of consideration transferred		11 000
Less share of FV of the net assets acquired:		
Share capital	10 000	
Retained earnings at acquisition	1 400	
	11 400	

NCI 20%	2 280
	13 280
Net assets	11 400
Goodwill	1 880

Adding that to the goodwill on the acquisition of the other group members gives a total of 20 000 + 1880 = 21 880.

B's equity at the date of disposal was $10\,000 + (12\,000 - (3/12 \times 7600)) = 20\,100$.[1]

NCI in B before disposal = $20\,100 \times 20\% = 4020$

NCI in B after disposal = $20\,100 \times 30\% = 6030$

Thus, NCI in B has increased by $6030 - 4020 = 2010$.

The proceeds of disposal were 1900.

The equity adjustment is, therefore, $2010 - 1900 = (110)$.

The closing NCI can be determined as a simple percentage of B's equity:

$$22\,000 \times 30\% = 6\,600$$

Alternatively, the figure can be calculated as:

NCI as at date of acquisition

Share capital	2 000
Retained earnings as at acquisition	280
Post-acquisition profits to 31 December 20X7	600
20% × (12 000 − 1400 − 7600)	
NCI in profit for year ((7600 × 9/12 × 20%) + (7600 × 3/12 × 30%))	1 710
Adjustment from sale of shares	2 010
	6 600

Retained earnings are calculated as follows:

A Group Statement of financial position	54 400
B Statement of financial position	12 000
Cancelled pre-acquisition earnings (80% × 1400)	(1 120)
Adjustment from disposal of shares	(110)
NCI (280 + 600 + 1710)	(2 590)
Group retained earnings	62 580

The consolidated financial statements are as follows:

A Group
Consolidated statement of profit or loss
for the year ended 31 December 20X8

	$000
Revenue	181 300
Operating costs	(111 650)
Profit before tax	69 650
Income tax	(29 550)
Profit for period	40 100
Attributable to:	
Owners of the parent	38 390
NCI	1 710
	40 100

Note that the only implication of the disposal of shares for the consolidated statement of profit or loss is that the NCI owned 20% for the first nine months of the year and 30% for the remainder.

There are no gains or losses arising from the disposal in the group statement of profit or loss, and the subsidiary is still consolidated in full because A retains control.

A Group
Consolidated statement of financial position
as at 31 December 20X8

	$000
Goodwill on acquisition	21 880
Other assets	89 300
	111 180
Equity and liabilities	
Share capital	30 000
Retained earnings	62 580
	92 580
Liabilities	
NCI	6 600
Other liabilities	12 000
	18 600
	111 180

Again, B is consolidated in full because it remains a subsidiary despite the disposal.

A word about the Parent

The parent's individual statement of profit or loss will have to be restated in order to reflect a gain of:

	$000
Sale proceeds	1900
Carrying amount according to parent's statement of financial position ($11m × 1/8)	(1375)
Gross gain on disposal	525
Tax (in the event that a taxable gain arose from the disposal)	(0)
Net gain/loss to parent	525

The question simplified the calculations by stating that the parent had not yet recorded the disposal in its bookkeeping records. If the disposal had been recorded then the original cost of the investment would have had to be added back and the net gain eliminated from the parent's retained earnings.

Loss of Control

If the disposal reduces the parent's investment to the point where control has been lost then the former subsidiary can no longer be consolidated from the date of disposal.

The accounting adjustments treat the disposal as the sale of the group member to a third party. That means that the consolidated statement of profit or loss will carry a gain or loss on disposal. That is arrived at by offsetting, as shown here:

Consideration received	Net assets of subsidiary as at date of disposal
Fair value of any investment retained	Unimpaired goodwill (offset by NCI as at date of disposal)
Difference = gain/loss on disposal This difference will be presented separately on the face of the statement of profit or loss immediately after operating profit.	

Assuming that the disposal took place part of the way through the year, the consolidated statement of profit or loss will have to incorporate the subsidiary's results for the part of the year that it spent as part of the group. The presentation will depend on whether the disposal of the subsidiary constitutes a discontinued operation:

• If the disposal is *not* a discontinued operation then the group statement of profit or loss will consolidate the relevant proportion of the former subsidiary's results on a line-by-line basis.
• If the disposal *is* a discontinued operation then the results from prior to the disposal will be aggregated and added to profit after tax from continuing operations.

Total Disposal

The simplest case arises when the parent disposes of its entire investment in the subsidiary.

For example, let us revisit the A Group, but assume that A sold its entire holding in B for $18.9m on 1 October 20X8 and that there was a tax charge of $1.3m arising from this sale. The disposal did not constitute a discontinued business activity.

A has not yet recorded this disposal in its bookkeeping records.

Goodwill on acquisition = $1.88m (as before).

NCI as at disposal = $4.02m (as before).

Consideration received: $18.9m	Net assets of subsidiary as at date of disposal: $22.0m − ($7.6m × 3/12) = $20.1m
Fair value of any investment retained: nil	Unimpaired goodwill: $1.88m
	(offset by NCI as at date of disposal:) ($4.02m)
Difference = gain/loss on disposal: $0.94m − gain before tax The $1.3m tax liability also has to be added to the group tax charge.	

Retained earnings are calculated as follows:

A Group Statement of financial position	54 400
B Statement of financial position	12 000
Less B profit earned post-disposal (7600 × 3/12)	(1 900)
Cancelled pre-acquisition earnings (80% × 1400)	(1 120)
NCI (280 + 600 + 1140) *where 1140 = 7600 × 9/12 × 20%*	(2 020)
Gain before tax	940
Tax on gain	(1 300)
Group retained earnings	61 000

A Group
Consolidated statement of profit or loss
for the year ended 31 December 20X8

	$000
Revenue	174 850
Operating costs	(108 175)
Profit before tax	66 675
Gain on disposal of subsidiary	1 040
Income tax	(29 775)
Profit for period	37 940
Attributable to:	
Owners of the parent	36 800
NCI	1 140
	37 940

Revenues and operating costs comprise the A Group figures plus the first nine months' worth of the B figures.

Tax is calculated in the same manner, but also includes the additional tax charge on the disposal.

A Group
Consolidated statement of financial position
as at 31 December 20X8

	$000
Goodwill on acquisition	20 000
Other assets	82 300
	102 300

Equity and liabilities	
Share capital	30 000
Retained earnings	61 000
	91 000
Liabilities	11 300
	102 300

Disposal Costs Control, but a Trade Investment Retained

If a small number of shares is retained then the entries and the adjustments are virtually the same as for the outright disposal of a subsidiary. The only differences are that the remaining shares are carried at their fair value (as indicated above) and accounted for in accordance with IFRS 9. Also, any dividends received after the disposal of the controlling interest can be recognised as income in the consolidated statement of profit or loss.

No example is provided here because of the similarity between this form of divestment and outright disposal.

Disposal Costs Control, but Significant Influence is Retained

The final possibility is that the parent disposes of sufficient shares to lose control but retains sufficient shares to exercise significant influence. In that case, the investee would be an associate and will have to be accounted for as such from the date of disposal.

This is accounted for in a manner that is reminiscent of the outright disposal or the retention of a trade investment, except that the former associate must be accounted for as an associate from the disposal onwards.

Again, we will revisit the A Group. This time, we will assume that A sold 5m of its 8m shares for $14.5m on 1 October 20X8 and that there was a tax charge of $1m arising from this sale. The disposal did not constitute a discontinued business activity. The 3000 remaining shares had a fair value of $8m on 1 October 20X8.

A has not yet recorded this disposal in its bookkeeping records.

Goodwill on acquisition = $1.88m (as before).

NCI as at disposal = $4.02m (as before).

Consideration received: $14.5m	Net assets of subsidiary as at date of disposal: $22.0m − ($7.6m × 3/12) = $20.1m
Fair value of any investment retained: $8.0m	Unimpaired goodwill: $1.88m

	(offset by NCI as at date of disposal: $4.02m)

Difference = gain/loss on disposal:
$4.54m − gain before tax
The $1.0m tax liability also has to be added to the group tax charge.

Investment in associate:

Fair value of investment	8 000
Group share of post-acquisition retained earnings	570
	8 570

Retained earnings are calculated as follows:

A Group Statement of financial position	54 400
B Statement of financial position	12 000
Less B profit earned post-disposal (7600 × 3/12)	(1 900)
Cancelled pre-acquisition earnings (80% × 1400)	(1 120)
NCI (280 + 600 + 1140) *where 1140 = 7600 × 9/12 × 20%*	(2 020)
Gain before tax	4 540
Tax on gain	(1 000)
Associate – group share of post-acquisition earnings	570
Group retained earnings	65 470

A Group
Consolidated statement of profit or loss
for the year ended 31 December 20X8

	$000
Revenue	174 850
Operating costs	(108 175)
Profit before tax	66 675
Gain on disposal of subsidiary	4 540
Tax	(29 475)

Profit for period	41 740
Share of associate's profit	570
	42 310

Attributable to:

Owners of the parent	40 600
Associate	570
NCI	1 140
	42 310

A Group
Consolidated statement of financial position
as at 31 December 20X8

	$000
Goodwill on acquisition	20 000
Investment in associate	8 570
Other assets	77 900
	106 470

Equity and liabilities

Share capital	30 000
Retained earnings	65 470
	95 470

Liabilities

Other liabilities	11 000
	106 470

Summary

The acquisition and disposal of equity in subsidiary companies can require a number of adjustments, some of which may appear counter-intuitive. For example, goodwill is not affected by the subsequent purchase of further shares in a subsidiary, nor is it always cancelled when some of the shares are disposed of.

This chapter deals with the mechanics of the adjustments arising from acquisitions and disposals. The most important matter arising remains the need to provide clear workings that deal with calculating the figures efficiently.

As far as understanding the adjustments is concerned, it is important to be aware that the need to provide a square statement of financial position may mean that some of the results can be difficult to explain. Some of the corrections described are based on the assumption that acquisitions and disposals are effectively undertaken between the parent and the non-controlling interest.

Tutorial Questions

Question 1

The statements of financial position for Hold and Sub as at 31 December 20X6 are provided below:

	Hold $000	Sub $000
Investment in Sub	12 000	
Property, plant and equipment	66 000	10 000
	78 000	10 000
Current assets	42 000	6 000
	120 000	16 000
Equity		
Share capital	60 000	2 000
Retained earnings	22 500	10 000
	82 500	12 000
Current liabilities	37 500	4 000
	120 000	16 000

Hold paid $2m for 15% of Sub on 31 December 20X2.

The fair value of the 15% investment was $3.1m on 31 December 20X5.

On 31 December 20X5, Hold paid $7.6m for a further 60% of the equity of Sub.

On 31 December 20X6, the fair value of Hold's total investment in Sub was $12m. Hold has recognised the increase in the fair value in its retained earnings. (*Note: Think about the implications of this – can the group recognise a gain from the parent investing in a subsidiary?*)

The fair value of the non-controlling interest at 31 December 20X5 was $2.7m.

Sub's retained earnings at that date were $9.2m.

Prepare the consolidated statement of financial position for the Hold Group as at 31 December 20X6.

Question 2

The statements of financial position for Jolt and Bump as at 31 December 20X7 are provided below:

	Jolt $000	Bump $000
Investment in Bump	73 800	
Property, plant and equipment	197 000	40 000
	270 800	40 000
Current assets	46 000	28 000
	316 800	68 000
Equity		
Share capital	100 000	5 000
Retained earnings	178 800	57 000
	278 800	62 000
Current liabilities	38 000	6 000
	316 800	68 000

Jolt paid $42m for 70% of Bump on 31 December 20X1.

Jolt paid a further $15m for an additional 20% of the equity on 31 December 20X5.

The value attributed to Jolt's investment includes the results of the restatement of the investment's value to its fair value as at 31 December 20X7.

The fair value of the non-controlling interest at 31 December 20X1 was $13.5m.

Bump's retained earnings were $42m at 31 December 20X1 and $54m at 31 December 20X5.

Prepare the consolidated statement of financial position for the Jolt Group as at 31 December 20X7.

222222

Question 3

The statements of financial position for Major and Minor as at 31 December 20X9 are provided below:

	Major $000	Minor $000
Investment in Minor	66 000	
Property, plant and equipment	701 000	75 000
	767 000	75 000
Current assets	88 000	15 000
	855 000	90 000
Equity		
Share capital	300 000	12 000
Retained earnings	503 000	62 000
	803 000	74 000
Current liabilities	52 000	16 000
	855 000	90 000

Major purchased 80% of Minor on 31 December 20X4 for $80m.

At 31 December 20X4, Minor had retained earnings of $42m. Non-controlling interest had a fair value of $18m on that date.

On 31 December 20X7, Major sold 10% of Minor's equity for $14m. Minor's retained earnings were $54m at that date. The proceeds of disposal were debited to cash and credited to investment in Minor.

Prepare the consolidated statement of financial position for the Major Group as at 31 December 20X9.

Questions with Answers

Question 1

H paid €8m for 10% of B's equity on 31 December 20X4.

On 31 December 20X7, H paid €52m for a further 50% of B. At that date, H's 10% holding had a fair value of €10m and the remaining 40% of B's shares had a fair value of €45m. B's retained earnings were €40m.

H shows its investment in B at its fair value.

The statements of financial position for H and B as at 31 December 20X9 are as follows:

	H €000	B €000
Investment in B	75 000	
Property, plant and equipment	133 000	70 000
	208 000	70 000
Current assets	32 000	9 000
	240 000	79 000
Equity		
Share capital	100 000	20 000
Retained earnings	121 500	55 000
	221 500	75 000
Current liabilities	18 500	4 000
	240 000	79 000

Prepare the consolidated statement of financial position for the H Group as at 31 December 20X9.

Question 2

D purchased 60% of F's equity on 31 December 20X4 at a cost of £80m. On that date F's retained earnings were £35m and the fair value of its non-controlling interest was £58m.

D made a further payment of £20m for an additional 15% of F on 31 December 20X6. At that date, F's retained earnings were £62m.

D shows its investments at their fair value in its statement of financial position.

The two companies' statements of financial position are as follows as at 31 December 20X8:

	D £000	F £000
Investment in F	107 000	
Property, plant and equipment	230 000	90 000
	337 000	90 000

Current assets	38 000	26 000
	375 000	116 000
Equity		
Share capital	200 000	40 000
Retained earnings	143 000	70 000
	343 000	110 000
Current liabilities	32 000	6 000
	375 000	116 000

Prepare the consolidated statement of financial position for the D Group as at 31 December 20X8.

Question 3

The statements of financial position for Major and Minor as at 31 December 20X9 are provided below:

	Major $000	Minor $000
Investment in Minor	24 000	
Property, plant and equipment	701 000	75 000
	725 000	75 000
Current assets	130 000	15 000
	855 000	90 000
Equity		
Share capital	300 000	12 000
Retained earnings	503 000	62 000
	803 000	74 000
Current liabilities	52 000	16 000
	855 000	90 000

Major purchased 80% of Minor on 31 December 20X4 for $80m.

At 31 December 20X4, Minor had retained earnings of $42m. Non-controlling interest had a fair value of $18m on that date.

On 31 December 20X7, Major sold half of its investment in Minor for $56m. Minor's retained earnings were $54m at that date. The proceeds of disposal were debited to cash and credited to investment in Minor. The remaining 40% holding is sufficient to give Major significant influence over the running of Minor. It is assumed that the remaining 40% holding was worth $56m at the date of disposal.

Prepare the consolidated statement of financial position for the Major Group as at 31 December 20X9.

Endnote

1. We subtract 3/12 of the profit earned by B for the year from B's retained earnings because the disposal occurred three months before the year end.

Reference

IASB (2010) IFRS 9 *Financial Instruments*.

FOREIGN CURRENCIES

Contents

Learning Objectives

After studying this chapter, you should be able to:

- discuss the importance (or lack of importance) of translation risk;
- translate transactions and balances of individual companies at the appropriate rate or rates;
- translate the financial statements of foreign subsidiaries for consolidation purposes;
- discuss the political and economic forces that have shaped accounting standards for translation of foreign currency balances;
- discuss the creative accounting issues that have arisen with respect to currency mismatching.

Introduction

Given the prevalence of multinational groups of companies, it should hardly be a surprise that the translation of overseas subsidiaries' financial statements into the parent company's reporting currency is regarded as an important issue.

The fact that exchange rates fluctuate means that figures can change when translated and then retranslated at a later date. When those changes are recognised they will affect the shareholders' equity, regardless of whether they are taken to the statement of profit or loss or directly to reserves.

The history of the accounting treatment of foreign currencies has been driven by concerns about reporting currency losses. There are several competing methods available to standard-setters and the one that has been accepted is the one that yields the smallest exposure to exchange differences.

The Basic Problem with Currencies

We live in a global economy and international trade is commonplace. Exchange rates between currencies tend to fluctuate, with very few exceptions.[1] Changing rates mean that there can be more than one rate at which to translate a transaction or a balance. For example, suppose a French company purchases materials costing 100 000 Danish krone (DKK[2]) on credit from a Danish supplier when the exchange rate is DKK7.5 to the euro. The rate increases to 7.6 by the time the balance is settled and the materials remain in inventory at the year end, by which time the rate is DKK7.7 to the euro. That makes it necessary to decide upon the rate (or rates) at which the company should record the purchase, the settlement of the trade payable and the cost of the inventory remaining at the year end.

The treatment of this transaction could have significant implications for the recognition of gains and losses arising from currency movements. If the asset of inventory is valued at its historical rate as at the date of purchase then it will be worth DKK100 000/7.50 = €13 333. If it is restated to the year end rate then the inventory will be worth DKK100 000/7.70 = €12 987. If we choose the closing rate over the historical rate, we will have to recognise a loss on this asset of €13 333 − €12 987 = €346.

Much of the debate surrounding foreign currency translation has been motivated by the possibility of gains and losses arising from the choice of rate.

A Brief Word about Currency Risk

A detailed discussion of currency risk is really a topic for a finance textbook rather than an accounting text. It is worth spending a minute or two on the different risks that can arise, however, if only because there can be some overlap between accounting and finance in this area. Currency risks can basically be divided between three categories:

- economic risk
- transaction risk
- translation risk.

These risks have been listed in decreasing order of importance and in decreasing order of complexity. In other words, translation risk is the least important but it is also the most easily understood. That can mean that it attracts a disproportionate amount of attention. Unfortunately, translation risk is also associated with financial reporting and that is why we must have some understanding of it.

Economic risk is the risk that changing exchange rates will have an impact upon future cash flows. That can arise for a variety of reasons, but the problem can be very subtle and difficult to measure. For example, a Dutch theme park may lose business if the euro strengthens so that it becomes more expensive for a foreign tourist from outside the Eurozone to visit the Netherlands. It will be very difficult to measure the direct impact of the strengthening euro on demand because there could be other factors at work.

Transaction risk is the risk that a receivable or payable will change in value because of a currency movement. We saw an example of that when our French company owed a sum that was payable in Danish krone. The euro strengthened before the balance was settled and so the payable was worth less than when the purchase was first recorded. Transaction risks can arise in the short term from receivables and payables and can also arise on long-term deposits and loans.

Translation risk arises because figures in the statement of financial position can change in value because of exchange rate movements. The resulting bookkeeping adjustments to the numbers may require the recognition of currency gains and losses, but these movements have very little meaning in themselves. That is the key point. Translation is not the same as conversion. It may be that a currency movement will lead to both transaction and translation risk but in that case the two risks should be considered separately: the fact that more of the home currency has to be used to settle a foreign currency balance (transaction risk) is far more important than the fact that a different number appears in the statement of financial position for that balance (translation risk).

One of the standard texts on foreign currency management discusses the different risks and describes translation risk in the following terms (Shapiro, 2010, ch. 10):

> The resulting exchange gains and losses are determined by accounting rules and are paper only.

The problem that has affected accounting for foreign currency balances has been that translation gains and losses are generally highly visible. That means that company directors have often gone to quite significant lengths to deal with translation risks. That has often harmed the company. For example, a company that had a long-term loan outstanding might be tempted to buy a financial instrument that will gain in value if the book value of the loan increases and reduce in value if the loan declines. That will mean that any translation loss on the loan will be offset by a gain on the instrument and vice versa. The problem is that the translation gain will exist only on paper, whereas the loss on the instrument will be a real loss that will impose a genuine economic loss on the company.

The Choice of Rates

Broadly speaking, any figure can be translated at one of two rates: the closing rate as at the year end; and the historical rate that was in force when the balance was created.

If a figure is translated at the historical rate then the exchange rate is fixed for the life of the balance. If closing rates are used then subsequent movements in the exchange rate will affect the book value and that will create currency gains and losses. Those will have to be presented in the financial statements.

IAS 21 *The Effects of Changes in Foreign Exchange Rates* (IASB, 2005) distinguishes three currencies:

- **Functional currency** is the currency of the primary economic environment in which the entity operates.
- **Presentation currency** is the currency in which the financial statements are presented.
- **Foreign currency** is a currency other than the functional currency of the entity.

Most companies will use their functional currency as their presentation currency, although it would be possible for a company to select a presentation currency on the basis of convenience to shareholders if the functional currency was not widely known and understood.

Accounting for Individual Transactions

There are two main situations in which translation is necessary: when a company has a transaction that is denominated in a foreign currency; and when a foreign entity must have its financial statements translated to a parent's presentation currency for consolidation purposes.

When an entity enters into a foreign currency transaction, IAS 21 requires that it be recorded at the exchange rate in force as at the date of the transaction.

Any balances in the books at the end of the accounting period (and any subsequent account periods if the balances remain) should be translated as follows:

• Foreign currency monetary items are translated at the closing rate.
• Non-monetary items that are measured in terms of historical cost in a foreign currency are translated at the historical rate as at the date of the transaction.
• Non-monetary items that are measured at fair value are translated at the historical rate as at the date of the valuation.

So, a UK company that borrowed USD4m from a US bank on 1 July 20X3 will translate the loan at the rate in force on that date in order to enter it into the books. The loan is a monetary item, so it will be retranslated at the rate in force at the year end of 31 December 20X3 and again at the rate in force at each year end thereafter until the loan has been repaid.

If the company used the cash from the loan to acquire an item of equipment then the cost will be translated at the rate in force on the purchase date. Equipment is a non-monetary item and so no adjustment will be made for changing exchange rates at subsequent year ends.

If the equipment is revalued or impaired, then a UK company will almost certainly restate its value in terms of GBP and so there will be no further need to consider currency rates in relation to the equipment. In the unlikely event that any subsequent revaluation is expressed in terms of USD, then the valuation will be translated at the rate in force on date of the valuation.

Exchange differences can arise at reporting dates and also at the settlement of a monetary amount. Gains and losses arising from exchange differences are recorded in the statement of profit or loss.

So, if the rate in force when the equipment was purchased was USD1.50/£ (GBP) then both the asset and the loan would be recorded on 1 July 20X3 as:

Debit Equipment at cost (USD4.0m/1.5)　　　GBP2.7m
　　　Credit Loan　　　　　　　　　　　　　　　　　　GBP2.7m

At 31 December 20X3, the equipment will be shown at cost of GBP2.7m and that translation rate will not change. The depreciation charge on the equipment will be calculated as a proportion of the GBP2.7m and will not be affected by currency movements.

If the rate has changed to USD1.40/GBP by 31 December 20X3, then the loan will be translated at that rate and valued at USD4.0m/1.40 = GBP2.9m. The increase on the book value of the loan will be shown as a currency loss of GBP2.9m − GBP2.7m = GBP0.2m in the statement of profit or loss for the year ended 31 December 20X3.

If the loan is repaid on 1 July 20X4 when the rate has changed to USD1.35/GBP then the value repaid will be USD4.0m/1.35 = GBP3.0m. There will be a further loss of GBP3.0m − GBP2.9m = GBP0.1m that will appear in the statement of profit or loss for the year ended 31 December 20X4.

Even this simple example highlights the possibility of gains and losses arising on monetary items. The directors could be a little frustrated that the rates for non-monetary items remain fixed while those on the liabilities fluctuate, even when there is a close association between the asset and the liability. In our example, a strengthening of the USD against the GBP will lead to the value of the loan increasing, so there will be a loss, but there will be no offsetting increase in the book value of the equipment and so the liability is effectively unhedged. This translation loss has no significance in and of itself, but the shareholders might still be concerned that a loss has reduced their reported earnings.

IAS 39 *Financial Instruments: Recognition and Measurement* (IASB, 2010), which is discussed in Chapter 8, deals with hedge accounting. In certain circumstances it would be possible to account for offsetting assets and liabilities in such a way that gains and losses cancelled one another. IAS 21 does not modify the requirements of IAS 39 in any way, so there are no particular foreign currency issues associated with hedge accounting.

The Translation of a Foreign Entity's Financial Statements

The second situation in which translation is necessary is when a group of companies has one or more members whose presentation currency is different from that of the parent. That makes it necessary to translate the member's financial statements before they can be consolidated with those of the rest of the group. This is, by far, a larger issue in terms of the debate concerning currency translation and so we will explore the different techniques that can be applied to the translation of the subsidiary's financial statements before we turn to the rules.

In theory, there are three main approaches that can be used to translate a foreign subsidiary's statement of financial position:

- The **closing rate** method uses the closing rate for all assets and liabilities.
- The **current/non-current** method translates current assets and liabilities at the closing rate and non-current assets and liabilities at their historical rates.
- The **monetary/non-monetary** method translates monetary assets and liabilities at the closing rate and non-monetary assets and liabilities at their historical rates.

The choice of method will have implications for the recognition of translation gains and losses. Closing rate has an inbuilt tendency to hedge gains and losses because most foreign subsidiaries will have both assets and liabilities, and a gain on one will tend to be offset by a loss on the other and vice versa. The same is generally true of current/non-current because non-current liabilities will tend to be matched against non-current assets. There is greater exposure from monetary/non-monetary because liabilities will be restated in line with exchange differences whereas most assets will tend to be non-monetary so they will be translated at their historical rate.

The **temporal method** is a fourth approach that relates the translation rate to the underlying accounting treatment of the item. If a balance is expressed in historical units of currency then the balance will be translated at the historical rate. If the balance is expressed at a current valuation then it will be translated at the closing rate. If the underlying accounting basis is historical cost accounting, then any assets shown at cost less depreciation will be translated at the rate in force when they were purchased. If the assets were revalued then the rate will be as at the valuation date. Any monetary assets will be translated at the closing rate because they will be stated in terms of year end currency.

If the accounts are based on pure historical cost accounting then the temporal method will produce results that are very similar to those of the monetary/non-monetary method. In the unlikely event that the figures are based on replacement cost or current purchasing power accounting then all of the figures in the underlying statements will be expressed in year end currency and so the temporal method will apply the closing rate to virtually everything.

The fact that the temporal method is consistent with the underlying accounting treatment gives it a strong theoretical justification, but it is unpopular with preparers because of the exposure that it creates to exchange losses.

For example, Subone is a foreign subsidiary company of a UK group that owns a plot of land in its home country. Subone's presentation currency is the euro. Subone's statement of financial position as at 31 December 20X5 is shown below:

	€m
Property	30
Inventory	8
Trade receivables	5
Bank	3
	16
Total assets	46
Equity	16
Non-current liability	30
	46

The company did not enter into any transactions during the year to 31 December 20X6 and so all of the euro balances remain unchanged at the end of the following year.

The following exchange rates were in force:

When property acquired	€1.60/GBP
When inventory acquired	€1.40/GBP
At 31 December 20X5	€1.30/GBP
At 31 December 20X6	€1.20/GBP

If we translate the figures using the closing rate method then the following figures are obtained:

Subone
Statements of financial position
as at 31 December

	€m	20X5 Closing rate	20X5 GBPm	20X6 Closing rate	20X6 GBPm
Property	30	1.3	23.1	1.2	25.0
Inventory	8	1.3	6.2	1.2	6.7
Trade receivables	5	1.3	3.8	1.2	4.2

Bank	3	1.3	2.3	1.2	2.5
	16		12.3		13.4
Total assets	46		35.4		38.4
Equity (balancing figure)	16		12.3		13.4
Non-current liability	30	1.3	23.1	1.2	25.0
	46		35.4		38.4

The fact that there were no transactions means that the equity figure has changed because of translation gains or, in this case, equity has increased from GBP12.3m to GBP13.4m, so there has been a translation gain of GBP13.4m − GBP12.3m = GBP1.1m.

Translating the figures using the temporal method gives a different story:

Subone
Statements of financial position
as at 31 December

	€m	20X5 Temporal rate	GBPm	20X6 Temporal rate	GBPm
Property	30	1.6	18.8	1.6	18.8
Inventory	8	1.4	5.7	1.4	5.7
Trade receivables	5	1.3	3.8	1.2	4.2
Bank	3	1.3	2.3	1.2	2.5
	16		11.8		12.4
Total assets	46		30.6		31.2
Equity (balancing figure)	16		7.5		6.2
Non-current liability	30	1.3	23.1	1.2	25.0
	46		30.6		31.2

Under the temporal method, the equity figure has declined by GBP7.5m − 6.2m = GBP1.3m. Thus, there has been a loss on translation. This has arisen because the book values of property and inventory have remained unchanged in the face of the strengthening euro, but the book value of the liabilities has increased.

The theoretical advantages and disadvantages of the temporal and closing rate methods will be discussed later. It will be helpful to consider the application of the rules in IAS 21, which requires the closing rate method, in some detail, before doing so.

IAS 21 and Translation of Foreign Entity Financial Statements

IAS 21 requires a variation on the closing rate method for the translation of a subsidiary's financial statements.

In principle, the basic translation process is quite straightforward:

- Assets and liabilities are translated at the closing rate.
- Income and expenses in the statement of profit or loss are translated at the average rate in force throughout the year. (Strictly, they should be translated at the actual rates in force when the transactions occurred, but the average rate can be used provided that produces an acceptable approximation.)
- Translation gains and losses go to equity, not to the statement of profit or loss. They will be shown in other comprehensive income and there could be a separate equity balance for accumulated exchange gains and losses.

The reality is that the use of closing rates leads to some fairly complicated adjustments. These arise because the figures brought forward from the previous period, which were shown in the previous year's financial statements at last year's closing rate, must now be restated at this year's closing rate. Those adjustments can affect a host of figures, including goodwill on consolidation and retained earnings brought forward.

The fact that the figures in the statement of profit or loss are translated at the average exchange rate for the year, while the figures in the statement of financial position are shown as at the closing rate means that there has to be a further adjustment in order to ensure that the statement of profit or loss and the statement of financial position articulate.

The most confusing aspect of the following example is that the double-entry bookkeeping would start to become very confusing if the adjustments were stated in terms of debits and credits. The secret to avoiding confusion as to why the statement of financial position balances, is to remember that closing net assets = opening net assets + recognised profit − dividends. The adjustments relating to the restatement of opening net assets are taken directly to equity, as a credit for a gain or a debit for a loss. The process of translating the corresponding asset and liability balances at the closing rate will automatically complete double entry.

The following example will be used to illustrate the process.

Helm, an Irish company, paid GBP78.0m for 80% of the equity of Subtwo, a British company, on 31 December 20X8. Subtwo's retained earnings at that date were GBP17.3m. The fair value of the non-controlling interest as at that date was GBP15.6m.

On 31 December 20X8 the exchange rate was €1.4/GBP.

On 31 December 20X9 the rate had changed to €1.6/GBP.

The average rate for the year ended 31 December was €1.5/GBP.

The statements of financial position for Helm and Subtwo for the year ended 31 December 20X9 were as follows:

Statements of comprehensive income for the year ended 31 December 20X9

	Helm	Subtwo
	€m	GBPm
Revenue	120.0	61.7
Costs	(62.0)	(37.0)
Profit before tax	58.0	24.7
Tax	(12.0)	(9.0)
Profit for year	46.0	15.7

Statements of financial position as at 31 December 20X9

	Helm	Subtwo
	€m	GBPm
Investment	109.2	
Other assets	200.0	103.0
	309.2	103.0
Share capital	120.0	50.0
Retained earnings	89.2	33.0
	209.2	83.0
Liabilities	100.0	20.0
	309.2	103.0

Helm would have recorded the payment in its own currency at the exchange rate prevailing at that time, GBP78.0m × 1.4 = €109.2m. As far as Helm is concerned, the investment is a non-monetary asset and so the cost will not be affected by any subsequent movements in exchange rates. It is necessary to restate the goodwill calculation using closing rates for consolidation purposes, which requires an adjustment to the cost of the investment. Any increase or decrease in the valuation of the investment at cost will be matched by an increase or decrease in group reserves.

The Helm Group appears to value non-controlling interest at fair value, so the goodwill calculation is as follows:

Goodwill

	GBPm
Cost of investment	78.0
NCI at fair value	15.6
	93.6
Share capital	(50.0)
Retained earnings	(17.3)
Goodwill	26.3
Group share of goodwill = 78.0 − (80% × (50.0 + 17.3))	24.2	92%
NCI share = 15.6 − (20% × (50.0 + 17.3))	2.1	8%

We are already familiar with this goodwill calculation, but we have to split the goodwill between the parent and the non-controlling interest (NCI) so that we can deal with the exchange gain or loss on retranslation as at the closing rate on 31 December 20X9:

	€m
Total translated at closing rate of €1.4/GBP = 26.3 × 1.4	36.8
Total translated at closing rate of €1.6/GBP = 26.3 × 1.6	42.1
Exchange gain	5.3
Group share (92% × 5.3)	4.9
NCI share (8% × 5.3)	0.4

Retranslating the goodwill figure requires that we retranslate the parent's cost of investment in the subsidiary:

Gain or loss on retranslation of cost of investment

	€m
Cost of investment at acquisition rate of €1.4/GBP = 78.0 × 1.4 =	109.2
Cost of investment at closing rate of €1.6/GBP = 78.0 × 1.6 =	124.8
Exchange gain to group reserves	15.6

We calculate non-controlling interest in the usual way, but must translate that figure using the closing rate:

Non-controlling interest

	GBPm
Fair value at acquisition	15.6
NCI share of post-acquisition retained earnings (20% × 33.0 − 17.3)	3.1
	18.7
	€m
Translated at closing rate of €1.6/GBP	29.9

Finally, we calculate group retained earnings:

Group retained earnings

	€m	GBPm
Parent	89.2	
Group share of subsidiary post-acquisition retained earnings		12.6
Translated at closing rate of €1.6/GBP = 12.6 × 1.6	20.2	
Gain on retranslation of Helm's investment in Subtwo	15.6	
	125.0	

Technically, we could stop here and prepare the statement of financial position, but it is potentially desirable to separate currency gains from other profits. In order to do that, we require some further calculations in order to determine the gains and losses arising from translation differences.

Firstly, Subtwo's opening net assets were effectively carried forward at the opening rate as at the beginning of the year. We need to restate those figures at the closing rate.

Secondly, the statement of profit or loss for the year ended 31 December 20X9 will translate Subtwo's figures at the average rate for the year of €1.5/GBP, but the statement of financial position will include the profit for the year translated at the closing rate of €1.6/GBP.

Finally, we need to show the effect of the retranslation of goodwill on the retained earnings.

Pulling these adjustments together provides us with our exchange differences for the year:

Group exchange difference

	Total €m	Group €m	NCI €m
Opening net assets at opening rate ((GBP50.0m + GBP17.3m) × 1.4)	94.2		
Opening net assets at closing rate ((GBP50.0m + GBP17.3m) × 1.6)	107.7		
Exchange gain (split 80%:20%)	13.5	10.8	2.7
Profit for year			
GBP33.0m − GBP17.3m = 15.7m at average rate of 1.5	23.6		
GBP15.7m at closing rate of 1.6	25.1		
Exchange gain (split 80%:20%)	1.5	1.2	0.3
Goodwill adjustment (see above)	5.3	4.9	0.4
Total adjustments	20.3	16.9	3.4

We can now check that our figures are correct by determining the closing balance on group profits as follows:

Reconciliation of group retained earnings

	€m
Helm	89.2
Group share of post acquisition profit at average rate = 80% × (33.0 − 17.3) × 1.5	18.9
	108.1
Group share of exchange differences	16.9
	125.0

This figure agrees with our earlier figure for group retained earnings, so the numbers articulate and the statement of financial position should balance. It also permits us to show a separate equity figure for the effect of translation differences as opposed to other gains and losses.

We can now prepare the main financial statements. In the statement of profit or loss, most of the figures are obtained by adding the parent figure to the subsidiary figure, which has been translated at the average rate of €1.5/GBP. So, revenue = 120.0 + (61.7 × 1.5) = €212.6m.

The exchange gains for the year total €20.3m, including the NCI share of €3.4m. These gains are treated as other comprehensive income. The NCI in total comprehensive income = 20% × profit of GBP15.7m, translated at the average rate of €1.5/GBP, plus the NCI share of exchange differences, which equals €3.4m. That equals (20% × 15.7) × 1.5 + 3.4m = €8.1m.

Helm Group
Consolidated statement of comprehensive income
for the year ended 31 December 20X9

	€m
Revenue	212.6
Costs	(117.5)
Profit before tax	95.1
Tax	(25.5)
Profit for year	69.6
Other comprehensive income	
Exchange gains on net investment	20.3
Total comprehensive income	89.9
Attributable to:	
Parent	81.8
Non-controlling interest	8.1
	89.9

The same logic gives us the figures that remain to be calculated for the statement of financial position. These are generally the parent figure, plus the subsidiary's figure translated at the closing rate of €1.6/GBP. So, other assets = 200 + (103 × 1.6) = €364.8m.

Helm Group
Consolidated statement of financial position
as at 31 December 20X9

	€m
Goodwill	42.1
Other assets	364.8
	406.9
Share capital	120.0
Retained earnings	108.1
Currency reserve	16.9
	245.0
Non-controlling interest	29.9
	274.9
Liabilities	132.0
	406.9

The workings in this question were simplified by the fact that the consolidation occurred at the end of the first year of the group's life. In subsequent years there will be an opening balance on the currency differences account. That opening balance would be difficult to determine without quite a significant amount of additional information relating to the preceding years. The focus in this chapter is on the principle and so subsequent years will not be considered, although the logic is unchanged.

It would be possible to produce a similar set of workings for the translation of a set of financial statements using the temporal method. Such detailed workings would be redundant, however, if the primary objective is simply to compare and contrast the results using temporal versus closing rate. Both methods lend themselves to relatively simple translation of the statements provided it is acceptable to insert a balancing figure in order to arrive at the closing equity figure.

The Background to Regulation

Most of the debate concerning accounting for foreign currencies has related to the choice between the temporal and closing rate methods, and much of that debate has been driven by the political and economic consequences of greater exposure to translation risk under the temporal method. In a sense, that battle has been well and truly won and there has been very little ongoing debate and discussion.

Nobes (1980) reviews the debate that has driven the development of a standard for foreign currency translation. His paper commences with a warning that:

> much of the argument for and against particular methods, on both sides of the Atlantic, seems to be based on the acceptability of their effects on the consolidated historic [*sic*] cost profits of large companies under the exchange rate and inflation conditions that exist in that particular country at that particular time. Partly for this reason, there are several recent writings in the US (where the temporal method has been in use) against the temporal method.

Nobes identifies arguments for and against the different treatments, as shown in Table 13.1.

The US Financial Accounting Standards Board (FASB) issued Statement of Financial Accounting Standards No. 8 (FAS 8) *Accounting for the Translation of Foreign Currency Transactions and Foreign Currency Financial Statements* in 1975. The standard required the use of the temporal method. FAS 8 was based upon considerable research and theoretical justification and was regarded as one of the best researched and supported standards ever issued. Unfortunately, the standard proved unpopular because it was published at a time when the US dollar was weak and so many companies felt that they were being forced to hedge against translation losses. Such behaviour may have been unjustified, but it was still prevalent and so FAS 8 was withdrawn.

FAS 52, Statement of Financial Accounting Standards No. 52, *Foreign Currency Translation* was issued by the FASB in 1981. In contrast to FAS 8, it was widely regarded as one of the least well supported standards ever issued. It required the use of the closing rate method in the face of demands to reduce exposure to translation risk.

FAS 52 claims that the need to maintain the relationships within individual group members' financial statements requires the use of the closing rate method, but that argument ignores the whole point of translation, namely the need to consolidate the group members' financial statements in order to present their results as a single economic entity. If they are, indeed, independent entities whose separate balances have to be kept distinct, then they should not really be consolidated.

An empirical study of the impact of foreign currency translation differences on share prices (Louis, 2003) found that the markets appear to focus more on economic risk. The broad finding is that companies that report translation gains tend to suffer an abnormal loss in terms of their share price performance, and vice versa. That is logical because the strengthening of a foreign subsidiary's currency will tend to harm sales because export customers will have to pay more and

Table 13.1 Accounting for foreign currencies

Method	Arguments for and against
Current/non-current	Current/non-current has the advantages that gains and losses on non-current liabilities are not recognised when exchange rates fluctuate. Arguably, that avoids the recognition of spurious currency changes because there is every possibility that movements on any given currency will cancel over time. That argument may have had some validity in the past because governments tended to maintain the values of their currencies within fairly narrow bands. That is no longer the case and so there is less reason to believe that currency gains and losses will tend to cancel themselves over time. Current/non-current also has the effect of linking non-current assets and liabilities (for example, when a loan is taken out to finance the acquisition of an asset). While that may have a practical advantage in terms of hedging, there is no logical reason to translate current and non-current assets and liabilities at different rates.
Monetary/non-monetary	Monetary/non-monetary has the practical drawback of leaving non-current liabilities exposed to currency fluctuations with no corresponding and offsetting exposure on non-current assets. It has been argued that this creates an inconsistency because a subsidiary whose currency strengthens will report translation losses on non-current liabilities, even though the subsidiary's strengthening currency will have the effect of increasing profits when they are translated into the parent's currency. The inconsistency argument was voiced at a time when the US dollar was weakening steadily in the 1970s. At that time, the US accounting regulations imposed by FAS 8 *Accounting for the Translation of Foreign Currency Transactions and Foreign Currency Financial Statements* required the use of the temporal method, whose results were very similar to those of the monetary/non-monetary method when it was applied to historical cost financial statements.

Table 13.1 (*Continued*)

Method	Arguments for and against
The temporal method	The temporal method can be accounted for on theoretical grounds because it has the effect of valuing non-monetary assets at the same cost in the consolidated financial statements, regardless of whether they have been purchased by the parent or by a subsidiary. If, say, a US parent company buys a machine from a German supplier, it will be translated at the rate in force on the date of the purchase. If the same machine had been purchased on the same date by a German subsidiary instead then the temporal method would still translate the purchase at that rate.
	This argument may be refuted on the basis that the economic and commercial environments are different in the US and Germany, and so the purchase of the same machine by both entities should not be regarded as comparable events that should be accounted for identically.
	Effectively, this means that the temporal method treats every transaction as if it was being entered into directly by the group in the parent's currency.
	Monetary balances are carried at their closing rates. In the case of non-current balances, future rates as at the dates of settlement would be preferred, but it could be argued that current rates are the best available predictor of future rates.
	When inventory is valued at the lower of cost and net realisable value then the temporal method deals with that in a theoretically consistent manner. Historical costs are translated at historical rates and net realisable values at current rates.
	The temporal method can even adapt seamlessly to a change of accounting basis. For example, a current value approach such as replacement cost or current purchasing power would lead to all balances being expressed in terms of current values and the temporal method would translate them all at the closing rate.

(*continued*)

Table 13.1 (*Continued*)

Method	Arguments for and against
Closing rate	It can be argued that a foreign subsidiary is not merely an income-generating unit that exists to remit dividends to the parent. Arguably, a foreign subsidiary is an autonomous business that should be viewed as a separate entity and so it should be viewed in terms of its net worth. That would suggest that it is desirable for all of the subsidiary's balances to be translated at the same rate.
	There is an obvious counter-argument to this in that the whole definition of the parent–subsidiary relationship hinges on control and the consolidation is about combining the group members' figures to reflect a single economic entity.
	One potential drawback to the closing rate method is that it may result in translated balances that do not reflect either the historical cost to the group or a valuation. They are simply the product of two unrelated numbers.
	Indeed, the temporal method can distort relationships between figures to the extent that a profit expressed in the subsidiary's local currency can be translated as a loss in the parent's currency. The closing rate applies the same rate to each figure and so the relationships are maintained.
	That argument ignores the fact that anybody who is interested in the interpretation of the subsidiary's performance and financial position can simply obtain the local financial statements in the subsidiary's local currency. The translated results are combined with those of the other group members and so there is no particular reason for their internal consistency to be maintained.

Source: Nobes (1980)

imported goods will be less expensive on the domestic market. The author argues that this phenomenon implies bad accounting because it is indefensible that a gain should be reported in circumstances that will reduce future profits. The author's argument implies a misunderstanding of the purpose of accounting because financial statements are generally not concerned with reporting on future performance. Furthermore, the paper's results could underline the arguments expressed at the beginning of this chapter to the effect that translation risk has no particular relevance in itself. The capital markets do not appear to penalise companies that report currency losses. Instead, their share prices tend to rise in the expectation that the competitive environment will be a little more conducive to making profits. Presumably, that rise would occur regardless of the reported gain or loss on currency translation because the share price is ultimately a reflection of future cash flows, which are unaffected by translation gains and losses.

Currency Translation and Creative Accounting

IAS 21 requires that currency gains and losses on the translation of subsidiary financial statements go to equity in order to prevent the reported earnings figures from being distorted. Gains and losses arising in the financial statements of individual companies go to the statement of profit or loss. That might seem a little inconsistent, but it is important to make individual companies take their gains and losses to the statement of profit or loss because of a problem that arose when all gains and losses went directly to equity. This was due to a technique called 'currency mismatching' that made it easy to overstate reported profit.

Currency mismatching was remarkably simple. It relied upon a simple economic relationship between interest rates and expected currency movements. Interest rates on loans and deposits in strong currencies tend to be low. Conversely, currencies that are expected to decline tend to be associated with very high rates of interest. No rational person would choose to invest or deposit funds in a weak currency unless the interest being paid was high enough to compensate for the declining value of the principal sum deposited. There is no need to attach such a premium to a rate applied to a strong currency.

One infamous case occurred in the 1980s when a company called Polly Peck used a form of currency mismatching to boost profit. Polly Peck exploited this phenomenon by borrowing funds in German Deutschmarks[3] and Swiss francs. The cash was then deposited in weak currencies such as the Turkish lira. The statement of profit or loss showed the interest received and paid and, unsurprisingly, there was a substantial surplus. There were currency losses because the strong currency loans were appreciating in value and the weak currency deposits were declining, but the rules that were in force at the time meant that those losses went directly to equity.

Polly Peck was a major accounting scandal in its day. Paradoxically, the currency mismatching aspect was visible to any reader who knew where to look. It is a relatively simple matter to average the opening and closing figures for deposits and borrowings to arrive at a crude estimate of net debt. Dividing that estimate into net interest paid should result in a realistic borrowing rate. If the result is suspiciously low then there may have been some distortion because of currency mismatching, although care should be taken because averaging out the opening and closing balances on loans and deposits ignores the possibility the balances changed significantly during the year; for example, the loans could have been repaid shortly after the start of the year and fresh loans taken out shortly before the year end.

By the time Polly Peck collapsed, most of its publicly traded shares were held by private individuals. Despite it being a major quoted company, none of the shares were held by institutions. One possible interpretation of that fact is that the more sophisticated shareholders could see that the company's accounting policies were overstating profits, and quietly sold their holdings.

This loophole no longer exists, but it is an interesting footnote to the whole question of the regulation of accounting. Quite apart from the specific question of whether losses should be treated as expenses or equity adjustments, there are issues about whether accounting regulators should consider the needs of all readers of financial statements or whether they should aim to inform the most sophisticated readers.

Hyperinflation

IAS 29 *Financial Reporting in Hyperinflationary Economies* (IASB, 2001) deals with the treatment of financial statements that are expressed in a functional currency that is the currency of a hyperinflationary economy. Inflation is the natural tendency for prices to rise over time, but it can become so severe that information based on prices from different times becomes misleading.

IAS 29 provides some benchmarks that can be used to identify hyperinflationary economies. These include:

- the general population of that country prefers not to hold local currency and instead prefer real assets or a stable currency;
- wages and prices are index linked;
- cumulative inflation rate over three years exceeds 100%.

Chapter 7 showed how a set of financial statements that have been prepared using historical cost accounting can be restated in terms of current purchasing power in order to deal with the effects of inflation. IAS 29 requires that a subsidiary whose figures have been distorted by hyperinflation should use this method to restate its figures before they are consolidated.

Summary

The translation of foreign currency balances has been a controversial area, particularly in the context of the translation of foreign subsidiaries' financial statements for consolidation purposes.

Company directors are generally concerned that translation losses will prove unacceptable to the shareholders. That may be because the shareholders misunderstand the nature of the bookkeeping adjustments that are involved or it may be because companies that have been exposed to translation losses have been known to hedge against those losses at considerable expense. The shareholders may be concerned that the directors will engage in such dysfunctional behaviour in the face of a potential loss.

The closing rate method is firmly established as the translation method of choice because it has an inherent hedge against translation losses. Its popularity persists despite the serious theoretical shortcomings of the technique. Indeed, it is quite widely accepted that closing rate has been selected because it has the most favourable economic consequences.

Tutorial Questions

Question 1

A shareholder has come to the annual general meeting of the parent company of a multinational group that is based in the UK. The shareholder has asked about the cost of a hotel that was purchased in the centre of Moscow by the group's Russian subsidiary for RUB400m. When the hotel was purchased, the exchange rate was 0.023GBP/RUB. The closing rate was 0.018GBP/RUB. The group values property at cost less depreciation. The asset's value in the subsidiary's financial statements is RUB392m. The shareholder believes that commercial property has not changed in terms of roubles and that a realistic valuation would be of the order of RUB385m to 400m.

(a) Calculate the value at which the hotel will be shown in the group's consolidated financial statements.
(b) Comment on the relevance of the figure derived in (a) above to a shareholder of the group.

Question 2

A French company purchased an Antonov cargo aircraft from an Indian company for INR 935 million on 1 January 20X2. On the date of purchase, the exchange rate was 69.1INR/€.

The French company depreciates aircraft at 25% per annum on the reducing balance basis.

The exchange rate on 31 December 20X2 was 67.2INR/€ and on 31 December 20X3 it was 66.8INR/€.

On 31 December 20X3, the French company contacted the aircraft's Ukrainian manufacturer and requested a valuation of the aircraft. The manufacturer insisted on providing this information in its own currency. The aircraft was valued at UAH172m on that date, when the exchange rate was 1 UAH = 0.096€.

Calculate the figures that will appear in respect of this aircraft in the French company's financial statements for the years ended 31 December 20X2 and 20X3, assuming that the manufacturer's valuation is incorporated into the financial statements.

Question 3

A Spanish company has a Tunisian subsidiary. The Tunisian subsidiary's statements of financial position for the previous two years are shown below:

	As at 31 December 20X8	As at 31 December 20X7
	TND000	TND000
Property, plant and equipment	15 000	16 000
Current assets		
Inventory	250	230
Trade receivables	400	390
Bank	80	30
	730	650
	15 730	16 650
Equity	12 210	13 170
Non-current liabilities	3 000	3 000
Current liabilities	520	480
	15 730	16 650

Property, plant and equipment comprise a plot of land that cost TND10m on 31 December 20X3 and equipment that was purchased on 31 December 20X4. No property, plant and equipment has been purchased or sold since then.

Inventory was purchased one month before the respective year ends.

The loan was taken out on 31 December 20X5.

The subsidiary has never paid a dividend, nor has it issued any further shares since its acquisition.

The following exchange rates have been obtained:

	TND/€
31 December 20X3	4.1
31 December 20X4	3.4
31 December 20X5	3.1
30 November 20X7	2.8
31 December 20X7	2.7
30 November 20X8	2.1
31 December 20X8	2.0

Required

(a) Translate the statements to euros using:
   (i) the closing rate method
   (ii) the temporal method.
(b) Determine the subsidiary's profit:
   (i) in TND
   (ii) using the closing rate method
   (iii) using the temporal method.
(c) Comment on the results.

Question 4

Use the following information to prepare a set of consolidated financial statements for the Hold Group.

Hold, a Norwegian company, acquired 80% of the equity of Sub, a Polish company. Hold's presentation currency is the Norwegian krone (NOK) and Sub's is the zloty (PLN).

Hold paid PLN52.1m for 80% of Sub's equity on 31 December 20X5. Sub's retained earnings were PLN17.0m on that date. The non-controlling interest was valued using the proportion of net assets method.

The following exchange rates have been obtained:

31 December 20X5	NOK0.65/PLN
Average rate for the year ended 31 December 20X6	NOK0.61/PLN
31 December 20X6	NOK0.56/PLN

Sub did not pay any dividends during the year ended 31 December 20X6. The latest financial statements for Hold and Sub are as follows:

Statements of profit or loss for the year ended 31 December 20X6

	Hold NOKm	Sub PLNm
Revenue	488.0	113.0
Costs	(124.0)	(74.0)
Profit before tax	364.0	39.0
Tax	(24.0)	(18.0)
Profit for year	340.0	21.0

Statements of financial position as at 31 December 20X6

	Hold NOKm	Sub PLNm
Investment	33.9	
Other assets	324.0	146.0
	357.9	146.0
Share capital	90.0	40.0
Retained earnings	127.9	38.0
	217.9	78.0
Non-current liabilities	100.0	60.0
Current liabilities	40.0	8.0
	357.9	146.0

Question 5

A South American aircraft manufacturer makes substantial sales to overseas customers. One major customer has purchased four aircraft on three months' credit and priced in the customer's home currency, with delivery of the aircraft two months prior to the year end.

(a) Distinguish economic, transaction and translation risk as faced by this manufacturer.
(b) Explain how it could be argued that translation risk is irrelevant when a movement on the exchange rate will clearly affect the cash from the receivable when it is settled.

Questions with Answers

Question 1

Uno is a Swedish manufacturing company. The company's latest draft statement of financial position is as follows:

Uno
Statement of financial position
as at 31 December 20X6

	SEK000
Property, plant and equipment	8 900.0
Investment in Pine	2 000.0
	10 900.0
Current assets	
Inventory	500.0
Trade receivables	300.0
Bank	100.0
	900.0
Total assets	11 800.0

Share capital	6 000.0
Retained earnings	2 730.0
	8 730.0
Non-current liabilities	2 700.0
Current liabilities	
Trade payables	250.0
Tax	120.0
	370.0
	11 800.0

Pine is a British company. Uno paid GBP200 000 for 100% of Pine's share capital on 2 March 20X6. This transaction was funded with a GBP200 000 loan, which is included in Uno's non-current liabilities. The exchange rate was SEK10/GBP when the acquisition took place. At 31 December 20X6 the exchange rate was SEK9.5/GBP.

Uno's inventory includes goods that cost €42 000 from a Belgian supplier at a time when the exchange rate was SEK8.1/€. These goods are all stated at cost, although one-third of the goods have been damaged in storage and will have to be sold for SEK1 000. The Belgian supplier has not yet been paid. The closing exchange rate is SEK8.3/€

No adjustments have been made in respect of any of the foregoing information. The draft financial statements are based on the original costs recorded in the statements.

Required

Restate Uno's statement of financial position and calculate the gain or loss on translation.

Question 2

A Chinese company has a Dutch subsidiary. The subsidiary's euro statements of financial position are shown on the next page:

Lion
Statements of financial position

	As at 31 December 20X8	As at 31 December 20X7
	€000	€000
Property, plant and equipment	31 000	32 000
Current assets		
Inventory	400	420
Trade receivables	520	490
Bank	70	50
	990	960
	31 990	32 960
Equity	26 580	27 770
Non-current liabilities	5 000	4 800
Current liabilities	410	390
	31 990	32 960

Lion's property, plant and equipment consist partly of land and buildings that cost €20.0m on 31 December 20X4. The book value of the land and buildings was €18.8m on 31 December 20X7 and €18.4m on 31 December 20X8. The remainder of the property, plant and equipment comprises equipment that was purchased on 31 December 20X5 for €16.0m.

Lion's inventory turns over at a consistent rate of two months.

The following exchange rates have been obtained:

	CNY/€
31 December 20X4	6.7
31 December 20X5	7.0
31 October 20X7	7.7
31 December 20X7	7.9
31 October 20X8	8.2
31 December 20X8	8.5

(a) Translate Lion's statements of financial position to CNY using both the temporal and the closing rate methods, and determine the profit that has been earned under both methods.

(b) Calculate the gearing and liquidity ratios using both sets of figures from your answer to (a) above and comment on the relevance of each.

Question 3

Hub, a German company, paid GBP25.0m on 31 December 20X7 for 75% of the equity of Spoke, a British company.

Spoke's retained earnings were GBP7.0m on 31 December 20X7. The remaining 25% of the shares had a fair value of GBP8.0m on that date. Hub values non-controlling interest on the basis of fair values.

The following exchange rates have been obtained:

31 December 20X7	€1.5/GBP
Average rate for the year ended 31 December 20X8	€1.4/GBP
31 December 20X8	€1.3/GBP

Spoke has not paid a dividend since joining the Hub Group.

Hub is preparing its consolidated financial statements:

Statements of profit or loss for the year ended 31 December 20X8

	Hub €m	Spoke GBPm
Revenue	330.0	38.5
Costs	(154.0)	(22.0)
Profit before tax	176.0	16.5
Tax	(24.0)	(4.5)
Profit for year	152.0	12.0

Statements of financial position as at 31 December 20X8

	Hub €m	Spoke GBPm
Investment	37.5	
Other assets	510.0	68.0
	547.5	68.0

Share capital	150.0	20.0
Retained earnings	162.5	19.0
	312.5	39.0
Non-current liabilities	200.0	26.0
Current liabilities	35.0	3.0
	547.5	68.0

Required:

Prepare the financial statements of the Hub Group.

Endnotes

1. For example, the United Arab Emirates has pegged the value of its Dirham to the US Dollar in order to prevent any exchange risks from trade denominated in the US currency.
2. All currencies have a three-letter code that is used for international currency trading. This chapter will use those codes for the sake of clarity. An exception will be made for the euro because there is a unique and easily understood symbol for that currency.
3. These events occurred before the introduction of the euro.

References

FASB (1975) Statement of Financial Accounting Standards No. 8, *Accounting for the Translation of Foreign Currency Transactions and Foreign Currency Financial Statements*.

FASB (1981) Statement of Financial Accounting Standards No. 52, *Foreign Currency Translation*.

IASB (2001) IAS 29 *Financial Reporting in Hyperinflationary Economies*.

IASB (2005) IAS 21 *The Effects of Changes in Foreign Exchange Rates*.

IASB (2010) IAS 39 *Financial Instruments: Recognition and Measurement*.

Louis, H. (2003) The value relevance of the foreign translation adjustment. *The Accounting Review* **78**(4) pp. 1027–1047.

Nobes, C.W. (1980) A review of the translation debate. *Accounting and Business Research* **10**(4) pp. 421–431.

Shapiro, A.C. (2010) *Multinational Financial Management*. Chichester: John Wiley & Sons.

INTERNATIONAL ACCOUNTING

Contents

Learning Objectives

After studying this chapter, you should be able to:

- discuss the significance of the differences between systems of accounting;
- identify the effects of culture on accounting;
- discuss the problems associated with harmonising accounting in the EU;
- describe the problems associated with obtaining final convergence between the US and the IASB;
- discuss the implications of exporting accounting expertise to the former Soviet countries when they were in transition.

Introduction

The international comparison of accounting practices has been a major area of study for many years. Business cultures differ dramatically between countries and so the needs and relative importance of different stakeholders can change too. For example, many countries have traditionally relied upon bank lending for business finance while others depend more on equity. Lenders and shareholders have different needs. National cultures can also play a role. For example, if there is limited access to higher education in a given country then it is possible that it would be unrealistic to expect a sophisticated accounting system.

The development of IFRS has had a confounding effect on these differences. The whole point of having a global set of accounting standards is that the preparers of financial statements will use the same standards, despite the cultural and other factors that have led to the differences mentioned previously. The ultimate objective of the harmonisation of accounting is that all companies will prepare financial statements that are comparable, regardless of their country of origin.

One of the problems that has delayed the global introduction of IFRS is that the development of accounting standards is regarded as a matter of national sovereignty. The US has shown some reluctance to embrace IFRS as the de facto standard for accounts preparation. To an extent, the history of the transition from a command economy to capitalism by the Soviet Union highlights that concern. During the early stages of the transition there was a substantial investment in sponsoring the implementation of IFRS, with many perceiving that as an important element of underpinning the changes that had occurred.

International Differences

The classification of national accounting practices was once a major area in accounting research (a detailed overview of this literature can be found in chapter 3 of Nobes & Parker, 2012). The basic starting point for this research arises from the fact that accounting figures differ from country to country and that these differences can arise for a variety of reasons. For example:

• Bank finance is used more heavily in some countries, which may result in accounting statements being prepared in a more conservative manner to meet the needs of lenders. Countries that rely more heavily on equity may place greater emphasis on providing shareholders with a more representative report on performance and so conservatism may be less of a feature.

• Some countries have a tradition of an independent and highly educated accountancy profession. Others have a tradition of detailed supervision of accounting by the government. Each approach will have implications for the flexibility of regulation and the manner of enforcement.

• Different legal systems will influence the manner of regulation. Code law countries tend to have more prescriptive laws and regulations that must be obeyed. Common law countries have a greater emphasis on principles and may be more flexible.

• Different levels of education may have an effect on the extent to which accountants can be expected to cope with complicated regulations.

The effects of these different factors were studied in a number of ways, with a view to drawing some conclusions about the nature and the extent of the differences that arise internationally or to determine their causes. For example, Nobes (1983) proposed the classification shown in Figure 14.1, based on a clustering of accounting practices that was then explained by means of an examination of the legal and economic factors that led to the similarities and differences.

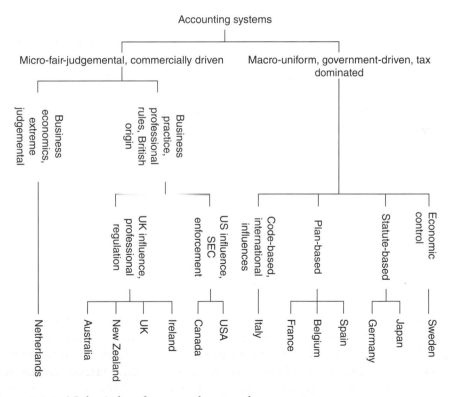

Figure 14.1 Nobes' classification of national accounting practices
Source: Nobes, 1983

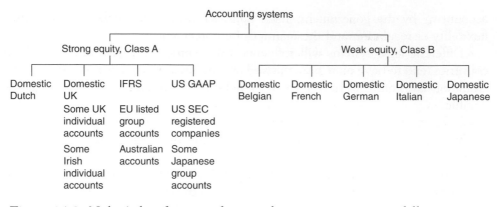

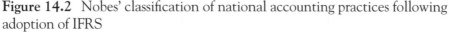

Figure 14.2 Nobes' classification of national accounting practices following adoption of IFRS
Source: Nobes, 1998

To an extent, this research has been overtaken by events. When Nobes revisited this study in 1998, he found that the adoption of IFRS had changed the nature of the differences (Figure 14.2).

In this context, 'domestic' means that the companies are unlisted and so the financial statements are largely for local use by shareholders within the countries in question. If only those practices relating to listed companies were classified then the model would leave only financial statements prepared under IFRS and those prepared under US GAAP.

Effectively, over a relatively short period of time, the widespread adoption of IFRS around the world has led to an agreed set of standards for most non-US listed companies. That does not necessarily guarantee that an Australian accountant will implement IFRS in exactly the same way as an Irish or a Dutch accountant, so national differences may remain, but these are likely to be far less significant thanks to the fact that the same accounting standards will be applied in all cases.

Culture and Accounting

Accounting varies from country to country. That is hardly surprising because of the variety of social and economic differences that can affect the development of accounting practices. Taken at face value, the differences will have been eliminated by the widespread adoption of IFRS around the world, but accounting standards are subject to interpretation and so there can be no guarantee that a set of financial statements prepared in, say, Denmark will be directly comparable to those of a similar business based in France.

It is possible that cultural differences will affect the preparation of financial statements in different countries, even when they have all adopted IFRS as the basis for their regulation. It is difficult to generalise about a country's approach to accounting, however, because there are such significant differences between accountants within any given country.

One way to approach the comparison of accounting systems is to set out a framework for the discussion of national cultures. If cultural differences can be identified and measured then it should be possible to investigate the ways in which those differences affect accounting.

Hofstede

Geert Hofstede laid the groundwork for a significant body of sociological research when he analysed a large database of employee value scores collected by IBM during the period from 1967 to 1973. IBM operated globally and so it was possible to draw upon the fact that the company employed many thousands of staff in scores of countries. Hofstede's research continued, with the data set being replicated and extended in the years that followed.

Hofstede's contribution amounts to offering researchers a starting point with respect to cultural values. Other authors have taken Hofstede's work as a starting point for the analysis of the effects of culture on the attitudes of airline pilots, undergraduate students, civil service managers and a host of other groups.

Hofstede's earliest work isolated four cultural dimensions that could be used to distinguish cultural differences:

- power distance
- individualism
- masculinity
- uncertainty avoidance.

A fifth dimension, long-term orientation, was added after the initial studies were extended to include Chinese employees.

Each dimension is effectively a continuum and it is possible to plot norms or averages for any given society in terms of each dimension (Table 14.1).

Hofstede's work lends itself to the development of cultural descriptions that provide the starting point for more detailed study or comparison. For example, China has high scores for long-term orientation and tolerance of power distance and a low score for individualism.

Table 14.1 Hofstede's cultural dimensions

Cultural dimension	How it can be used to distinguish cultural differences
Power distance	All societies are unequal in the sense that leaders have greater power than followers. That can be true of organisations and other institutions such as the family. Societies differ in terms of the extent to which leaders demand and followers tolerate this inequality.

Individualism	Individualism is the opposite of collectivism.
	    In individualist societies the ties between individuals are loose. Individuals take care of themselves and their immediate families.
	    Members of collectivist societies are bound into strong, cohesive groups. These could take the form of extended families. These relationships demand loyalty and, in return, members are supported and protected by the group.

Masculinity	Hofstede found that women's values differ less between societies than do men's values.
	    Men's values vary from culture to culture, from very assertive and competitive at one extreme to modest and caring (and similar to women's values) at the other.
	    The masculinity dimension captures the extent to which the masculine traits associated with assertiveness prevail over more caring feminine traits.
	    There tends to be a less pronounced difference between the values adopted by men and women in more feminine countries. The gender differences tend to be more pronounced in more masculine countries.

Uncertainty avoidance	Societies differ in their tolerance of uncertainty and ambiguity.
	    Uncertainty-avoiding cultures tend to have strict laws, rules, safety and security measures. They also tend to be associated with a belief that there is a single absolute 'truth'.
	    Members of uncertainty-avoiding societies also tend to be more emotional.
	    Uncertainty-accepting cultures are more tolerant of opinions that are different from what they are used to. They try to have as few rules as possible. They tend to take a more relativist view of 'truth'.

Long-term orientation	Values associated with long-term orientation are thrift and perseverance. Values associated with short-term orientation are respect for tradition, fulfilling social obligations, and protecting one's 'face'.

Table 14.2 Gray's accounting values

Value	Features
Professionalism versus statutory control	A preference for the exercise of individual professional judgment and the maintenance of professional self-regulation as opposed to compliance with prescriptive legal requirements and statutory control.
Uniformity versus flexibility	A preference for the enforcement of uniform accounting practices between companies and for the consistent use of such practices over time as opposed to flexibility in accordance with the perceived circumstances of individual companies.
Conservatism versus optimism	A preference for a cautious approach to measurement so as to cope with the uncertainty of future events as opposed to a more optimistic, laissez-faire, risk-taking approach.
Secrecy versus transparency	A preference for confidentiality and the restriction of disclosure of information about the business only to those who are closely involved with its management and financing as opposed to a more transparent, open and publicly accountable approach.

Source: Gray, 1988

Gray

Gray (1988) proposed four hypotheses that draw upon Hofstede. These hypotheses were offered as a starting point for the use of Hofstede in theorising comparative studies into the effects of culture on accounting.

Gray identified four 'accounting values', shown in Table 14.2.

These values are linked to Hofstede using the following hypotheses (H):

• H1: The higher a country ranks in terms of individualism and the lower it ranks in terms of uncertainty avoidance and power distance, then the more likely it is to rank highly in terms of professionalism.

• H2: The higher a country ranks in terms of uncertainty avoidance and power distance and the lower it ranks in terms of individualism, then the more likely it is to rank highly in terms of uniformity.

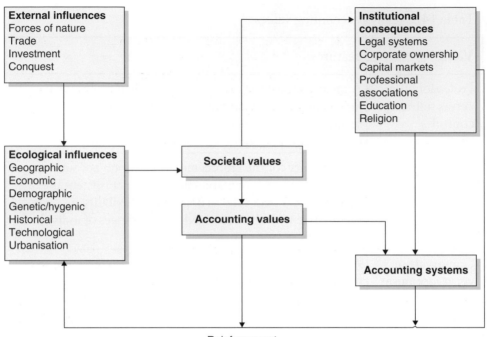

Figure 14.3 Gray's framework
Source: Gray, 1988

• H3: The higher a country ranks in terms of uncertainty avoidance and the lower it ranks in terms of individualism and masculinity, then the more likely it is to rank highly in terms of conservatism.

• H4: The higher a country ranks in terms of uncertainty avoidance and power distance and the lower it ranks in terms of individualism and masculinity, then the more likely it is to rank highly in terms of secrecy.

Gray's framework goes beyond simply claiming that accounting is driven by culture. He provides the diagram in Figure 14.3 to explain the links between the factors that can influence not only society but also the accounting systems within any given society.

In essence, Gray argues that societal values drive accounting values, which, in turn, drive accounting systems. There is feedback and reinforcement in these relationships, with accounting ultimately feeding back into the societal values.

Studies using Gray

Gray provides a defensible starting point for the study of the impact of culture. For example, Chanchani and Willett (2004) used Gray as the basis for a comparison of the accounting values in New Zealand and India. The authors cited a variety of studies that have drawn upon Gray, but claimed that their paper was the first to actually put it to the test in terms of gathering empirical evidence with which to investigate Gray's hypotheses.

Chanchani and Willet gathered information from both users and preparers of financial statements in New Zealand and India, using an 'accounting values survey' instrument. This posed a number of assertions such as 'profits and assets should be valued downwards in case of doubt' and sought a response on a seven-point Likert scale that ranged from 'strongly agree' to 'strongly disagree'. The assertions dealt with conservatism, uniformity, secrecy and professionalism.

The objective of this study was not really about exploring differences between accounting in the two countries. Rather, it was about testing Gray's framework as a basis for conducting such comparisons. On balance, Chanchani and Willett found some basis for adopting the Hofstede–Gray framework, but cautioned that the very act of developing their research instrument around Gray's arguments risked biasing their results in favour of his position.

Gray's model has also been criticised for over-simplifying the relationships at work and the resulting accounting values. For example, Heidhues and Patel (2011) compare and contrast their understanding of German culture and its accounting systems with those proposed by Hofstede and Gray, and claim that the models that have been offered are inaccurate. Gray, in particular, falls into the trap of describing another country's accounting systems on the basis of perceptions and preconceived ideas that have been influenced by his UK background. Heidhues and Patel's point is not, of course, that Gray is wrong about Germany in particular but that it is necessary to develop a much more intimate and detailed understanding of an accounting system before one can offer suggestions as to its operation.

IFRS and the European Union

The European Union (EU) has been working towards the harmonisation of very different accounting systems for quite some time. The original version of Nobes' classification had the member states spread across the range of systems that he had identified. Some of the member states had code law legal systems (e.g. France), while others had common law systems (e.g. Ireland). Some states' major corporations were financed largely by equity (e.g. the UK), while others were heavily dependent upon bank finance (e.g. Germany).

The first step towards harmonisation of accounting throughout the EU occurred with the adoption of the Fourth Council Directive 78/660/EEC of 25 July 1978. EU Directives must be incorporated into the laws of member states. The Fourth Directive set out a host of provisions concerning accounting rules that led to significant changes in every state. For example, the UK insisted that the Fourth Directive require that financial statements should give a true and fair view. That concept had no direct equivalent in many states, particularly code law countries where the rules were generally more prescriptive. In the same vein, the UK's Companies Act 1981, which incorporated the Fourth Directive into UK company law, introduced mandatory formats for the presentation of financial statements. Prior to this law, UK companies could present their financial statements in any format they wished, provided the disclosure requirements were met.

The Seventh Council Directive 83/349/EEC of 13 June 1983 also had significant implications for accounting. This Directive harmonised the legislation concerning consolidations, setting out a common definition of the parent–subsidiary relationship and establishing a common set of rules for the publication of group accounts by parents.

There were significant differences between the accounting systems in force across the EU before the introduction of these directives and so this harmonisation of company law represented a major achievement. However, the changes in the law across Europe did not resolve the significant differences in national cultures and their impact on accounting. The fact that the Fourth Directive provided detailed formats for the statements themselves led to a situation whereby income statements and statements of financial position looked the same when compared from country to country, but the basis upon which those figures had been prepared was often quite different.

Alexander (1993) provides a lucid discussion of the difficulties associated with communicating the idea of truth and fairness as an overriding concept to those member states whose laws had previously set out explicit rules. Apart from the difficulties associated with translating the phrase into other languages, the concept itself called for fundamentally different attitudes towards financial reporting. Alexander reported 'persistent rumours' of a confidential minute that had been passed at the request of German representatives to the effect that compliance with the detailed rules contained in the Fourth Directive would, in and of itself, lead to the presentation of a true and fair view.

With the passage of time, the needs imposed by the global financial markets have prevailed and an EU Regulation was passed in 2002 (Regulation (EC) No 1606/2002 of the European Parliament and of the Council of 19 July 2002 on the application of international accounting standards), which required the use of IFRS by all listed companies in the EU. That regulation came into force in 2005. To an extent, the requirement to report under IFRS was motivated by the fact that many listed companies were seeking dual listings and were reporting in terms of either IFRS or US GAAP in order to reduce the cost of raising finance internationally.

This adoption of IFRS has raised a number of issues that have been studied by a variety of researchers. The standardisation of accounting throughout the EU is, in and of itself, a significant matter because of the size of the European economy and the impact on the financial reporting practices of a large number of significant companies. There are also opportunities to observe the implications of switching to IFRS, which has attracted the attention of a number of US academics. The next section will discuss the question of the convergence between US and IFRS GAAP, which has been a controversial matter for US regulators.

The classic approach to the study of new accounting disclosures involves looking at capital market reactions. For example, Armstrong *et al.* (2010) examined the European stock market reactions to a number of events that shed light on the likelihood of the adoption of IFRS as mandatory throughout the EU. They observed the following capital market reactions:

- The prospect of the mandatory adoption of IFRS caused a positive reaction for companies that were perceived as publishing lower quality earnings information. The switch to IFRS would, presumably, reduce information asymmetry and enhance investors' confidence.
- Companies in code law countries had a negative reaction, suggesting that their investors were concerned about the difficulties associated with the enforcement of IFRS for companies that were accustomed to the more structured and prescriptive regulation implied by code law.
- There were positive reactions for companies that were publishing high-quality information before the adoption of IFRS, which suggested that their investors foresaw net benefits from convergence to IFRS.

Such a result does not, in itself, demonstrate that IFRS will enhance financial reporting, but there does appear to be evidence that the capital markets perceived some benefits. Interestingly, for different reasons, Armstrong *et al.* found that those benefits were perceived for a range of companies, not just those with a reputation for publishing either poor-quality or high-quality information.

Jermakowicz and Gornik-Tomaszewski (2006) surveyed preparers of financial statements for EU-listed companies at the time of the implementation of mandatory reporting in terms of IFRS. They asked about the approach these companies were taking to conversion, the impact of adopting IFRS on the financial statements and the perceived benefits and challenges of implementing IFRS.

The responses can be summed up as follows:

• A majority of respondents had adopted IFRS for more than just consolidation purposes – which probably suggests that it makes little sense for listed companies that are forced to report their consolidated financial statements in terms of IFRS to prepare their own individual company accounts in terms of local accounting standards.

• The process of switching to IFRS was perceived as costly, complex, and burdensome. It should be noted, however, that the response rate was only 27% and so it may be that those preparers who were most exercised by the implications of switching to IFRS were also the most likely to complete the research instrument.

• Preparers did not believe that the switch to IFRS would lower their companies' costs of capital.

• Respondents accepted that the more comprehensive the adoption of IFRS, the greater the costs of switching and also the greater the benefits that can be expected from convergence. These expectations are rather intuitive because a less comprehensive approach would require less time and effort and would compromise the expected benefits.

• Respondents expected the switch to IFRS to increase volatility in reported financial results.

• Preparers envisaged significant challenges to arise because of the complexity of IFRS, the lack of guidance on implementation and differences in interpretation.

• A majority of respondents would not adopt IFRS if not required by the EU Regulation.

The move to IFRS has had a significant impact on many companies' financial statements. For example, Spain has developed a new series of Spanish Accounting Standards that are based upon IFRS. These new standards apply to all companies, both quoted and unquoted. Implementation became mandatory during a 12-month period from 1 January 2007 to 1 January 2008, which gave many companies some discretion as to the period in which they would switch. Early studies suggest that accounting figures are very different under the new rules, with a significant impact on many accounting ratios (Fitó, Gómez & Moya, 2012).

IFRS and the US – The Convergence Project

The IASB and the US Financial Accounting Standards Board (FASB) have been working together since 2002 to achieve convergence of IFRS and US GAAP. The US has been working towards the adoption of IFRS, but has yet to make the final step of implementing IFRS in place of its own standards.

FASB and the IASB have invested a great deal of time and effort in the convergence of their standards in the interests of developing high-quality, compatible accounting standards that could be used for both domestic and cross-border financial reporting. The two boards have signed formal undertakings in the Norwalk Agreement, which was issued in 2002, and a subsequent Memorandum of Understanding between the IASB and the FASB, which was originally issued in 2006 and updated in 2008.

The most tangible result of these documents has been the conduct of a number of joint projects, with both boards working to reach agreement on a variety of specific matters. For example, IFRS 2 *Share-based Payment* (IASB, 2010) and FASB's Statement No. 123 *Share-Based Payment* (FASB, 1993) are essentially the same document.

FASB has yet to reach the point where it will adopt IFRS in their totality. Indeed, a report on the convergence project leaves room for ongoing discussion and debate (IASB & FASB, 2012):

The phrase international convergence of accounting standards refers to both a goal and the path taken to reach it.

FASB reaffirms its commitment to the goal of a single set of global accounting standards. However, the journey along the path to that goal continues. Both FASB and the IASB must continue to 'improve' both US GAAP and IFRS with the intention of eliminating the differences between them.

The convergence project is viewed as continuing through joint projects to develop common standards.

The US seems to regard the development of a set of global standards as desirable, but the problem seems to be the risk to national sovereignty if that will arise from the outright adoption of IFRS. For example, in the aftermath of the 2008 financial crisis it was felt that the FASB was better placed to act swiftly in the defence of US interests.

The issues arising from adoption of IFRS are explored in detail in a two-part paper that might reflect much of the institutional reluctance to making the final commitment to IFRS (Hail, Leuz & Wysocki, 2010a; 2010b). The first part describes the costs and benefits of adopting IFRS from a US point of view. The authors appear to be broadly of the opinion that there will be some benefit from the adoption of IFRS, but there will be significant costs and so the overall net benefit will be slender. In particular, US GAAP is of such a high quality as it stands that switching to IFRS would do very little to improve matters.

The second paper discusses the political and institutional matters arising from convergence. One major concern is the fact that 'foreign governments and interest groups' exercise an undue influence on the IASB and, consequently, the formulation of IFRS. In the past, the development of IFRS has been heavily influenced by the needs of 'outside investors' in countries such as the UK, Australia, and the United States. While that would imply that the US has little to fear from convergence, there is a threat that the direction followed by the IASB could be influenced more by 'insider' or 'stakeholder' economies.

The development of IFRS has been heavily influenced by US GAAP for many years. Long before the Norwalk agreement it was often apparent that new IFRS often bore a close similarity to corresponding FASB standards. Despite that, it is possible to demonstrate that there are significant differences between FASB and IFRS financial statements. One way to demonstrate that is to exploit the fact that US rules permit foreign companies that are cross-listed on local and US stock exchanges to choose between reporting under either IFRS or US GAAP. Before 2007, it was necessary for companies that chose to report under IFRS to reconcile net income and equity to the figures that would have been reported under US rules. Such reconciliations provide the basis for an empirical analysis of the differences between the two versions of GAAP – if the reconciling items are large, then so must be the differences between the standards. For example, one study reported that return on equity is, on average, five percentage points higher under IFRS than under US GAAP (Henry, Lin & Yang, 2009). It could be argued that such studies have limited value in terms of informing US preparers of the differences that they might expect in the event of a switch to IFRS. The problem is that the legal and other factors that affect the preparation of financial statements could also have affected the reconciliations. A US company preparing financial statements under IFRS may not find that the differences between the resulting numbers are as pronounced.

Exporting Accounting – Accounting in Transition

The Cold War between East and West was possibly the defining feature of 20th century history. When the former Soviet Union moved away from socialism and towards capitalism there was a sudden rush to export Western accounting principles as one aspect of making this change permanent and to assist Western corporations in establishing a presence in the newly formed Commonwealth of Independent States (CIS).[1]

The EU saw the changes sweeping through the Soviet Union as both a threat to economic and political stability in Europe and an opportunity to develop trading links with the economies which were expected to emerge from this process. A number of initiatives were developed in order to assist with the establishment of democracy and the development of a market economy.

The Technical Assistance to the CIS (TACIS) programme was one such initiative, which ran from 1991 to 2006. It provided grant finance for the transfer of know-how to 12 countries of the former Soviet Union, and Mongolia. In so doing, it aimed to foster the development of market economies and democratic societies.

The EU listed six priority areas for this programme:

- support for institutional, legal and administrative reform;
- support for the private sector and assistance for economic development;
- support for addressing the social consequences of transition;
- development of infrastructure networks;
- promotion of environmental protection and management of natural resources;
- nuclear safety.

It is intriguing that the reform of accounting (which was part of the support for institutional, legal and administrative reform) is mentioned in the same list of priorities as nuclear safety.

The United Nations Conference on Trade and Development (UNCTAD) was established in 1964 as the principal organ of the United Nations General Assembly in the field of trade and development. Its main goals are to maximise the trade, investment and development opportunities of developing countries, and to help them face challenges arising from globalisation and to integrate into the world economy on an equitable basis. UNCTAD was also influential in assisting the development of accounting in the CIS.

One of UNCTAD's programmes was entitled 'Accountancy Reform in Economies in Transition'. This aimed to assist countries in transition:

- to enhance the technical capabilities of the staff in the Ministry of Finance to undertake accounting and auditing reforms;
- to ensure that accounting reforms meet the needs of the country;
- to ensure that internationally accepted accounting principles are used;
- to ensure that the reforms incorporate the strengths of the existing accounting systems; and
- to train public and private accounting practitioners in the implementation of accounting and auditing reforms.

The activities undertaken in support of these objectives took three main forms:

- the provision of technical expertise in the revision of the national chart of accounts and in drafting new or revised accounting and auditing laws and regulations;

• the training of government officials and private sector practitioners in the new reforms (usually by developing suitable materials and then providing intensive training for local trainers); and

• assistance in the development of professional bodies of accountants and auditors in order to provide an ongoing infrastructure for continuing the reforms achieved.

The belief that Western-style accounting would encourage the economic and political changes in the former Soviet Union to remain permanent is highlighted in the following editorial piece written by the then president of the Institute of Chartered Accountants in England and Wales (Chamberlain, 1993):

> But there is more at stake than self-interest. I do not think it is an exaggeration to say that, without a vigorous accountancy profession in Central and Eastern Europe, respected and understood by managers in the public and private sectors, the prospects for stability and prosperity in the former centrally-planned economy countries are very uncertain.

Before the economic and political changes of the 1990s, accounting in Eastern Europe and the Soviet Union was very heavily biased towards the production of information for central economic planning. Typically, the central statistical office and ministry of finance provided a uniform plan of accounts that had to be adhered to by all enterprises (Jaruga, 1990). The fundamental assumptions underlying accounting practices were based around the accurate maintenance of bookkeeping records, supported by the physical inventory of assets. Accounting statements contained very little detail, but the records themselves were of immense value to central planners. Indeed, the whole purpose of accounting and record-keeping was to supply central planners with economic data.

Accounting had a very poor reputation, with one report (Smirnova, Sokolov & Emmanuel, 1995) ranking accountancy in 91st place in terms of prestige on a list of 92 professional occupations. The former socialist system had placed most of its efforts in the development of economic models for managing enterprises as elements of the wider economy. Educating local accountants was partly intended to raise the profile of accounting as the basis for performance measurement.

The complexities associated with assisting countries to make the transition to a Western style of financial reporting are reported by the participants of a team who were engaged in facilitating reform in Romania (King *et al.*, 2001). The interactions between different areas of regulation, such as the links between accounting and tax law or the need to establish working arrangements between the professional accountancy bodies and the government, led to some rather delicate and complicated negotiations. The successful export of accounting could not have happened without the active support of key players in the countries under reform.

Summary

The international comparison of accounting has always been a fruitful area for academic research. National differences can be measured and explained. Differences are generally due to cultural influences that have driven the approaches taken to the development and enforcement of accounting requirements.

These comparative studies are likely to continue, but the move towards the global adoption of IFRS will mean that many of the differences will be more subtle than before and will require a little more care in their evaluation. The pressures imposed by the globalisation of financial markets have encouraged the adoption of IFRS, almost regardless of the accounting traditions that were previously in place.

The US has not yet embraced IFRS, despite the fact that the IASB's standards have traditionally been heavily influenced by those of the US and in recent years many important accounting standards have been developed using joint working parties from both FASB and IASB. There is an active dialogue that will, hopefully, enable the US to adopt IFRS in the same way that many other countries have done.

The possibility of exporting accounting ideas has been illustrated to effect by the response of many agencies to the opportunities created by the transition of the former Soviet states. There were many initiatives to develop Western-style accounting institutions. These appear to be motivated by a desire to create societies that were open to many of the values that are accepted in the West.

Tutorial Questions

Question 1

Discuss the advantages and disadvantages of having a common set of accounting standards that apply to all entities that prepare financial statements, regardless of their nationality.

Question 2

Look up Hofstede's classification of culture for your home country and consider whether you believe that Gray's hypotheses would provide an appropriate starting point for a study of accounting.

Question 3

It has been suggested that the US may be reluctant to adopt IFRS fully because of concerns about national sovereignty. Discuss the validity of this suggestion. Do you believe that the concerns are justified?

Question 4

Discuss the logic that the adoption of IFRS will encourage the former members of the Soviet Union to remain committed to capitalism.

Question 5

Discuss the difficulties that would have been faced by the experts who were engaged to assist the CIS states with their transition to IFRS.

There are no additional questions with answers in this chapter.

Endnote

1. This section is based partly on the experiences of the authors of this text, who were but two of the many Western academics who were pressed into service in assisting with the development of accounting institutions in the East and with the training of teachers and academics.

References

Alexander, D. (1993) A European true and fair view? *European Accounting Review* 2(1) pp. 59–80.

Armstrong, C.S., Barth, M.E., Jagolinzer, A.D. & Riedl, J. (2010) Market reaction to the adoption of IFRS in Europe. *Accounting Review* **85**(1) pp. 31–61.

Chamberlain, M. (1993) Fulfilling a vital role in Eastern Europe. *Accountancy* **112** (1202) p. 10.

Chanchani, S. & Willett, R. (2004) An empirical assessment of Gray's accounting value constructs. *International Journal of Accounting* **39**(2) pp. 125–154.

FASB (1993) Statement No. 123 *Share-Based Payment.*

Fitó, A., Gómez, F. & Moya, S. (2012) Choices in IFRS adoption in Spain: Determinants and consequences. *Accounting in Europe* **9**(1–2) pp. 61–83.

Gray, S.J. (1988) Towards a theory of cultural influence on the development of accounting systems internationally. *Abacus* **24**(1) pp. 1–15.

Hail, L., Leuz, C. & Wysocki, P. (2010a) Global accounting convergence and the potential adoption of IFRS by the US (Part I): Conceptual underpinnings and economic analysis. *Accounting Horizons* **24**(3) pp. 355–394.

Hail, L., Leuz, C. & Wysocki, P. (2010b) Global accounting convergence and the potential adoption of IFRS by the US (Part II): Political factors and future scenarios for US accounting standards. *Accounting Horizons* **24**(4), pp. 567–588.

Heidhues, E. & Patel, C. (2011) A critique of Gray's framework on accounting values using Germany as a case study. *Critical Perspectives on Accounting* **22**(3) pp. 273–287.

Henry, E., Lin, S. & Yang, Y. (2009) The European–US 'GAAP Gap': IFRS to US GAAP Form 20-F reconciliations. *Accounting Horizons* **23**(2) pp. 121–150.

IASB (2010) IFRS 2 *Share-based Payment*.

IASB & FASB (2012) *IASB–FASB Update Report to the Financial Stability Board Plenary on Accounting Convergence*, 5 April.

Jaruga, A.A. (1990) Accounting functions in socialist countries. *British Accounting Review* **22**(1) pp. 51–78.

Jermakowicz, E.K. & Gornik-Tomaszewski, S. (2006) Implementing IFRS from the perspective of EU publicly traded companies. *Journal of International Accounting, Auditing and Taxation* **15**(2) pp. 170–196.

King, N., Beattie, A., Cristescu, A–M. & Weetman, P. (2001) Developing accounting and audit in a transition economy: the Romanian experience. *European Accounting Review* **10**(1) pp. 149–171.

Nobes, C.W. (1983) A judgemental international classification of financial reporting practices. *Journal of Business Finance and Accounting* **10**(1) pp. 1–19.

Nobes, C.W. (1998) Towards a general model of the reasons for international differences in financial reporting. *Abacus* **34**(2) pp. 162–187.

Nobes, C. & Parker, R. (2012) *Comparative International Accounting* (12th ed.). Harlow: Pearson.

Smirnova, I.A., Sokolov, J.V. & Emmanuel, C. (1995) Accounting education in Russia today. *European Accounting Review* **4**(4) pp. 833–846.

ACCOUNTING FOR THE ENVIRONMENT

Contents

Learning Objectives

After studying this chapter, you should be able to:

- discuss the implications of accounting for natural resources;
- discuss the content of a typical sustainability report prepared under the Global Reporting Initiative's Sustainability Reporting Guidelines;
- discuss the factors that may motivate corporate social reporting;
- discuss the accounting issues arising from carbon trading.

Introduction

Traditional accounting pays little or no attention to the externalities inflicted on society and on the environment by the commercial activities of profit-making entities. It has been recognised for many years that these externalities exist and that they may even have the potential to bring about death and destruction on a massive scale. Few individuals, if any, can be unaware of the arguments concerning global warming and other threats.

One issue that has not been agreed upon is the question as to whether accounting has a role in addressing the social and ecological threats arising from economic activities. This chapter opens with an account of the dangers associated with attaching monetary values to natural resources. The very act of doing so may be responsible for the attitude that the undermining of employees' rights or the harming of the environment are justified by the wealth being created in the process of doing so.

Sustainability can be defined in a host of different ways. The Global Reporting Initiative, a not-for-profit organisation that seeks to encourage useful and transparent sustainability reporting, has offered a set of guidelines (Global Reporting Initiative, 2011) that give the basis for a sound and comprehensive report that can be audited by an external reviewer.

One problem associated with accounting for sustainability is that most enterprises are responsible for a mixture of costs and benefits and so there may not be a valid basis for identifying entities that create a net cost or benefit. One response to this has been the allocation of allowances for emission of greenhouse gases. Requiring companies to report on the single issue of whether or not they have met their specific limits on emissions enables governments to work towards an overall improvement in performance in that one area. The flexibility that is offered to buy and sell emissions allowances has led to the creation of an active market in surplus allowances and that has created an accounting conundrum in the process.

A Story About a Tree

Hines (1991) wrote a brief but insightful story about her relationship with the rubber tree in her garden. She had considered digging the tree up to prevent its fast-growing roots from damaging her house, but realised that many other plants depended upon the tree for both shade and shelter and that much of her enjoyment of her garden depended upon retaining the tree.

She considered the implications of her dilemma concerning the tree for her understanding of accounting (Hines, 1991):

Nature is excluded from accounting calculations. And how could it be otherwise? All in nature are interdependent: my little rain forest cannot be bounded and separated from the Rubber Tree. It depends on the Rubber Tree. As I do. People are part of nature, aren't they? But accounting, like any language, names, bounds and thus separates.

Hines discussed the implications of attaching a financial value to her tree, so that she might better understand the implications of keeping it for the sake of protecting her garden despite the risk of root damage to her house. She concluded that attaching such a financial valuation would lead to a change of attitude on her part because she would quickly find it difficult to justify keeping the tree on the basis of its notional value when that was compared with the net present value of the plumbing work required to repair the pipes that would be damaged by its roots.

Her paper concludes (Hines, 1991):

It seems to me that the best thing I can do for nature, as a person who is an 'expert' in financial accounting-speak, and thus its limitations, is to speak my love of nature; to call attention to the limitations of the planetary-wide financial accounting language, and to make an issue of refusing to speak of nature in this language of numbers. It seems to me that, if other 'experts' in accounting around the planet were openly to speak out, in all kinds of forums, to all kinds of audiences, about the limitations of accounting, thus demystifying it and reducing its power to entrance people, this would constitute a powerful addition to a too-slowly changing planetary consciousness.

It is in the name of Net Profit, Budget Surplus and Gross National Product that the natural environment in which we all co-exist is being destroyed. Those who speak this language have more social power to influence thinking and actions than they perhaps realise, or utilise.

Elements of Accounting and Nature

This chapter aims to explore the idea that accounting may have a role in making businesses accountable for the damage that they cause to the environment. This potential has been the subject of academic research, and many companies choose to account for their impact on the environment. There is no conscious political agenda beyond that, although it is acknowledged that some readers may already have an interest in green issues.

The discussion of the impact of human activity on the planet is beyond the scope of this text. There is little or no need to defend the argument that manufacturing and travel consume scarce and irreplaceable resources, such as fossil fuels, and also create emissions that are (at least potentially) harmful. The problem with addressing such damage through accounting has been identified by Hines. Financial reporting is bounded by the definitions of the elements of financial statements, primarily assets and liabilities:

• An asset is a resource controlled by the entity as a result of past events and from which future economic benefits are expected to flow to the entity.
• A liability is a present obligation of the entity arising from past events, the settlement of which is expected to result in an outflow from the entity of resources embodying economic benefits.

The first problem is that these definitions depend upon the identification of an entity. The whole point of identifying an accounting entity is to place boundaries that separate the matters that will be accounted for from those that will not. For example, the atmosphere is not a resource controlled by any one entity and so polluting the atmosphere does not impair or consume any assets controlled by the entity. Thus, the pollution is defined as costless.

Love Canal

Tinker's (1985) analysis of the Love Canal story highlights the failure of traditional accounting to recognise social costs. A failed canal project was abandoned, leaving a mile-long trench. A chemical manufacturer, a major employer in the area, purchased the trench and used it to dump waste chemicals. The company claimed that the chemicals were dangerous only if 'touched or swallowed'. Some time later, the company filled in the trench and sold the land to the city, which built houses and a school on the site. Over the following years it became increasingly obvious that the chemical residues that had been left behind were responsible for serious illnesses and the incidence of birth defects. Eventually, the government had to step in and purchase residents' homes to enable them to move away from the area.

Tinker highlights the fact that conventional accounting did not recognise any costs in the manufacturer's financial statements while the trench was being used as a dump. There were some financial penalties, but Tinker pointed out that even those did not necessarily reflect the full cost of the harm that was inflicted on local residents and the final cost to the state in moving the local community and rectifying the site.

Creating a Role for Accounting

The potential role for accounting in corporate social reporting was explored in a groundbreaking book by Gray, Owen and Maunders ('GOM') called *Corporate Social Reporting*, first published in 1987. The authors describe the role of social reporting as:

> the process of communicating the social and environmental effects of organizations' economic actions to particular interest groups within society and to society at large.

GOM acknowledge that the question of social responsibility is, in itself, contested. They identify five positions, shown in Table 15.1.

Table 15.1 GOM's five positions on social responsibility

Position	Features
Pristine capitalists	Hold the extreme view that corporations exist to create wealth for their shareholders and should not incur costs or forgo revenues in order to pursue activities that are not consistent with that goal. Social responsibility amounts to obeying the law.
Expedients	Believe that long-term economic success requires the acceptance of a minimum level of wider social responsibilities. There are conflicting values and rights, and addressing those associated with social responsibility may prevent the imposition of more stringent regulation.
Proponents of the 'social contract'	It can be argued that businesses enjoy a licence to operate and that this licence is granted by society as long as the business acts in such a way as to be deserving of that licence. Basically, that requires the creation of some form of socially desirable output, whether that be jobs, products or some other commodity.

(*continued*)

Table 15.1 (*continued*)

Position	Features
Social ecologists	Argue that business activities have a negative impact on the environment and so they should accept some responsibility for rectifying the damage that they cause. This differs from the position of those describing the social contract in that social ecologists believe that business should wish to act in this way rather than because of the need to demonstrate a net benefit to society.
Socialists	Believe that business is instrumental in concentrating wealth in the hands of the capitalist class. Business should aim to redress the inequalities that have arisen and should work in the interests of a much wider range of stakeholders.

Source: Gray *et al.*, 1987

To an extent, these different views should be viewed as a continuum rather than a sequence of discrete positions. Individuals have to decide for themselves how they view companies' responsibilities. There are, potentially, further points beyond the socialist position. For example, deep ecologists believe that humans have no greater right to exist and prosper than any other species. Ecosystems are so fragile that they should not be tampered with for the sake of creating economic wealth (Gray, Owen & Adams, 1996). While this may be perceived as an extreme view from a political perspective, it is worth noting that Beck's (1992) study of the sociology of risk has achieved mainstream status and has highlighted the fact that the greatest threats to mankind are essentially man-made. Risks arising from natural disasters, though potentially serious in themselves, pale in comparison to the risks associated with nuclear power generation and the worst forms of pollution.

The diverging views on the responsibilities of businesses mean that it is unclear what the role of corporate social reporting (CSR)[1] should be or, indeed, who should be responsible preparing of reports. GOM highlight the potential role of accountants as follows (Gray *et al.*, 1987):

Nevertheless, three things are quite apparent: (a) social reports can be developed without accountants; (b) many ordinary practising accountants are convinced that CSR is none of their business, and yet (c) accounting academics and practitioners continue to exercise a commitment to the area as revealed by the astonishing plethora of CSR argument and research which is found in accounting literature.

This paradox concerning the potential role for accountants was reprised in a paper by Hopwood (2009):

Accounting has already started to be implicated in the consideration of environmental issues and the probability is that its involvement will develop further over the coming years. As greater acknowledgement is given to the role of human agency in the environmental sphere, the need for different approaches to both conceiving and acting upon human and organizational interaction with the environment has started to be recognized, albeit still far too slowly. There are, as a consequence, more signs of an emerging awareness that many aspects of human life are likely to change, even including accounting and other calculative systems. As changes occur in our concepts and focus of accountability for the environment, the demands for different flows of information, accounting and otherwise, are also likely to grow.

One of the most intriguing aspects of this paper is that it was written more than 20 years after the publication of GOM (Gray *et al.*, 1987) and yet it appears that there is still a sense that the accountant's role in CSR is still emerging. The question of whether accountants are best suited to preparing CSR information is a matter of debate. It could be argued that fully appreciating the issues that ought to be accounted for requires a technical understanding of the science in some cases (e.g. the impact of certain emissions) or of the ethics (e.g. health and safety and other employment issues such as child labour). Accountants cannot claim any particular expertise in terms of the technical issues associated with, say, climate change. On the other hand, accountants are skilled at communicating compli-cated ideas and at dealing with the information needs of different stakeholders. Also accountants are highly skilled in the whole area of audit and assurance and are, therefore, able to offer expertise in the verification and certification of external CSR reports.

Corporate Social Reporting in Practice

Companies often offer a considerable amount of information about their approach to social responsibility. For example, Nokia's 2011 sustainability report runs to 137 pages. It covers the company's performance in terms of both its impact on 'people' and on 'the planet'.

Nokia identifies key sustainability topics, but stops short of defining sustainability. Part of the problem with reporting in this area is that there is no universally accepted definition of sustainability. At one level, it might be possible to define the term in relation to consumption versus renewal. For example, it might be argued that ecosystems can cope with a certain amount of consumption. Fishing or logging will not necessarily cause long-term damage unless species are fished to the point of extinction or felled trees are not replaced by replanting. Sustainability can also incorporate much wider values than the capacity of ecosystems to regenerate themselves in the face of consumption or pollution. Human rights, particularly with respect to treating employees with respect and compassion, are also generally viewed as an element of sustainability.

Nokia identified nine 'key sustainability topics' that are classified between people and planet (shown in Table 15.2).

Nokia provides clear statements of intent on each of those issues and goes into considerable detail about the ways in which the company upholds human rights, both as a supplier and as an employer. For example, the company has clear

Table 15.2 Nokia's nine key sustainability topics

People	Planet
Customer satisfaction, privacy and safety	Environmentally leading product range
Economic impact	Green operations and facilities
Improving peoples' lives with mobile technology	Green supply chain and logistics
Labour and social issues in own performance	Take-back and recycling
Social and ethical performance in supply chain	

policies on a host of topics such as anti-corruption and labour rights. Employees at all levels receive formal training on those topics and there are reporting systems in place to ensure compliance by managers.

Nokia publishes several pages of key data to support the claims that it makes for itself. These tables include comparatives for the previous four years and cover a range of issues from greenhouse gas emissions to employee injury rates. Nokia also publishes data about its engagement with members of its supply chain, and so makes itself accountable for the broader implications of its manufacturing processes.

Nokia ensures the credibility of the information in its report in two ways. Firstly, it applies the Sustainability Reporting Guidelines published by the Global Reporting Initiative (2011). Secondly, Nokia has its sustainability report reviewed by the external audit firm that reports on its financial statements, and the auditor's report is published.

Motivations for Sustainability

Measuring the overall impact of an enterprise is complicated. For example, Hopwood, Unerman and Fries (2010) highlight the difficulties associated with measuring the impact of the construction industry. Manufacturing and delivering building materials results in the emission of a considerable quantity of greenhouse gases. These costs will, hopefully, be offset by the social benefits to be derived from the resulting buildings. The net cost or benefit may be further complicated by possibilities such as the destruction of natural habitats or other damage from building on the site. Finally, there will be complications arising from contested issues, such as the perennial question of whether new roads ease congestion and so reduce wastage of fuel and pollution or whether they encourage increased traffic and so exacerbate the problems that they were allegedly aiming to prevent.

Quite apart from the net cost of benefit in terms of sustainability, there is a parallel view that CSR can be motivated by commercial sensitivities. Hopwood et al. (2010) describe the factors that might come into play, shown in Table 15.3.

Hopwood et al. (2010) highlight a number of roles that accounting might have in embedding sustainability into the management process:

- identifying past and potential future social impacts and benefits;
- providing forward-looking information to formulate and implement strategic solutions;

Table 15.3 Possible commercial motivations of corporate social reporting

Commercial motivation	Role of CSR
Winning and retaining customers	Many customers take sustainability into account when making purchasing decisions, regardless of whether they are individual consumers, businesses or governments.
Competitive advantage, innovation and new products	The development of more environmentally friendly products may enable companies to be more competitive thanks to the willingness of consumers to pay a premium for sustainable products.
Attracting, motivating and retaining staff	This is hardly surprising, given that sustainability is often defined partly in terms of employee engagement and the provision of safe and secure working environments.
Managing risk	Certain political and regulatory risks may be reduced by managing the entity in a socially responsible manner.
Driving operational efficiencies and cost reduction	Improving sustainability can encourage waste reduction, which may reduce consumption of energy or materials. It may also reduce the costs of waste disposal and avoid fines or other penalties for failure to comply with the rules for waste management.
Maintaining licence to operate	An entity with a sound reputation for sustainability may find it easier to win contracts or negotiate barriers to expansion, such as obtaining planning permission.
Accessing capital	Many lenders and investors take account of sustainability when evaluating proposals.
Reputation and brand	Sustainable business practices can lead to an enhanced brand impact that can improve relationships with all stakeholders, not just customers. Conversely, failure to behave responsibly can create significant problems.

Source: Hopwood *et al.*, 2010

- support risk management through the identification of sustainability-related risks and opportunities; and
    - giving an account of sustainability policies and practices to third parties.

One consequence of these roles for sustainability is that organisations might wish to claim to be sustainable in order to enjoy the associated financial and commercial advantages. That may create the threat of partial, and therefore misleading, reports that create a misleading impression of managerial motives. For example, Cowper-Smith and de Grosbois (2011) reported inconsistency in the content of airline CSR reports. That lack of consistency hindered comparison.

Sustainability Reporting Guidelines

The Global Reporting Initiative (GRI) has published a set of Sustainability Reporting Guidelines (Global Reporting Initiative, 2011). The guidelines are based around the GRI Reporting Framework:

What to report	**How to report**
Standard disclosures	Principles and guidance
	Protocols

The standard disclosures consist of topics that are material to most organisations and are of interest to most stakeholders. These include the following:

- Strategy and analysis:
    - A statement from the CEO on the relevance of sustainability to the entity, including priorities, targets, etc.
    - A description of the entity's key impacts on sustainability and the associated challenges and opportunities.
- Organisational profile:
    - Information concerning the entity's location, products, size in terms of payroll, revenues and market capitalisation and so on.
- Report parameters:
    - Period covered.
    - Process for determining content, such as materiality and identification of stakeholders.
    - Boundary of the report (in other words, the identification of the economic entity that is being reported upon – Is it the whole of the group? Does it include joint ventures? and so on).

- ○ Data measurement techniques.
- ○ An index should be provided, linking the GRI standard disclosures to the content of the report to ensure that all of the standard disclosures have been provided.
- ○ It should be made clear whether any external assurance has been provided and, if so, the scope and basis of that assurance.
- Governance, commitments and engagement:
  - ○ Details of the overall governance arrangements, such as the composition of the board.
  - ○ Commitments to external initiatives should be described, such as memberships of associations that impose duties with respect to sustainability.
  - ○ The approach taken to stakeholder engagement, including the identification of the stakeholders who are engaged by the entity and the basis upon which each is engaged.
- Management approach and performance indicators:
  - ○ This section is organized by economic, environmental, and social categories.
  - ○ Each category includes a disclosure on management approach (headed 'Management Approach') and a corresponding set of core and additional performance indicators.
  - ○ The guidelines provide detailed guidance on the disclosures required under each of these headings.

The discussion of principles and guidance is intended to ensure transparency in reporting. To that end, there are principles for determining the content of the report and also the manner in which the disclosures should be presented.

The principles for determining content are:

- **Materiality:** The definition of materiality mirrors that for financial reporting. The report should reflect the entity's significant economic, environmental and social impacts. It should also disclose any information that would substantively influence the assessments and decisions of stakeholders.
- **Stakeholder inclusiveness:** The report should identify the stakeholders and should explain how their 'reasonable' expectations and interests have been met. Stakeholders should include those who can reasonably be expected to be affected by the entity's activities and also those who have the ability to affect the implementation of strategies.
- **Sustainability context:** The context includes matters such as the entity's impacts on regional ecosystems and the like; or employment information such as wage levels expressed in relation to national averages in the countries where it operates.

• **Completeness:** Information should be complete in terms of its coverage of material topics and indicators, and the report's boundary should be sufficiently inclusive to reflect the entity's significant economic, environmental, and social impacts.

The principles for determining quality are:

• **Balance:** The report should cover both positive and negative aspects in order to ensure a balanced assessment.
• **Comparability:** Information should be presented in a consistent manner so that disclosures can be compared with those of previous periods and also those of other organisations.
• **Accuracy:** In this context, the information has to be 'sufficiently' accurate. Some disclosures will require higher levels of accuracy than others.
• **Timeliness:** The report should be published on a regular schedule and should be made available in time for stakeholders to make informed decisions.
• **Clarity:** The information in the report should be clear and accessible to stakeholders.
• **Reliability:** The information that is disclosed should be verifiable.

The protocols provide definitions, compilation guidance and other information to assist report preparers and to ensure consistency in the interpretation of the performance indicators.

There is no specific requirement for an entity to apply the GRI Sustainability Reporting Guidelines, but it is to be hoped that many will choose to do so in order to demonstrate their commitment to meaningful sustainability reporting. The resulting reports should be far more credible if they have been prepared in accordance with the guidelines and it will be far easier for external reviewers to express an opinion on the report if they can compare it with a codified statement that sets out the form and content that define good practice.

The question of whether sustainability reports actually encourage genuine sustainable behaviour was discussed by Gray (2006). Gray quotes the definition of sustainable development offered by the United Nations World Commission on Environment and Development:

[Sustainable development] meets the needs of the present without compromising the ability of future generations to meet their own needs.

Gray (2006) argues that economic activity has already passed the point at which the planet's resources are being depleted beyond the point at which they might be able to renew or regenerate themselves, and that the global analysis of inequality demonstrates a lack of the social justice that lies at the heart of sustainability. Gray argues that sustainability reports miss the point, and quotes from BP's 2004 sustainability report (acknowledging that company's efforts to raise awareness of carbon footprinting):

> Thus does the concept of sustainability involve no apparent conflicts; it consists almost entirely of the company doing nothing particular about the planet or society beyond what might be thought of as best business practice. Phrases such as these succeed in switching our concern away from a business operating within the parameters of a sustained environment to the sustaining of the business assuming that the planet and society are sound . . . How the aspired-to utopia of a supportive environment might be reached in the face of a dying planet and increasing social injustice is not only not addressed but is actually linguistically excluded by the carefully chosen definition.

Carbon Trading

Sustainability reporting is by no means the only form that CSR can take. One alternative is the provision of more specific information concerning the emissions of greenhouse gases, most notably carbon dioxide. There is significant scientific evidence that such emissions have a major role to play in global climate change.

Greenhouse gases are released by a variety of natural processes and their concentrations fluctuate naturally. There is evidence that these natural cycles are linked to climate changes that have occurred over the millennia. The greater the concentration of those gases in the atmosphere, the greater the heat absorbed from the sun's rays and the hotter the mean temperature across the planet.

Since the Industrial Revolution, mankind has massively increased the quantity of greenhouse gas emissions, most notably through the combustion of fossil fuels. That has led to a massive increase in the concentration of greenhouse gases in the atmosphere and that appears to have caused an increase in mean temperatures. The overall effects of these changes are not necessarily fully understood, but there are arguments that global warming will accelerate and cause the destruction of entire ecosystems.[2]

Negotiations sponsored by the United Nations Framework Convention on Climate Change culminated in the Kyoto Protocol, which committed the major industrialised countries to reducing their carbon emissions. The targets for the overall reduction are complicated for a host of reasons; in particular, it can be argued that emissions are the result of both manufacturing and consumption. An increase in consumption of consumer goods in the West may lead to an increase in manufacturing activity in countries such as China, where many of those goods are created.

Compliance with the Kyoto Protocol is the responsibility of the governments who agreed to reduce emissions. Meeting these commitments requires changes to the behaviour of both consumers and companies. Practical steps for bringing about change include imposing financial costs on the emissions.

Carbon pricing arises from the process of setting allowances for emissions, with allowances invariably set so that emissions reduce. Under these circumstances, it is deemed acceptable for entities to purchase emission rights from other entities, thus encouraging greater flexibility and, perhaps, greater economic efficiency. Those who can reduce their emissions at the lowest cost are able to free up surpluses from their allowances, which can then be sold on to those who find compliance more difficult or expensive. For example, EU member states have imposed allowances upon companies operating within energy-intensive industries, such as electricity generation and steel manufacturing. Those companies are free to trade their allowances should they wish to do so.

Accounting for Carbon Trading

The EU scheme requires regulated companies to provide an annual return that discloses their emissions, their allowance and any extra allowances that they have purchased. There are financial penalties for breaching the total of allowances granted and bought in allowances, and the shortfall in extra allowance must also be purchased retrospectively, so that companies cannot choose to carry on as before and regard the penalty as a cost of doing business.

The predicted market mechanisms have quickly established themselves (see, for example, MacKenzie, 2009). It is not entirely clear whether the imposition of allowances has led to the reported reductions in emissions or whether that has been a partial result of economic downturns or changes that would have occurred in any case with the introduction of cheaper processes that have the side effect of being more environmentally friendly.

The accounting treatment of these emissions rights has been a rather fraught issue that has not been satisfactorily resolved as at the time of writing. The IASB's International Financial Reporting Interpretations Committee (IFRIC) published a draft interpretation, IFRIC 3 *Emission Rights*, in 2004 (IASB, 2004). The document was withdrawn in 2005 without replacement.

The reasons for this difficulty are due to the fundamentals of accounting for intangible non-current assets. IFRIC 3 required that the allowances be accounted for as intangible assets from the date on which they were granted. The fair values of those assets could be accounted for on the same basis as any other intangible accounted for under IAS 38 *Intangible Assets* (IASB, 2009), with the fair value of the asset being restated at the reporting date to reflect changing fair values. Unfortunately, gains on revaluation were taken to a revaluation reserve rather than the statement of profit or loss. The liabilities arising from the emissions were accounted for under the requirements of IAS 37 *Provisions, Contingent Liabilities and Contingent Assets* (IASB, 1998) with the liability being restated at fair value and movements going to the statement of profit or loss. Market forces were likely to push up the fair values of both assets and liabilities simultaneously, but the increases would not offset one another in the statement of profit or loss, and so IFRIC 3 led to allegations that it was making reported profits more volatile. (For a fuller discussion of this, see Cook, 2009.) The interpretation was withdrawn in 2005, leaving no clear standard in place for dealing with the balances arising from emissions allowances.

Summary

Businesses create wealth for their shareholders and their employees and they create valuable goods and services that benefit other stakeholders. They also create externalities in the form of social inequalities and harmful emissions. This chapter explored some of the issues arising from those externalities and, in particular, whether accountants have a role to play in their resolution.

The question of whether attaching monetary values to social and environmental costs and benefits does more harm than good is an intriguing one. It could be argued that attaching a notional cost to the value of, say, a serious industrial accident can lead to some very dangerous thinking about the extent to which such accidents should be tolerated when prevention is possible – albeit at a price.

There is guidance available to assist in the compilation and verification of sustainability reports. It may be open to debate as to whether accountants are best equipped to engage in this process. It might be argued that accountants have skills as communicators and auditors that make them the ideal people to lead in this process.

The freedom to buy and sell the rights to emit greenhouse gases has led to the creation of a significant and active secondary market. Unfortunately, the associated accounting issues have been rather difficult to resolve. Paradoxically, this – the one aspect of this chapter that demands a clear accounting argument – is the one topic that has not been open to resolution using accounting theory.

Tutorial Questions

Question 1

Download a sustainability report and be prepared to discuss the costs and benefits arising from that company's activities.

Did the company bring about a net cost or benefit from its activities?

Question 2

Discuss the implications for sustainability reporting of the growing tendency to outsource manufacturing to third-party factories located in developing countries.

Question 3

An airline is preparing a sustainability report and has decided to describe the reduction in emissions arising from the introduction of a more fuel-efficient aircraft that was purchased because it had lower running costs. Discuss the assertion that the airline should not claim that reduction as evidence of corporate social responsibility because it was motivated by increased profits.

Question 4

Discuss the implications for sustainability reporting of a car manufacturer introducing a hybrid vehicle that is powered by a combination of an electric motor when driving at slow speeds around town and a petrol engine for longer journeys. The car uses slightly more petrol, on average, than many small petrol-only cars.

Question 5

Discuss the assertion that sustainability reporting is a significant fee-earning opportunity for accountants.

There are no additional questions with answers in this chapter.

Endnotes

1. To avoid (or perhaps create) confusion, the abbreviation CSR is also used to refer to corporate social responsibility. This chapter focuses on reporting issues, and reports are one aspect of the way in which corporate social responsibility is discharged, so the distinction between the two uses of CSR is not as important as it could be in other contexts.

2. A detailed discussion of the scientific evidence underlying these theoretical arguments lies beyond the scope of this text. For the purpose of this chapter, it is sufficient that we accept that mankind is responsible for higher concentrations of greenhouse gases than have ever been created by natural processes and that this may be sufficient to bring about catastrophic climate changes.

References

Beck, U. (1992) *Risk Society – Towards a new modernity*. London: Sage.

Cook, A. (2009) Emission rights: From costless activity to market operations. *Accounting, Organizations and Society* **34**(3) pp. 456–468.

Cowper-Smith, A. & de Grosbois, D. (2011) The adoption of corporate social responsibility practices in the airline industry. *Journal of Sustainable Tourism* **19**(1) pp. 59–77.

Global Reporting Initiative (2011) *Sustainability Reporting Guidelines*. Version 3.1. Amsterdam: Global Reporting Initiative.

Gray, R. (2006) Does sustainability reporting improve corporate behaviour? Wrong question? Right time? *Accounting and Business Research* **36**(supplement) pp. 65–88.

Gray, R., Owen, D. & Adams, C. (1996) *Accounting and Accountability*. London: Financial Times/Prentice Hall.

Gray, R., Owen, D. & Maunders, K. (1987) *Corporate Social Reporting – Accounting and accountability*. Hemel Hempstead: Prentice Hall.

Hines, R. (1991) On valuing nature. *Accounting, Auditing & Accountability Journal* **4**(3) pp. 27–29.

Hopwood, A. (2009) Accounting and the environment. *Accounting, Organizations and Society* **34**(3–4) pp. 433–439.

Hopwood, A., Unerman, J. & Fries, J. (2010) Introduction to the accounting for sustainability case studies. In A. Hopwood, J. Unerman and J. Fries, *Accounting for Sustainability*. London: Earthscan.

IASB (1998) IAS 37 *Provisions, Contingent Liabilities and Contingent Assets*.

IASB (2004) IFRIC 3 *Emission Rights*.

IASB (2009) IAS 38 *Intangible Assets*.

MacKenzie, D. (2009) Making things the same: Gases, emission rights and the politics of carbon markets. *Accounting, Organizations and Society* **34**(3) pp. 440–455.

Tinker, T. (1985) *Paper Prophets*, Ch. 1. Frederick, MD: Beard Books.

WRITING A DISSERTATION

Contents

Learning Objectives

After studying this chapter, you should be able to:

- discuss the process of developing a dissertation topic and carrying out the work;
- manage the relationship with the dissertation supervisor;
- describe the structure of a typical dissertation.

Introduction

The dissertation is often an important element of the final assessment of a degree.

With the correct approach, it is possible to manage the writing and submission of a dissertation to get the best possible mark. There is no substitute for hard work, but that time and effort can be directed efficiently to obtain the best possible mark.

What is a Dissertation?

The precise rules concerning the form and content of a dissertation vary from course to course and so you will have to be careful not to confuse any advice offered in this chapter with the formal requirements against which you are going to be assessed. There are, however, some broad principles that can be applied to virtually any programme's requirements.

A dissertation is basically the written output from a research project that has been undertaken as an independent piece of work by a student. Dissertations are normally written in the final year of a degree programme. Writing a dissertation develops academic and research skills that could be of value to anybody who is interested in studying for a higher degree. Dissertations also develop more practical skills, such as the ability to manage a complex project and the ability to work to a deadline.

The form and content of dissertations vary tremendously between degrees at different universities. Nothing that is said in this chapter should be taken as an instruction to deviate from any formal or informal guidance given in a specific course. The advice that is provided here is based on the authors' experiences of supervising, marking and externally examining dissertations at a number of institutions, but every department and every university is different.

Dissertations are important because they tend to be very heavily weighted in two ways. That may be in the arithmetical sense of the dissertation mark being quite a substantial proportion of the final mark. It may also be in the sense that the examination board will often pay close attention to a dissertation mark in the case of a borderline student. If a student narrowly fails to get a particular class of degree, exam boards often ask whether the dissertation is strong enough to justify an adjustment. The fact that the dissertation is an individual piece of work means that it gives a deeper insight into the qualities displayed by the student and so it is a little more persuasive than a good mark in a taught class.

Dissertation Supervisors

The following discussion is one that will have to be expressed in the most general terms. Different universities and colleges have their own ideas about the amount of support that students are entitled to expect from their supervisors. Furthermore, individual supervisors often have their own ideas about what they are prepared to do in support of the students for whom they are responsible.

It is important to make the maximum possible use of the supervisor's support. Students usually find the process of writing a dissertation fairly challenging and they tend to require a fair amount of assistance in getting started. A supervisor should be able to reduce the risk of costly mistakes. For example, students often have good ideas that would be interesting studies but that would also prove impractical because they require access to information that, in the supervisor's experience, will be difficult to obtain.

You should get in touch with your supervisor at the first opportunity. Ideally, you will have thought about your topic and will have had some ideas about how best to study it. The first meeting will often involve discussing two or three possible areas of mutual interest and then you will be left on your own to explore the more promising areas. It is probably not a good idea to invest too much time and effort in an idea before that initial meeting in case your idea is one that is interesting but impractical – part of the supervisor's job is to point this out before significant amounts of time have been wasted.

It is important to agree a strategy for working with your supervisor. The dissertation is supposed to be an independent study and the supervisor is supposed to offer support and supervision rather than act as project manager. That said, the supervisor will not wish to be associated with a disaster that obtains a poor mark. It is in the interests of both the student and the supervisor to stay in touch so that the student can make the best possible use of any advice that can be offered.

Some departments have quite specific rules about the number of meetings that can be had with a supervisor, to avoid the common complaint that some students have an unfair advantage because their supervisors are more helpful than others. In that case, it is important to be clear about how to make the best use of the limited contact. If there are, say, five meetings available, then it is a good idea to schedule those for sensible points in the process. Otherwise, the tendency is for students to be reluctant to use their limited opportunities to meet and the supervisor loses track of progress. In other departments, it is left to the common sense of both parties to agree a sensible approach to staying in touch and there are no formal limits on contact.

It is important to remember that it is perfectly reasonable to ask for a supervisor to provide advice and feedback. That must always be done in a sensible and realistic manner. For example, there is very little point in submitting a full draft shortly before the deadline (when the supervisor will possibly be swamped with similar requests from other students) and expecting helpful feedback. Indeed, the value of feedback can sometimes diminish when the deadline is approaching because there is very little point in suggesting major changes if there is little time left in which to make them.

The supervisor will always be in a slightly delicate position because supervisors are often required to mark dissertations after they have been submitted. That can create a slight conflict of interest in dealing with students. The key is for both parties to be professional in their dealings with one another. Typically, the university will require a second member of staff to act as a second marker. The supervisor and the second marker will usually mark the dissertation independently and then agree a mark. Any disagreement will result in a third marker being asked for a view, or the external examiner will be asked to make a final decision on the mark.

The supervisor's role as an examiner means that it is a little unfair to ask for any assurances about the mark that a draft is likely to receive. The supervisor has to remain objective about the final mark, particularly given the need to agree a grade with a colleague and with the external examiner.

The Structure of a Dissertation

Broadly speaking, a dissertation comprises the following chapters:

- Introduction
- Method (and possibly methodology)
- Literature review
- Contribution/analysis/study
- Conclusion.

Each element will be discussed below, in a more logical sequence than their ordering within the dissertation.

Literature Review

In academic circles, 'literature' is the body of refereed papers that has been written in a particular area of study. The aim of any research project, whether it is a dissertation, a PhD thesis or a paper for publication in an academic journal, is to contribute to an existing body of literature. The starting point is, therefore, to set out the current state of knowledge on that topic so that the new findings can be shown in their proper context.

The literature that is selected will not necessarily be about the topic itself. For example, a dissertation that is about different approaches to accounting for depreciation might be based on a literature about accounting choice; or it could focus on a particular social theory that might be used to shed some light on the whole question of the impact of accounting on stakeholders. The supervisor should be able to suggest the direction that the literature review should take.

It is difficult to sum up what a good literature review looks like, but a poor one consists of a brief summary of each of the papers in the dissertation bibliography. The problem with that is that there is no real contribution; the papers probably came with perfectly clear summaries in their introductions and conclusions and so there is little point in restating those without adding some value.

A better approach might be to write about the meanings that can be drawn from the papers when they are taken together as a body of knowledge. For example, it might be possible to state that a particular accounting issue has been explored by means of questionnaires and by analysing comments in response to exposure drafts. A number of references should be stated after each type of study described to prove that these studies exist. Then it could be developed by stating what each style of research tells us. So, questionnaire-based studies might reveal a number of general findings that can be brought out and summarised, with two or three references after each point being made.

The best way to see how this effect can be achieved is to look at the section of any academic paper. A dissertation is basically a research project that should result in a report that will look very much like an academic paper.

Generally, the literature review will focus almost exclusively on academic papers. Your dissertation might draw upon other materials such as newspaper and magazine articles or web pages, but those are not literature.

Apart from pulling together the different arguments and findings, your literature review should offer some evaluation of the prior literature. It is perfectly acceptable to highlight the strengths and weaknesses of different styles of research. The objective is to leave the way open to your making a contribution to prior literature. Ideally, that will be supported by a summary of papers that use a similar method that has been evaluated in the literature review and found to have some value. The next step is to argue that a further study using that approach will be useful.

Contribution/Analysis/Study

An academic paper could involve the work of two or three academic authors, who have been supported by research assistants and funded by some third party who sponsors research. Dissertations can often be of publishable quality, but they need not reach that standard in order to attract a good mark.

The selection of a topic is a matter for discussion with your supervisor, although your own interests should also be taken into account. Some departments provide lists of topics that have been suggested by the teaching staff, and that may simplify matters. Certainly, it means that there is at least one person in the department who considers the study to be a practical proposition. If the compilation of such a list is not part of departmental policy then you may find that your supervisor is keen to discuss your ideas but will not provide anything more than broad guidance. It can be argued that it is the student's responsibility to identify the topic and that is part of the learning activity.

The key to writing the body of the dissertation is to ensure that it follows on from the literature review. Ideally, the literature review should set the scene by pulling together the existing state of knowledge according to the literature and should draw a conclusion to the effect that there is a need for further study in a particular area. The dissertation should then go on to provide such a study. There is no need to overdo that link, but it should be possible for the examiner to see that the dissertation is based upon prior literature.

One trick is to consider writing both the literature review and the analysis chapter in parallel. Initially, it will be necessary to focus on the literature review, but there may be times when it would be worth stopping to investigate the practicalities of a particular project. For example, there may be some speculative ideas that might be worth investigating at an early stage in order to decide whether they are practical possibilities. If a dissertation hinges on the availability of accessible data or the willingness of potential interviewees to make some time available then that should be investigated and followed up if necessary. Knowing that the data are not available or that the interviewee will not cooperate means that the idea will have to be changed to something that is more practical, and that will always be far easier at the early stages.

Having some tentative findings based on the early analysis of material may make it easier to target further readings, so the integration can be developed.

Your supervisor should be able to help you avoid any disasters at this stage. Students often feel that they can take it for granted that all of the research evidence that they require will be available to them. In many cases, that is a somewhat naïve assumption. For example, many students have interesting ideas that would be worth exploring as topics, but that will only be practical if they have the support of senior members of the accountancy profession. That support may be given if there is a personal link.[1] It is not unheard of for accountancy undergraduates to have social contacts that include qualified accountants and there is nothing inherently wrong about asking them to help. It is also possible that a final year student will have completed an internship within a firm of accountants and the firm may be willing to assist with the dissertation.

Your final mark is probably far more dependent upon the quality of the analysis and the link back to the research than upon the difficulty associated with gathering the data. For argument's sake, a well written analysis of the attitudes of fellow students towards a career in accountancy or of the manner in which language has been used in a company's annual report (both of which would be possible topics that did not require any external support) could attract a high mark if the literature review was to the point and indicated that the study had some merit. Conversely, a dissertation that drew weak conclusions based on high-quality data that had been gathered at considerable cost in terms of time and effort or ingenuity may not be that well received by the examiners.

There are many issues that can be explored using publicly available information. For example, accounting standard-setters frequently put comments received about draft regulations on their websites. That makes it possible to download a consider-able amount of material and to investigate, say, the direction that lobbying took on the draft standard. Respondents can be grouped into different categories and so the analysis can be fairly sophisticated.

Inventive topics can often be designed so that there is no risk whatsoever that the dissertation will come to a halt because of a lack of data or access. For example, a former colleague once supervised a dissertation in which the student had recorded the television news one evening and then analysed the programme from beginning to end, looking for instances where accounting (in its broadest sense) was visible in the day-to-day discussion of current events. There was no overt mention of financial statements in the entire bulletin, but there were reports about the economy and its effects on the employment market, the performance of the public sector health service (which raised questions about the measurement of that performance and the communication of that measure-ment) and so on. The final dissertation was of a very high quality and it received a high mark. It worked well because the supervisor was able to suggest some relevant readings as the basis for the literature review and the student was bright enough to make the links between those papers and the news stories, but the fact that the topic was self-contained meant that there was no need to rely on external support.

Method and Methodology

At some point in your dissertation you should describe the methods that have been used and link those to the quality and relevance of the findings. The point of this is to offer the ability to reflect on what the dissertation is capable of achieving. This often highlights shortcomings in the thought process.

For example, students often gather information from interested parties using questionnaires and interviews. Students often regard these as equivalents, but they are anything but. Interviews are an excellent way to explore the interviewee's responses to a particular set of questions on a particular issue. Interviewing three audit partners from a local office will provide insights that may not necessarily be generalisable to other partners in the same office, never mind the firm as a whole or all partners in all firms. That does not alter the fact that the interviewees expressed some thoughts in the context of structured interviews where they could seek clarification of any ambiguities and could be asked to explain or expand upon any interesting responses. Questionnaires will generally be far more rigidly structured and will generally be completed by a relatively large number of respondents. There is generally an expectation that questionnaire-based evidence will be viewed as representative of the population that has been surveyed and so factors such as non-response bias start to become quite important.

Thinking about method also raises questions about the manner in which assertions are supported. For example, if two sets of results are being compared then it is important to offer some statistical support for the claim that two averages are the same or different. That may require some discussion concerning the statistical tests that are appropriate. A study that links accounting numbers to share price performance may require the data to be analysed using advanced statistical techniques that require a host of assumptions that have to be tested for before the test can be applied. A study that analyses social data may be better conducted using non-parametric statistics that are inherently categorical rather than quantitative. For example, it is possible to compare the responses of first year students with those of third year students to a question that asks for the selection of an answer from a five-point scale (e.g. ranging from strongly disagree to strongly agree).

The discussion of the method may have to be revisited in the light of the results. For example, there is very little point in conducting a statistical analysis if there are very few responses. One of the authors second-marked a dissertation where the student had received only two responses to a very detailed questionnaire sent to a large number of audit partners. Rather than analyse each response in some detail, the student calculated 'average' responses and peppered his dissertation with comments such as '50% of respondents stated that ...', rather than being open and stating that the two respondents disagreed on a point, one saying X and the other saying Y.

It is worth considering the other limitations that methods can have. For example, if you download the comments on a draft IFRS then you can draw conclusions about what the authors of those comments said, but you may have to be careful when interpreting their arguments. For example, a respondent may argue against a draft standard by voicing technical concerns about its validity. The motivation behind the comment may be that the proposed standard will have a negative impact on reported profit, but it is unlikely that a respondent will ever make that comment in public. If the dissertation is concerned with what respondents *say* then the comments can be analysed without fear. If the analysis is concerned with what the respondents *mean* then it may be necessary to gather further evidence (or to revise the objective to focus on the content of letters of comment).

Finally, a quick word about methodology. Some research-led universities require an explicit comment about both method and methodology. Methodology is a higher level, more abstract statement concerning the approach that is being taken to the dissertation. Methodology is the coming together of *epistemology* (which is the question of how knowledge or understanding comes into being) and *ontology* (which is the question of how something can be said to be real or to exist).

If your supervisor expects you to make a formal statement concerning methodology then that will be made clear to you and you will be advised on how to analyse the epistemological and ontological positions that you are taking.

If you are not expected to discuss methodology then please take care not to confuse the two terms. Methodology is far more abstract than method. Anything that can be described simply, such as a statistical analysis or a survey, is a method.

Introduction and Conclusion

Your dissertation should begin with an introduction and end with a conclusion. These cannot be written until the rest of the dissertation has been completed and it is possible to reflect on the work that has been done and the contribution that it has made.

Both the introduction and conclusion are very important and they are typically under-developed. Many students appear to be overcome with false modesty when writing these chapters.

It is worth studying the introduction and conclusion of a typical published paper for clues as to what constitutes best practice.

The introduction sets out the objective of the dissertation and explains why that objective is important. The objective that is to be described is the one that is implied by the final version of the dissertation, not the intention at the start of the project. It is the nature of research projects that they tend to get adapted as time passes, both in dealing with problems and in pursuing fresh ideas that arise during the study. The primary purpose of the introduction is to engage the reader (who is also likely to be an examiner or marker) by explaining why the idea was worth pursuing. That may involve referring to press coverage, material in business magazines or ideas from academic literature.

The introduction can set out the basics of the methods used, the literature surveyed and the findings. It is a common mistake that a dissertation should be structured like a detective story, with the reader being kept in suspense until the very end. It is far more important to put the reader in a positive frame of mind by making it clear from the outset that the dissertation has a clear objective and that it achieves its stated objectives in a valid and coherent manner.

The conclusion is intended to provide the reader with confirmation that the dissertation has served some useful purpose. The focus is on the findings and their contribution to prior knowledge. This is an opportunity to reflect on the project and to highlight its value. From an academic point of view, the ability to provide a meaningful reflection is further evidence of understanding and competence. It builds upon the literature review and the analysis of the topic, and it provides a capstone.

The tone of the conclusion is a tricky balancing act. As has been mentioned, students are often overcome with a (possibly false) modesty and they often understate the point of the dissertation. That is better than the other extreme, in which the student claims to have conducted groundbreaking research of the highest order and made the world a better place in the process. Neither extreme is an adequate reflection and both should be avoided.

The conclusion should start from the basis that the objective was clearly specified in the introduction (and restated briefly at the beginning of the conclusion) and that the objective was achieved. In the process, the dissertation was a valuable learning activity for the student and has provided the reader with some insights that would not otherwise have been available. It is sufficient, for example, to state that a particular accounting issue has been explored through a case study that confirmed prior findings. The results will not change the direction of future research, but they have confirmed previous knowledge.

Sometimes students feel that they must spell out the limitations of their research. In a sense, that can be counter-productive if the limitations are expressed too forcibly. Nobody wishes to read a dissertation from beginning to end and then be told that the findings were worthless because the data were inadequate. The introduction and conclusion are supposed to be positive statements that support the body of the dissertation. Rather than list shortcomings, it may be possible to offer suggestions for further research. That could then contribute to the notion that the conclusion is a reflection. If, for argument's sake, the dissertation was based on a very small sample, then it would be possible to offer some conjecture on the benefits that might be obtained in the future if larger data sets become available.

Deadlines

Everything takes far longer than anticipated and that applies to dissertations too. The students who set out at the beginning of the year to write their dissertations in record time usually manage to complete a week or two before the final date without too much stress. The students who plan to start late and make up time as the deadline approaches usually end up suffering sleepless nights.

Deadlines are normally enforced with penalties for late submission. Those penalties are often relaxed in extreme cases of ill health, but only if they are relevant. For example, having a severe cold two weeks before the deadline may not be accepted as a reason to accept a late submission.

Most academics have anecdotes about problems with computers. It makes no sense whatsoever to have only a single copy of a vital file or folder, particularly if that is then stored on a memory stick that could be lost or damaged. It is not expensive to keep a secure copy on a separate machine or even on a web-based storage file that can be accessed in the event of a problem.

Similarly, there is very little likelihood that a deadline will be extended because of poor planning. If a dissertation requires the assistance of third parties then make sure that, say, interviews are scheduled well in advance. The deadline is unlikely to be extended because an interviewee was approached late and could not find a suitable time before the deadline.

It is also important not to get behind because of the pressures of other classes. The final year of a degree is often a busy time and students often need to make time between classes and essays to write their dissertations. It is very unlikely that a deadline will be relaxed because of pressure of other academic work.

Summary

The dissertation is an important part of the final year of many degree courses. It is important to understand the process of choosing a topic, reviewing the literature, analysing the issue and writing up the results.

With the right approach, the dissertation can become an enjoyable challenge. Many students go into their final year with a feeling of some apprehension about their dissertation and then find that the reality is far less stressful than the expectation.

It is possible to enjoy writing a dissertation. The only two secrets are to work closely with the supervisor and to schedule as much time as possible to work steadily throughout the year.

Endnote

1. One of the authors of this text once supervised a fascinating dissertation written by the niece of a very prominent industrialist, who was able to arrange for her to interview the finance director of the quoted company that he had founded and the partner in charge of the company's external audit.

Appendix: Answers to End-of-Chapter Questions

Chapter 3

Question 1

If it is assumed that the tax law is set by a democratically elected government then it is reasonable to assume that all citizens (including corporate citizens) are expected to pay a fair amount of tax. The cost of tax is essentially a contribution towards public spending.

It is realistic to argue that tax accountants have an important role to play in ensuring that those with complicated tax affairs pay the correct amount of tax, and no more. However, it could be argued that seeking out and exploiting loopholes in tax law simply means that wealthy individuals escape their responsibilities. That means either that public services may be underfunded or that other taxpayers will have to pay more.

On balance, there are aspects to tax planning that are within the spirit of the law. For example, advising the client to bring forward or delay the timing of transactions that would occur anyway is an acceptable way to manage the client's tax liability, as is taking tax into account when advising on the manner in which the project should be funded. It could be argued that a wholly artificial scheme that is designed to do nothing other than lead to an underpayment of tax is immoral.

Question 2

The accountant has a positive duty to the client to prevent the overpayment of tax. As discussed in the chapter, it could be argued that there is a limit to the extent to which a positive duty can impact upon the accountant's responsibilities. It is certainly not the accountant's formal responsibility to decide on the principle of whether a profit-making entity should pay tax or the effective rate at which that tax should be charged. That is a matter for an elected government.

The accountant has a negative duty to avoid breaching the letter of the law. It may also be that the professional status granted by society imposes a duty to obey the spirit of the law. It could be argued that the negative duty extends to ensuring that the client pays an amount that has been determined as fair by the elected government.

It might be argued that the accountant would be in breach of any contract that stated that the firm would minimise the company's tax liability if it overlooked an opportunity to do so. That said, the accountant should not be making contractual commitments to assist their clients to underpay tax.

Question 3

This is an open ended question that has two basic lines of argument.

It could be argued that moral development might be a significant element of the socialisation of its staff. In other words, an employee whose moral development is significantly different from the firm's norms might feel uncomfortable and might not be an ideal appointment. Given that moral development deals with the response to moral dilemmas, that member of staff could take a different view to any contentious issues and could prove disruptive.

The counter-argument is that using the DIT instrument to select staff will lead to the reinforcement of those norms. They will cost the firm the opportunity to have staff who might approach problems from a different direction and so the potential benefits from rethinking established norms may be lost. It may be, for example, that an intake of staff who operate at a more principled level may stimulate some fresh debates about the firm's role and its approach to professional work and the associated responsibilities.

Question 4

The basic issue here is whether the partner's independence could be compromised. The gift itself is unlikely to have any intrinsic value and will have cost very little to purchase. It is impossible to imagine that the shareholders or any other stakeholders would feel threatened by the fact that the audit partner accepted such a gift.

It is perfectly acceptable for auditors and their clients to have an amicable working relationship. Modest and proportionate entertaining, such as working lunches and even small 'token' gifts, are acceptable.

Chapter 4

Question 1

	Unadjusted figures	Adjusted figures
Return on capital employed	\$100m/(\$400m + \$250m) = 15%	\$102m/(\$400m + \$310m) = 14%
Gearing	\$250m/(\$400m + \$250m) = 38%	\$310m/(\$400m + \$310m) = 44%

The adjusted figures show a slight decrease in return on capital employed and a fairly significant increase in terms of gearing. In other words, the unadjusted figures make the company appear more profitable than it really is, as well as less risky.

Question 2

There is no definitive answer to this question.

Question 3

There is no definitive answer to this question.

Chapter 5

Question 1

There is no definitive answer to this question.

Question 2

There is no definitive answer to this question.

Question 3

Year ended 31 December 20X0
1000 − 86 − 125 = 789 employees are expected to be eligible.
   The fair value of the rights = 789 × \$11.00 × 1000 = \$8 679 000.

One third of the vesting period has passed, so to the liability to be recognised = $8 679 000 × 1/3 = $2 893 000.

Debit Staff costs	$2 839 000	
	Credit Provision for Share appreciation rights	$2 839 000

Year ended 31 December 20X1

1000 − 86 − 53 − 55 = 806 employees are expected to be eligible.
The fair value of the rights = 806 × $13.00 × 1000 = $10 478 000.
Two thirds of the vesting period has passed, so to the cost to be recognised = $10 478 000 × 2/3 = $6 985 333.

Debit Staff costs	$4 146 333	
	Credit Provision for Share appreciation rights	$4 146 333

Year ended 31 December 20X2

1000 − 86 − 53 − 48 = 813 employees were finally eligible.
The fair value of the rights = 813 × $14.50 × 1000 = $11 788 500.
The liability as at 31 December 20X3 was $11 788 500.

Debit Staff costs	$4 803 167	
	Credit Provision for Share appreciation rights	$4 803 167

If the rights were to be settled in equity rather than cash then the fair value as at the grant date would have been used throughout, instead of updating the figures for year end prices on an annual basis. The credits in the journals would have gone to an equity account rather than a liability account.

Chapter 6

Question 1

	€m
Present value of plan obligation at 1 January 20X7	650.0
Interest cost	50.7
Current service cost	124.0

Benefits paid	(128.0)
Actuarial (gain)/loss on obligation (balancing figure)	33.3
Present value of plan obligation at 31 December 20X5	730.0

	€m
Fair value of assets at 1 January 20X7	635.0
Expected return on plan assets	73.0
Contributions received	70.0
Benefits paid	(128.0)
Actuarial gain/(loss) on obligation (balancing figure)	(5.0)
Fair value of assets at 31 December 20X7	645.0

Question 2

	20X3 $m	20X4 $m	20X5 $m
Present value of plan obligation at start of year	1.20	1.07	1.01
Interest cost	0.10	0.10	0.09
Current service cost	0.14	0.12	0.11
Benefits paid	(0.51)	(0.50)	(0.49)
Actuarial (gain)/loss on obligation (balancing figure)	0.14	0.22	0.26
Present value of plan obligation at year end	1.07	1.01	0.98

	$m	$m	$m
Fair value of assets at start of year	1.10	0.95	1.20
Expected return on plan assets	0.11	0.10	0.12
Contributions received	0.77	0.75	0.72
Benefits paid	(0.51)	(0.50)	(0.49)
Actuarial gain/(loss) on obligation (balancing figure)	(0.52)	(0.10)	(0.06)
Fair value of assets at 31 December 20X7	0.95	1.20	1.49

Plan liabilities	1.07	1.01	0.98
Plan assets	(0.95)	(1.20)	(1.49)
Net liability	0.12	(0.19)	(0.51)

Statement of profit or loss expense

Interest cost	0.10	0.10	0.09
Current service cost	0.14	0.12	0.11
Expected return on plan assets	(0.11)	(0.10)	(0.10)
Actuarial (gain)/loss	0.66	0.32	0.30
Expense	0.79	0.44	0.40

Opening net liability	0.10	0.12	(0.19)
Expense	0.79	0.44	0.40
Contributions received	(0.77)	(0.75)	(0.72)
Closing net liability	0.12	(0.19)	(0.51)

Chapter 7

Question 1

Replacement cost

	HC	Index	RC	Realised holding gains
Opening inventory	6 000	164/150	6 560	
Purchases	80 000	164/164	80 000	
Closing inventory	(6 667)	164/177	(6 177)	
Cost of sales	79 333		80 383	1 050
Depreciation − premises	1 100	124/120	1 137	37
Depreciation − equipment	1 800	201/180	2 010	210
				1 297

	HC	Index	RC	Unrealised holding gains
Premises	53 900	127/120	57 044	3 144
Equipment	7 200	223/180	8 920	1 720
Inventory	6 667	179/177	6 742	75
				4 939

D
Replacement cost statement of profit or loss
for the year ended 28 February 20X5

	$	$
Sales (all cash)		124 000
Cost of sales	(80 383)	
Wages	(11 000)	
Depreciation – premises	(1 137)	
Depreciation – equipment	(2 010)	
Interest	(4 734)	
Operating expenses		(99 264)
Replacement cost operating profit		24 736
Realised holding gains		1 297
Unrealised holding gains		4 939
Replacement cost profit		30 972

D
Replacement cost statement of financial position
as at 28 February 20X5

	$	$
Property plant and equipment		
Premises		57 044
Equipment		8 920
		65 964
Current assets		
Inventory	6 742	
Bank	20 000	
		26 742
		92 706
Equity		
Share capital		30 000
Retained earnings		16 972
		46 972

Non-current liabilities
    Mortgage on premises   37 734
Current liabilities
    Trade payables   8 000
                                     92 706

Current purchasing power	HC	Index	CPP
Gain or loss on net monetary assets			
Opening net monetary assets	(40 000)	225/200	(45 000)
Sales	124 000	225/212	131 604
Purchases	(80 000)	225/212	(84 906)
Wages	(11 000)	225/212	(11 675)
Interest paid on 31 August	(2 367)	225/212	(2 512)
Interest paid on 28 February	(2 367)	225/225	(2 367)
Dividend	(14 000)	225/225	(14 000)
Predicted net monetary assets/			
(liabilities)			(28 856)
Closing net monetary assets			
Bank			20 000
Mortgage			(37 734)
Trade payables			(8 000)
			(25 734)
Gain on net monetary assets			3 122
Interest			
Paid 31 August	2 367	225/212	2 512
Paid 28 February	2 367	225/225	2 367
			4 879

D
Current purchasing power statement of profit or loss
for the year ended 28 February 20X5

	HC		Index	CPP	
	$	$		$	$
Sales (all cash)		124 000	225/212		131 604
Opening inventory	6 000		225/200	6 750	

Purchases	80 000	225/212	84 906
Closing inventory	(6 667)	225/223	(6 727)
Cost of inventory consumed	79 333		84 929
Wages	11 000	225/212	11 675
Depreciation – premises	1 100	225/200	1 238
Depreciation – equipment	1 800	225/200	2 025
Interest	4 734		4 879

Total expenses	97 967	104 746
Operating profit	26 033	26 858
Gain on net monetary assets		3 122
		29 980

D
Current purchasing power statement of financial position as at 28 February 20X5

	HC $	$	Index	CPP $	$
Property plant and equipment					
Premises		53 900	225/200		60 638
Equipment		7 200	225/200		8 100
		61 100			68 738
Current assets					
Inventory	6 667		225/223	6 727	
Bank	20 000			20 000	
		26 667			26 727
		87 767			95 465
Equity					
Share capital		30 000	225/200		33 750
Retained earnings		12 033			15 980
		42 033			49 730
Non-current liabilities					
Mortgage on premises		37 734			37 734
Current liabilities					
Trade payables		8 000			8 000
		87 767			95 464

There is a rounding difference because all figures are rounded to the nearest $1.

Real terms

	HC	CPP	Gain due to inflation
	$	$	$
Unrealised holding gains due to general inflation			
Premises	53 900	60 638	6 738
Equipment	7 200	8 100	900
Inventory	6 667	6 727	60
			7 698

Realised holding gains due to general inflation

	$
Historical cost operating profit	26 033
CPP operating profit	26 858
Realised gain due to inflation	(825)

Real holding gains

	$
Realised RC holding gains	1 297
Unrealised holding gains	4 939
Due to inflation − unrealised	(7 698)
Due to inflation − realised	825
Real holding loss	(637)

Share capital is expressed in CPP terms.

D
**Real terms statement of profit or loss
for the year ended 28 February 20X5**

	$	$
Sales (all cash)		124 000
Cost of sales	(80 383)	
Wages	(11 000)	
Depreciation − premises	(1 137)	
Depreciation − equipment	(2 010)	
Interest	(4 734)	
Operating expenses		(99 264)
Replacement cost operating profit		24 736

Real holding loss		(637)
Gain on net monetary assets		3 122
Real terms profit		27 221

D
Real terms statement of financial position
as at 28 February 20X5

	$	$
Property plant and equipment		
Premises		57 044
Equipment		8 920
		65 964
Current assets		
Inventory	6 742	
Bank	20 000	
		26 742
		92 706
Equity		
Share capital		33 750
Retained earnings		13 221
		46 971
Non-current liabilities		
Mortgage on premises		37 734
Current liabilities		
Trade payables		8 000
		92 705

There is a rounding difference because all figures are rounded to the nearest $1.

Chapter 8

Question 1

Cash flows attributable to bond element:

Date	Cash flow	Discount factor 7%	DCF
31 December 20X1	500 000	0.935	467 500
31 December 20X2	500 000	0.874	437 000

31 December 20X3	500 000	0.817	408 500
31 December 20X4	500 000	0.764	382 000
31 December 20X5	10 500 000	0.714	7 497 000
			9 192 000

If these cash flows had been received from a straightforward debt instrument then they would have been worth £9 192 000.

The equity element of the instrument is worth £10 000 000 − £9 192 000 = £808 000.

The statement of profit or loss will show a finance charge of £9 192 000 × 7% = £643 440.

The statement of financial position will show a non-current liability of £9 192 000 + £643 440 − £500 000 = £9 335 440.

The statement of financial position will also show an equity balance of £808 000.

Question 2

The fact that the shares are redeemable, with no discretion on the part of the issuer, means that they should have been classified as a liability.

The company has effectively borrowed £7 700 000 − £53 000 = £7 647 000 at 7%.

The annual coupon payment = £5m × 6% = £300 000.

The statement of profit or loss will show a finance charge of £7 647 000 × 7% = £535 290.

The statement of financial position will show a liability of £7 647 000 + £535 290 −300 000 = £7 882 290.

Question 3

Date	Balance at start of year	Finance charge at 12%	Cash flow	Balance at end of year
Year 1	3 630 000	435 600	150 000	3 915 600
Year 2	3 915 600	469 872	150 000	4 235 472
Year 3	4 235 472	508 257	150 000	4 593 729
Year 4	4 593 729	551 247	5 150 000	(5 024)

The figures for the finance charge should be shown in the statement of profit or loss as an expense.

The balance at the end of the year will appear in the statement of financial position as a non-current liability at the end of years one and two and as a current liability at the end of year three.

By the end of year four the liability should have been reduced to zero. The small negative balance is a rounding error that will have to be cancelled.

Chapter 9

Question 1

This question is looking for an explanation of the adjustments and cancellations that are required when preparing consolidated financial statements.

Question 2

The basic problem is that subsidiary companies are sometimes used to borrow on behalf of the group and so excluding some subsidiaries has been a very effective method of off-balance sheet financing.

Some groups may also have had subsidiaries that were engaged in activities from which the group wished to distance itself. There could have been problems with risk and volatility or the business may have been one that might affect the company's reputation.

Question 3

The main problem is that the group is an economic entity, but it has no formal legal identity. That means that the consolidated financial statements may prove misleading when considering entering into any form of relationship with a group member. For example, the directors of the holding may not necessarily act to save a subsidiary that runs into difficulty. Even if they want to, there could be practical problems such as a bank balance held by an overseas subsidiary being subject to exchange controls that limit the group's ability to repatriate the cash.

There are further complications that will quickly become apparent if you read a real set of group accounts. Different group members will operate in different industries and that may be sufficient to make it difficult to make sense of a single set of financial statements that presents a complicated undertaking in its entirety.

Chapter 10

Question 1

Goodwill

	$000
Investment in S	30
Share capital acquired	(14)
Retained earnings acquired	(7)
Goodwill on acquisition	9

Retained earnings

R	38
S – group share of post-acquisition earnings	5
	43

R Group
Consolidated statement of financial position
as at 31 December 20X9

	$000
Property, plant and equipment	50
Goodwill	9
Current assets	12
	71
Share capital	28
Retained earnings	43
	71

Question 2

Cost of control

Investment in U	8500	Share capital	2500
Fair value of NCI	900	Retained earnings	1500
		Property, plant and equipment	200
		Goodwill	5200
	9400		9400
Goodwill	5200		

Debit Retained earnings	30	
Credit Inventory		30
Debit Retained earnings	32	
Debit NCI	8	
Credit Property, plant and equipment		40

Non-controlling interest

Property, plant and equipment	8	Cost of control	900
Bal c/d	1 492	Share of post-acq. profits	600
	1 500		1 500
		Bal b/d	1 492

Retained earnings

Cost of control	1 500	Bal b/d	15 000
Non-controlling interest	600	Bal b/d	4 500
Inventory	30		
Property, plant and equipment	32		
Bal c/d	17 338		
	19 500		19 500
		Bal b/d	17 338

T Group
Consolidated statement of financial position
as at 31 December 20X6

	$000
Non-current assets	
Property, plant and equipment	24 620
Goodwill	5 200
	29 820
Current assets	
Inventory	2 540
Trade receivables	1 650
Bank	450
	4 640
	34 460

Equity	
Share capital	10 000
Retained profits	17 338
	27 338
Non-controlling interest	1 492
Total equity	28 830
Non-current liabilities	
Loans	1 500
Current liabilities	
Trade payables	2 800
Tax	930
Overdraft	400
	4 130
	34 460

Question 3

V Group
Consolidated statement of profit or loss
for the year ended 31 March 20X0

	£000
Revenue	42 100
Cost of sales	(24 550)
Gross profit	17 550
Other expenses	(7 000)
Operating profit	10 550
Tax	(1 500)
Profit for the year net of tax	9 050
Profit attributable to:	
Owners of the parent	7 600
Non-controlling interest	1 450
	9 050

Revenue = £25 000 + 19 000 − 1900 = £42 100
Cost of sales = £15 300 + 11 000 − 1900 + 150 = £24 550

Chapter 11

Question 1

I's effective interest in N is 60% × 60% = 36%

Goodwill on acquisition of J

	€000
Investment	1500
Fair value of non-controlling interest	510
Fair value of net identifiable assets	(1720)
Goodwill on acquisition of J	290

Goodwill on acquisition of N

	€000
Investment	850
Fair value of non-controlling interest	400
Fair value of net identifiable assets	(1090)
Goodwill on acquisition of N	160

Non-controlling interest

	J	N
As at date of acquisition	510	400
Interest in post-acquisition reserves		
40% × (1400 − 820)	232	
64% × (1090 − 640)		288
Non-controlling interest	742	688
Total non-controlling interest		1430

Retained earnings − I	1275
Group share of J = 60% × (1400 − 820)	348
Group share of N = 36% × (1090 − 640)	162
	1785

I Group
Consolidated statement of financial position
as at 31 December 20X6

	€000
Property, plant and equipment	6500
Goodwill	450
	6950

Current assets	410
	7360
Share capital	2000
Retained earnings	1785
	3785
Non-controlling interest	1430
Total equity	5215
Non-current liabilities	1850
Current liabilities	295
	7360

Question 2

Y's effective interest in V is 75% × 60% = 45%

Goodwill on acquisition of G

	$000
Investment	12 000
Fair value of non-controlling interest	1 500
Fair value of net identifiable assets	(7 900)
Goodwill on acquisition of G	5 600

Goodwill on acquisition of V

	$000
Investment	8 000
Fair value of non-controlling interest	3 900
Fair value of net identifiable assets	(3 200)
Goodwill on acquisition of V	8 700

Non-controlling interest

	G	V
As at date of acquisition	1 500	3 900
Interest in post-acquisition reserves		
25% × (4350 − 900)	863	
55% × (2700 − 2200)		275
Non-controlling interest	2 363	4 175
Total non-controlling interest		6 538

Retained earnings — Y	10 460
Group share of G = 75% × (4350 − 900)	2 588
Group share of V = 45% × (2700 − 2200)	225
	13 273

Y Group
Consolidated statement of financial position
as at 31 December 20X5

	$000
Property, plant and equipment	20 800
Goodwill	14 300
	35 100
Current assets	2 550
	37 650
Share capital	10 000
Retained earnings	13 273
	23 273
Non-controlling interest	6 538
Total equity	29 810
Non-current liabilities	6 600
Current liabilities	1 240
	37 650

Question 3

Cost of control — F			
Investment	600	Share capital	416
		Retained earnings	60
		Goodwill c/d	124
	600		600
Goodwill b/d	124		

T's effective interest in C = 40% + (80% × 40%) = 72%

Cost of control – C

Investment	500	Share capital	360
Investment (80% × 450)	360	Retained earnings	65
		Goodwill c/d	435
	860		860
Goodwill b/d	435		

Non-controlling interest – F

		Share capital	104
Bal c/d	166	Retained earnings	62
	166		166
		Bal b/d	166

Non-controlling interest – C

Investment	90	Share capital	140
Bal c/d	98	Retained earnings	48
	188		188
		Bal b/d	98

Retained earnings

Cost of control	60	Bal b/d	510
Cost of control	65	Bal b/d	310
Non-controlling interest	62	Bal b/d	170
Non-controlling interest	48		
Bal c/d	755		
	990		990
		Bal b/d	756

T Group
Consolidated statement of financial position
as at 31 December 20X9

	£000
Property, plant and equipment	1410
Goodwill	559
	1969

Current assets	
Inventory	490
Trade receivables	740
Cash	170
	1400
	3369
Share capital	1800
Retained earnings	755
	2555
Non-controlling interest	264
Total equity	2819
Current liabilities	550
	3369

Question 4

Goodwill on acquisition of H

	€000
Investment	1200
Fair value of non-controlling interest	520
Fair value of net identifiable assets	(1100)
Goodwill on acquisition of H	620
Unrealised profit on inventory	20
60% to group profit	12
40% to NCI	8
Cash in transit	28
Increase bank and decrease receivables by 28	
Decrease receivables and payables by 17	

Non-controlling interest

	€000
As at date of acquisition	520
Interest in post-acquisition reserves	
40% × (710 − 300)	164
Less unrealised profit	(8)
	676

Investment in associate

	€000
Initial investment	570
Group share of post acquisition profit 40% × (1890 − 400)	596
Goodwill on acquisition of V	1166
Retained earnings − U	1343
Group share of H = 60% × (710 − 300)	246
Less unrealised profit	(12)
Group share of B = 40% × (1890 − 400)	596
	2173

U Group
Consolidated statement of financial position
as at 31 December 20X6

	€000
Property, plant and equipment	2450
Goodwill	620
Investment in associate	1166
	4236
Current assets	
Inventory	650
Trade receivables	1700
Bank	399
	2749
	6985
Share capital	3000
Retained earnings	2173
	5173
Non-controlling interest	676
Total equity	5849
Current liabilities	
Trade payables	1136
	6985

Chapter 12

Question 1

Investment in B	€000
Fair value of 10% at date of acquisition of control	10 000
Fair value of 50% investment	52 000
Fair value of controlling interest	62 000
Further capital gain — to be eliminated as a consolidation adjustment	13 000
	75 000

Goodwill calculation	€000
Fair value of investment consideration	62 000
Fair value of non-controlling interest	45 000
Fair value of net assets	(60 000)
Goodwill	47 000

Retained earnings at 31 December 20X9	€000
H	121 500
Gain on investment in subsidiary	(13 000)
Group share of post-acquisition earnings	9 000
	117 500

Non-controlling interest	€000
Fair value at date of acquisition	45 000
NCI share of post-acquisition earnings	6 000
	51 000

H Group
Consolidated statement of financial position
as at 31 December 20X9

	€000
Goodwill	47 000
Property, plant and equipment	203 000
	250 000
Current assets	41 000
	291 000

Share capital	100 000
Retained earnings	117 500
	217 500
Non-controlling interest	51 000
Total equity	268 500
Current liabilities	22 500
	291 000

Question 2

Investment in F	£000
Fair value of 60% at date of acquisition of control	80 000
Further investment	20 000
Fair value of controlling interest	100 000
Further capital gain — to be eliminated as a consolidation adjustment	7 000
	107 000

Goodwill calculation	£000
Fair value of investment consideration	80 000
Fair value of non-controlling interest	58 000
Fair value of net assets	(75 000)
Goodwill	63 000

Non-controlling interest at 31 December 20X6 before further acquisition	£000
Fair value of NCI at acquisition	58 000
NCI share of post-acquisition earnings 40% × (62 000 − 35 000)	10 800
	68 800

Non-controlling interest at 31 December 20X6 after further acquisition	£000
Fair value of NCI at acquisition	58 000
NCI share of post-acquisition earnings 25% × (62 000 − 35 000)	6 750
	64 750

Decrease in non-controlling interest	4 050
Cost of additional investment	(20 000)
Loss − taken to retained earnings	(15 950)

Retained earnings at 31 December 20X8	**£000**
D	143 000
Gain on investment in F	(7 000)
Adjustment on additional investment	(15 950)
Group share of post-acquisition earnings	
1 January 20X5 − 31 December 20X6 (60% × (62 000 − 35 000))	16 200
Group share of post-acquisition earnings	
1 January 20X7 − 31 December 20X8 (75% × (70 000 − 62 000))	6 000
	142 250

Non-controlling interest	**£000**
As at 31 December 20X5	64 750
NCI share of post-acquisition earnings	2 000
	66 750

D Group
Consolidated statement of financial position
as at 31 December 20X8

	£000
Goodwill	63 000
Property, plant and equipment	320 000
	383 000
Current assets	64 000
	447 000
Share capital	200 000
Retained earnings	142 250
	342 250
Non-controlling interest	66 750
Total equity	409 000
Current liabilities	38 000
	447 000

Question 3

Goodwill calculation	$000
Fair value of investment consideration	80 000
Fair value of non-controlling interest	18 000
Fair value of net assets	(54 000)
Goodwill	44 000

No gain or loss on disposal has been shown in the parent's financial statements.

NCI as at date of disposal	$000
Fair value as at date of acquisition	18 000
NCI share of post-acquisition profits	2 400
	20 400

Consideration received	56 000	Minor's net assets at disposal	66 000
Fair value of investment retained	56 000	Unimpaired goodwill	44 000
		NCI as at disposal	(20 400)
	112 000		89 600
Difference – gain on disposal	22 400		

Investment in associate	$000
Fair value	56 000
Group share of post-acquisition earnings	3 200
	59 200

Retained earnings	$000
Major	503 000
Group share of Minor's profits while a subsidiary 80% × (54 000 − 42 000)	9 600
Group share of Minor's profits while an associate 40% × (62 000 − 54 000)	3 200
Equity adjustment on disposal	22 400
	538 200

Major Group
Consolidated statement of financial position
as at 31 December 20X9

	$000
Investment in associate	59 200
Property, plant and equipment	701 000
	760 200
Current assets	130 000
	890 200
Share capital	300 000
Retained earnings	538 200
	838 200
Current liabilities	52 000
	890 200

Chapter 13

Question 1

Loan for purchase of Pine

		SEK000
As stated	GBP200 000/10.00	20.0
At closing rate	GBP200 000/9.50	21.1
Loss		(1.1)
Trade payable		
As stated	€42 000/8.1	5.2
At closing rate	€42 000/8.3	5.1
Gain		0.1
Inventory shown at fair value		
Cost of damaged inventory	€42 000/3 = €14 000	
As stated	€14 000/8.1	1.7
At closing rate	€14 000/8.3	1.0
Total loss		(0.7)

The loss on the inventory is complicated by the fact that some of the loss is due to the write-down of the inventory and some is due to changes in the exchange rates. Normally, inventory will be shown at its historical cost and so changes to rates will not make a difference, but the inventory shown at net realisable value is valued at the closing rate (which is automatically applied in this case because the inventory will be disposed of for SEK1000).

All of the gains and losses will go to retained earnings, so the adjusted figures are as follows:

	SEK000
Property, plant and equipment	8 900.0
Investment in Pine	2 000.0
	10 900.0
Current assets	
Inventory	499.3
Trade receivables	300.0
Bank	100.0
	899.3
Total assets	11 799.3
Share capital	6 000.0
Retained earnings	2 728.3
	8 728.3
Non-current liabilities	2 701.1
Current liabilities	
Trade payables	249.9
Tax	120.0
	369.9
	11 799.3

Question 2

Closing rate

	As at 31 December 20X8			As at 31 December 20X7		
	€000	Rate	CNY000	€000	Rate	CNY000
Property, plant and equipment						
Land and buildings	18 400	8.5	156 400	18 800	7.9	148 520
Equipment	12 600	8.5	107 100	13 200	7.9	104 280
	31 000		263 500	32 000		252 800
Current assets						
Inventory	400	8.5	3 400	420	7.9	3 318
Trade receivables	520	8.5	4 420	490	7.9	3 871
Bank	70	8.5	595	50	7.9	395
	990		8 415	960		7 584
	31 990		271 915	32 960		260 384
Equity (balancing figure)	26 580		225 930	27 770		219 383
Non-current liabilities	5 000	8.5	42 500	4 800	7.9	37 920
Current liabilities	410	8.5	3 485	390	7.9	3 081
	31 990		271 915	32 960		260 384

Temporal

	As at 31 December 20X8			As at 31 December 20X7		
	€000	Rate	CNY000	€000	Rate	CNY000
Property, plant and equipment						
Land and buildings	18 400	6.7	123 280	18 800	6.7	125 960
Equipment	12 600	7.0	88 200	13 200	7.0	92 400
	31 000		211 480	32 000		218 360
Current assets						
Inventory	400	8.2	3 280	420	7.7	3 234
Trade receivables	520	8.5	4 420	490	7.9	3 871
Bank	70	8.5	595	50	7.9	395

	990		8 295	960		7 500
	31 990		219 775	32 960		225 860
Equity (balancing figure)	26 580		173 790	27 770		184 859
Non-current liabilities	5 000	8.5	42 500	4 800	7.9	37 920
Current liabilities	410	8.5	3 485	390	7.9	3 081
	31 990		219 775	32 960		225 860

Under the closing rate method, profit = CNY225 930 000 − CNY219 383 000 = CNY6 547 000.

Under the temporal method, profit = CNY173 790 000 − CNY184 859 000 = (CNY11 069 000).

The yuan has been steadily devaluing against the euro, which means that the temporal method has permitted the euro liabilities to appreciate without any offsetting gains on assets.

The ratios under the two translation methods are:

	Closing rate		Temporal	
	20X8	20X7	20X8	20X7
Gearing	42 500/ (225 930 + 42 500) = 16%	37 920/ (219 383 + 37 920) = 15%	42 500/ (173 790 + 42 500) = 20%	37 920/ (184 859 + 37 920) = 17%
Current ratio	8415/3458 = 2.4:1	7584/3081 = 2.5:1	8295/3458 = 2.4:1	7500/3081 = 2.4:1

The smaller profits under the temporal method mean that gearing is higher, so the company appears to be more risky under the temporal method.

The temporal method also leads to a lower value for inventory, given the direction of the changing rates. That reduces current assets without affecting current liabilities. That is not sufficient in this case to affect the current ratio to any great extent, but the ratios are a little lower.

Question 3

Goodwill

	GBPm
Cost of investment	25.0
NCI at fair value	8.0
	33.0
Share capital	(20.0)
Retained earnings	(7.0)
Goodwill	6.0

Group share of goodwill = $25.0 - (75\% \times (20.0 + 7.0)) =$	4.8	80%
NCI share	1.2	20%

	€m
Total translated at opening rate of €1.5/GBP	9.0
Total translated at closing rate of €1.3/GBP	7.8
Exchange loss	(1.2)

Gain or loss on retranslation of cost of investment

	€m
Cost of investment at acquisition rate of €1.5/GBP	37.5
Cost of investment at closing rate of €1.3/GBP	32.5
Exchange loss to group reserves	(5.0)

Non-controlling interest

	GBPm
At acquisition	8.0
NCI share of post-acquisition retained earnings	3.0
$(25\% \times (19.0 - 7.0))$	
	11.0

	€m
Translated at closing rate of €1.3/GBP	14.3

Group retained earnings

	€m	GBPm
Parent	162.5	
Group share of subsidiary post-acquisition retained earnings		9.0

Translated at closing rate of €1.3/GBP	11.7		
Loss on retranslation of investment	(5.0)		
	169.2		

Group exchange difference

	Total €m	Group €m	NCI €m
Opening net assets at opening rate ((GBP20.0m + GBP7.0m) × 1.5)	40.5		
Opening net assets at closing rate ((GBP20.0m + GBP7.0m) × 1.3)	35.1		
Exchange loss (split 75%:25%)	(5.4)	(4.1)	(1.3)
Profit for year			
12.0m at average rate of 1.4	16.8		
12.0m at closing rate of 1.3	15.6		
Exchange gain (split 80%:20%)	(1.2)	(1.0)	(0.2)
Goodwill adjustment (see above)	(1.2)	(1.0)	(0.2)
Total adjustments	(7.8)	(6.1)	(1.7)

Reconciliation of group retained earnings

	€m
Parent	162.5
Group share of post-acquisition profit at average rate = 75% × 12.0 × 1.4	12.6
	175.1
Group share of exchange differences	(6.1)
	169.0

Income statements
for the year ended 31 December 20X8

	Hub €m	Spoke GBPm
Revenue	330.0	38.5
Costs	(154.0)	(22.0)
Profit before tax	176.0	16.5

	Tax	(24.0)	(4.5)
	Profit for year	152.0	12.0

Statements of financial position as at 31 December 20X8

	Hub €m	Spoke GBPm
Investment	37.5	
Other assets	510.0	68.0
	547.5	68.0
Share capital	150.0	20.0
Retained earnings	162.5	19.0
	312.5	39.0
Non-current liabilities	200.0	26.0
Current liabilities	35.0	3.0
	547.5	68.0

INDEX